The Art
of Managing
Everyday Conflict

The Art of Managing Everyday Conflict

Understanding Emotions and
Power Struggles

Erik A. Fisher and Steven W. Sharp

Westport, Connecticut
London

Library of Congress Cataloging-in-Publication Data

Fisher, Erik A., 1966–

    The art of managing everyday conflict : understanding emotions and power
  struggles / Erik A. Fisher and Steven W. Sharp

    p. cm.

  Includes bibliographical references and index.

  ISBN 0-275-98184-3 (alk. paper)

    1. Interpersonal conflict. 2. Conflict (Psychology) 3. Control (Psychology)
  4. Emotions—Social aspects. 5. Conflict management. I. Sharp, Steven W.
  II. Title.

HM1121.F57 2004

303.6'9—dc22   2003066140

British Library Cataloguing in Publication Data is available.

Library of Congress Catalog Card Number: 2003066140
ISBN: 0-275-98184-3

First published in 2004

Praeger Publishers, 88 Post Road West, Westport, CT 06881
An imprint of Greenwood Publishing Group, Inc.
www.praeger.com

Printed in the United States of America

The paper used in this book complies with the
Permanent Paper Standard issued by the National
Information Standards Organization (Z39.48-1984).

10 9 8 7 6 5 4 3 2

Illustrations by Scott Simpson

Dedication

This book is dedicated to my brother, Gorman, who perhaps taught me more about life since he has left this world; to my parents for teaching me perseverance and ambition through success and failure; to my sisters for their unconditional support and belief in me; to my wife for being my champion, my partner, my guide, and my friend; and to my clients, who have been my most significant mentors and scholars. I thank John Gale, Norm Skala, Patti Pohlman, Kevin Thompson and Bob Phillips for being teachers in my life who believed in my vision when I could not see. And finally, I could not have done this without the experience, help and support of Steven and Samantha Sharp, who helped this manuscript become a published reality. Agape.

Erik A. Fisher, Ph.D.

I dedicate this book to my grandmother, Virginia Sharp, whom I think of as a second mother. Her unwavering love and belief in me, no matter what I've tried to accomplish, has had an immeasurable influence upon me and my life. I thank my mother and father, Ann Campbell and Wayne Sharp, for the love, support, kindness and care that they have provided to me throughout my life. I offer a special thanks to Jeanie Kezo and Scott Simpson for their considerable efforts in this project, and to my friends at Ink Tank who have traveled on this journey with me. To my wife, Samantha: I owe you more than I can ever repay; "wife" is such a small word to convey all that you mean to me. In closing, I thank Erik Fisher for including us in this project and allowing us to share in this wonderful journey.

Steven W. Sharp

Contents

Contents

Illustrations

Preface

Man's mind, once being stretched by a new idea, never regains its
original dimensions.

—Oliver Wendell Holmes

The motivation for writing this book arose out of working with many
clients in practice and teaching them to examine conflicts, to see how
conflicts affect them, their lives, and their relationships. In viewing
these conflicts, it is important to understand how they are often inter-
mingled with our personal sense of power and our emotions. The idea
of power, and how we use it, are involved in most interactions in our
lives, and the struggle for power often begins at the moment of birth.

This text seeks to help the reader to avoid conflicts when possible and
deal with them productively when they do occur. The key to diffusing
many of the conflicts we encounter in our day-to-day lives involves
understanding our emotions and our sense of power. In the process of
understanding how power affects our relationships with others, first it
is important to understand how our personal manipulations of power
affect us. To help others understand the role of power in their lives, the
key is to help them to see the logical relationships between their perceptions of power, the emotions they were presenting to others, and the
underlying emotions.

We, as humans, are complex animals; we learn and adopt very complex behavioral, language, and emotional patterns. We experience
many levels and layers of emotion that we (often unknowingly) use to
cover up other emotions. We also modify our perceptions to protect our
image from others and ourselves. The ties between our emotions and

our sense of power are so intricate that it is easy to overlook the relationship between the two. As such, we are often unaware of the connections between power and emotion. This book seeks to help the reader to identify those relationships in order to have the choice to change patterns that we often feel helpless to change.

Philosophy teachers often pose various dilemmas to their students for discussion and evaluation. One such dilemma provides an opportunity to consider the two models of power covered in this book—the hierarchical and equity models. This philosophical conundrum is called the Commoner's Dilemma. The following story is one of many different versions.

Consider a pasture where farmers can bring their cattle to graze. The field is just large enough to sustain all the cattle if each farmer allows his cattle to eat only enough to survive. In doing this, all the cattle will survive, but none will become fat enough to bring high prices at the market. If, however, one or more of the farmers decide to allow their cattle to graze enough to become fat, then it is likely that another farmer's cattle will starve to death.

The dilemma arises when a farmer questions the price he will receive for his cattle at market if they maintain their size compared to the price they would bring if he allowed them to overgraze. In fattening his cattle, the other cattle stand a chance of starving, but he may make more money. If he limits how much his cattle graze, as the others do, all should survive, yet the farmer may have more competition when selling his cows.

When the farmer considers the issue of how much to allow his cattle to graze, he may also realize that the other farmers have to make the same decisions. This situation could lead to feelings of fear and mistrust between him and the other farmers. If his feeling of mistrust becomes too great, he may decide to overgraze his cattle to protect himself. Many other issues tie into this dilemma. It may be interesting to think about this dilemma and reconsider it as you continue to read.

Throughout this book, I will challenge you to examine how you approach your past, present, and future. There are questions at the end of most chapters and you may find it helpful to jot down some notes in response to these questions. In doing so, you may question your emotions, realize how often people feel powerless, and begin to understand the emotions and defenses we use to protect ourselves. I do this in an attempt to open the reader's eyes to the choices made in our world every day.

In reading this book, you will learn to understand your emotions and the emotions of others, and it will be very important to use your newly found power wisely. When someone learns a new skill, they may be tempted to try to use it in order to advance their own power at the expense of others. If we try to use this skill for that purpose, it often does more harm than good, not only for that individual but also in their relationships. As you will learn, the manipulation of emotions can cause a great deal of harm. Although feeling hurt can contribute to our growth, if our pain emerges in an unproductive manner, it can foster more hurt and pain, and delay the healing process.

This book seeks to teach people to understand themselves, their feelings, their conflicts and their personal sense of power. I do not intend to incite people to go out and try to change the world. If, however, we can understand ourselves more clearly, we will likely see ways in which the world reflects our own flaws. As we correct our own flaws, our reflection of the world around us will likely change to demonstrate those changes within ourselves.

ON USAGE

1. This book's "I" is Erik Fisher, whose practice and experience is its basis. 2. We have chosen to avoid either sexist language or awkward, repetitious "he/she" or "his or her" or the like, by the use of "they" and "their" in their place. 3. The names and identities of the persons and specific case information referenced in the examples contained in this book have been altered to protect the privacy of actual persons.

1

Introduction

Power is the ultimate aphrodisiac.
—Henry Kissinger

TEACHING OBJECTIVES

- Provide a framework for understanding power issues
- Explain relationship between power and emotion
- Discuss historical basis of power struggles
- Increase self-awareness to personal power issues

It was late in March when Suzanne came home with a shopping bag and Glen, her husband, greeted her coolly. After five years of marriage, Suzanne knew when he was unhappy and she was sure that the shopping bag had a lot to do with his reaction to her. Glen kept a tight rein on the finances since taking the job over after she'd allowed a couple of checks to bounce because of oversights. "Anyone can make a mistake," she told herself, and it bothered her that he took the responsibility of managing the finances away from her. However, she felt embarrassed and ashamed over her mistake and did not fight to keep the job.

She knew money was always tight around the end of the month, but with his company banquet approaching, she felt she needed a new dress. Glen looked at the bag and then glared at her. He slowly shook his head and walked away. Without saying a word, he could somehow incite her pulse to race, her cheeks to flush, and summon a feeling of rage that she sometimes felt pressed to control. They often argued over money; matters as seemingly trivial as whether to buy ground round or ground chuck could lead to a shouting match. "He's just a greedy, selfish man," Suzanne sometimes told her friends after one of their bouts. "She just goes through money without a care in the world," Glen told his friends when the topic of their wives' spending habits arose. However, is the situation just that simple?

Since the dawn of time, life has been about a struggle for power. Our ancestors fought for survival. History shows this, and we can look at the animal kingdom to see that this is true. As time passed, we fought battles over such issues as arrogance, ignorance, and bigotry. Charles Darwin has helped advance our understanding of the struggle for power. Darwin's theories on natural selection assert that strength and power are two attributes that can often ensure a species' survival. To a human's way of thinking, animals are brutal in their process of selection. However, are we willing to look closely at ourselves to see how we self-select and determine our power? If we were to look as closely at the world as it "really" is, what would we feel, and would we want to change our ways?

How often do we hear, "history repeats itself"? If we look through the fabric of time, it is likely that we would see that the same conflicts cease to end; there are only different players. A struggle for power causes conflict. This conflict is often born out of a fear of someone overpowering us. We may sense that this struggle happens between people, but it often happens within each person.

If we choose to view situations so that we learn about our power, we must see ourselves with a fair and honest eye. We must also be willing to accept whatever truth we find. We can look to the past for answers, but how would we react to the truth if we found it? Would these current patterns continue, or would they end? It is our collective choice to continue these power struggles, even though they cause pain. These patterns continue in the history of the human race and in the history of each of us.

While not wanting to admit it to ourselves, we often feel powerless to change the path of our life. What seems to shape the course of our lives? Most of us would say our parents, spouses, friends, money, and the government hold key roles. We feel unable to alter the way our parents, spouse or friends treat us. We cannot change the price of the food we eat or the amount of taxes we pay. Some feel that we live in a world of crime and evil. They no longer feel safe going out at night or walking through a darkened parking lot alone. We do not even feel we can trust the candy given to our kids by the neighbors on Halloween. This perspective creates an image of an unkind world filled with cruel and evil people who control us and make us victims.

Even when we see others living in a world like the one we "dream" of, we choose not to move forward. But why? What holds us back? Do politicians, bad parents, troubled teens, criminals, or terrorists stop us from having the life we want? We give so many others the power to affect our worldview, when, for each of us, we live in a world that we have created. Yet, we may still feel powerless to change it.

WHAT IS POWER?

What is this thing we call "power," and where do we find it? Does it come from others, or from within us? To determine where we get our power, we must first define it. *Webster's New World Dictionary* provides the following definitions:

> 1. ability to do, act, or produce 2. a specific ability or faculty 3. great ability to act or affect strongly; vigor; force; strength 4. the ability to control others; authority; sway; influence 5. the capacity to exert physical force or energy 6. a person or thing having great influence, force or authority.

Many see power as being strong, successful, or victorious over a person, people or thing. We often associate it with strength. *Powerful* is a word we use to convey that a person has strength or authority over other people. The word *power* describes a range of feelings from weak and power*less* to strong and power*ful*.

In short, power consists of a range of feelings, perceptions, or emotions. In order to feel or perceive power, we have to experience life. To gain the perception of a level of power at any moment, we have to feel. You may say, "I am powerful." or you may say, "I feel powerful!" and come closer to the truth. Power is a state of feeling at a moment in time that can change in an instant. The feeling of power can ebb and flow with other feelings, circumstances, and situations. If I state that I *am* powerful, then I should always be powerful. States of being are much more constant than states of feeling, which can fluctuate rapidly and often. When you look at power this way, you can see that all experiences of power must involve emotion of some sort.

Clearly, there is a close relationship between power, feelings, and emotion. We call our feelings different things: thoughts, attitudes, and/or perceptions; we learn to ignore them. Many people think of emotions as a pointless and unneeded part of life. Whether we want to believe it or not, our power and our emotions are connected. The sooner we recognize this relationship, the sooner we can understand why we act as we do.

WHERE DO WE GET POWER?

At the instant of birth—and likely before—we begin our search for power. Some argue that the unborn child feels the emotions of the parents, and may even feel his own emotions; we begin to feel our power from these emotions. The power we attribute to each emotion is often learned through society and, most importantly, through the family.

We are animals that learn through our behaviors and their consequences. As early as birth, we may experience rewards and/or consequences from the act of being born. One such reward may take the form of having a warm, caring environment. A newborn may sense that warmth and affection are a reward for a difficult journey that involved cold metal tools and stern voices. We are unable to remember the events of being born. Nevertheless, some argue that memories of birth are often rooted within our subconscious, which may set the stage for power struggles throughout our life.

After birth, we gain rewards from our environment. We receive food, love, physical touch, a clean body and clean clothes, smells, sounds, warmth, soothing voices; and we often feel punished if we do not receive these things. Either an infant enjoys the rewards of feeling safe, secure and comfortable or is unrewarded and feels sadness, fear, loneliness, anger, and neglect. During or following his expression of emotion, in whatever form, the child receives a response from the environment. The response may be one the child wants, such as being held, fed, or spoken to, or one that is unwanted such as being ignored, struck, or shouted at.

We continue to develop our sense of personal power from these early experiences. From these experiences, we begin to think that we are empowered by others.[1] Other people must notice our power for it to exist. This is why kids (and some adults) will do just about anything to get attention. Kids often like to gain attention by "making a big splash." When we give a child attention, we acknowledge his power. Our beliefs that we get our power from others form the beginning of dependency. If we feel we only gain power through other people, we may develop defiant and avoidant behaviors and attitudes to resist this need. There is also likely some genetic influence on our behaviors and search for power, but no one knows how much.

HISTORY OF POWER

What does history teach us about power? Consider the statement, "those who have won the wars have written the histories." History has been written (or re-written for that matter) by those who were in political power. In this vein, history is not so much about recording the truth, but a means of recording the perceptions, ideas, and beliefs of the victor. History shows us that it is impossible for one person to hold all the power, and the greedy often lose in the end. People we think of, historically, as being powerful are often associated with emotions such as confidence, arrogance and pride. Terms like determination, anger, defiance, rage, sarcasm, humor, humility, and peace also describe emotions we often associate with powerful people. Besides these emotions, we see powerful people using logic as a tool to manipulate their power and influence others. Powerful people avoid showing emotions that others may view as weak. People of power shy away from outward displays of vulnerability, failure, frustration, guilt, shame, doubt, jealousy, or envy. We see, from history, that society views people who show these emotions as being weak.

Over time, we have learned another interpretation of the "golden rule": "He who has the gold makes the rules." Sometimes power comes from what a person has. If I am thirsty, the person who has water has more power than I. However, there is a flaw in this philosophy because we often do not see what gives us power. I have the power to choose to drink their water or to search for other sources. When people have things that we want, we often feel that they abuse their power and take advantage. They may misuse their power by either hoarding what they have, or by raising the cost of what they have if they are willing to part with it.

As an example, let's consider a conflict between two neighbors, Jack and Ted. Jack has an apple tree close to his property line. When the apples are ripe, some fall to the ground. Ted grabs a few apples from the ground to take home. Jack sees Ted take the apples and accuses him of stealing. Ted explains that apples left on the ground rot very quickly and that he did not think Jack would miss a few. But Jack argues that they are not Ted's to take. Jack takes the apples from Ted's hands and walks away. This incident begins a conflict that lasts for years. The neighbors stop talking, and they forbid their children from playing with each other. Jack builds a fence between the two properties. They continue to argue and fight until Ted's family moves away, taking their anger, hatred and hurt with them.

Such conflicts can exist in various magnitudes. Some of these have worldwide implications. Throughout time, wars have erupted over many things such as land, water, food, gold, oil, religion, beliefs, etc. In each of these situations, the object (land, religion, water, oil...) served as the source of power, not the owner of the "thing"; however, each individual collectively fought the war. Without the belief in the power of the object we are fighting for, there would be no cause for the conflict.

Think back to Suzanne and Glen and the hard feelings surrounding her purchase of a new dress. Glen wants to share his fear and concern over not being able to pay bills with his wife. He may not want to tell her what is going on because of certain thoughts or feelings he has. Glen may feel the stress of being the "breadwinner" or arrogance in his ability to "fix" everything. Still, what if he fails in his role of breadwinner? Maybe he has never failed at providing for his family, but what if he does now? Glen risks facing his fear of feeling vulnerable, stupid, and weak. Providing for his family gives him a strong source of power. Suzanne may lose confidence in him if he admits his feelings to her. He might fear that if she lost faith in his ability to provide, she would leave him (fear of rejection), because he could not meet their needs and offer a sense of security.

This inner conflict causes a feeling of guilt, shame, fear, sadness, and remorse to overcome him. Glen then feels more insecure about sharing these emotions. He feels the need to show his strength by reassuring Suzanne of his competence in handling the finances. If she pressures him, he may resort to sarcasm, anger, and rage. These outbursts are reactions to his effort to protect his feelings of vulnerability. Glen ignores the building emotions and continues to struggle. Fear may cause him to resort to unprofessional and/or illegal means to pay the bills. This ill-gotten money can cause him more problems. He fears capture and feels guilt, shame, sadness, failure, etc. Logic is his main defense. Therefore, he tries to rationalize and justify his actions. The outcome may vary, but these emotional patterns are common. Expressions of emotions and defenses create struggles for power; these occur within the emotions that we feel. There are also power issues between Glen and Suzanne.

I often tell clients and audiences, "The existence of all emotions in humans is universal; it is what we do with the emotions that makes us different." Although we all have the capacity to feel all emotions, there are individuals (such as sociopaths) who can effectively mask certain emotions to the point of near non-existence. In other words, we all have the same emotions, but our experiences in life teach us to use and show the emotions differently, or not at all. There is no good, bad, right, or wrong about it. It just is the way it is.

SUMMARY

The common threads of emotion run through conflict and this book explains these relationships. It is often easier to understand our conflicts with others than our inner conflicts. Being able to recognize the conflicts within ourselves enables us to resolve the conflicts occurring on the outside. Often, conflicts arise when we give our power away in some form. It is worth mentioning that I do not believe that others can forcefully take our power.

If we grew up in a society where everyone learned that they were equally empowered, why would there be conflict? At the root of all conflict is a perceived inequity in power. When involved in a conflict, we only see things through our own eyes, often not realizing the other person's point of view. We each have the power to continue a conflict for as long as we feel there is an inequity. We all know the cliché that says, "Knowledge is power." I hope you choose to use the knowledge provided by this book with care and wisdom.

QUESTIONS

1. How do you feel about your personal power? Do you wish you had more?
2. Do you often feel motivated to succeed in order to hold onto your current level of power?
3. In hindsight, can you think of times when you might have put your emotions to better or more productive use instead of the way you actually utilized them?

Consider your responses to these questions and make a note of them in your journal.

Hierarchical Power Systems and How They Cause Conflict

Power never takes a step back—only in the face of more power.
—Malcolm X

TEACHING OBJECTIVES

- Explain hierarchical model of power
- Provide examples of hierarchical power issues
- Inform on the nature of conflict and inequity
- Explain the nature of status power versus internal perceptions of power

Consider the differences in the power structure of a corporate office and that of a therapy group. In a corporate office, there is a pecking order wherein everyone has a clear place. Each person has a position that may give him or her authority over others, but they must be accountable to those higher in the power structure. In a group therapy environment, all participants are equal. They all have thoughts and experiences to relate, and the intent is to have a situation wherein everyone benefits mutually from the sharing of thoughts and experiences offered by each member. These two separate power models form the basis for the ones we will examine in this book: the hierarchical system and the equity system. The hierarchical system maintains that everyone has a different level of power. This "status power" may change depending on the system they are in (for example, family, school, work, friends). A hierarchical system is what has been imposed on most of the world in which we live. What do I mean by "imposed"? The people who created the hierarchy are commonly the most powerful in the hierarchy. Through manipulation, position, or status, they have been able to manipulate the system.

The concept of the hierarchical system in our society comes from the idea that each person in the hierarchy has a different status and a different amount of power. When you put each person in order in terms of their level of power, you have built a hierarchy. The person at the top of the hierarchy often determines the amount of power that each person in the hierarchy will receive. The goal of most people is to figure out how to get the most power possible.

Perhaps it is best to think of personal power as a ball of energy. In many ways, each of us is made of energy that we can choose to expend, save, or give away. In most cases, however, we believe that we have only limited energy. Thinking this way may lead us to try to hold on to it or try to find ways to obtain more energy from others.

In Figure 2.1, a different circle or ball of energy represents a person. The size of each circle shows the level of their feelings of status power. In most hierarchical systems, each person is supposed to maintain status in the system. If a person's power is threatened, they will likely resist. As such, a change in a person's status is not generally voluntary. Instead, power changes when someone with more power alters the power of one or more members of the system. For example, Chris tells

Figure 2.1 Hierarchical Power Model Conceptualization

Joan, her second-oldest child, that she is "in charge" to watch the younger children while she and the eldest child run an errand. Another example occurs when a boss promotes someone and that person goes from being a worker to supervising her former coworkers. As such, people learn to search their external environment for recognition of power instead of looking within and trusting their own internal belief in their power.

STATUS IN HIERARCHIES

If we want higher status, but we have no support for this increase, we may try to reduce other people's perception of power. Joan, in the previous example, calls her big brother names the next time he is in charge of them because she feels she lost her power. She resents her brother for assuming the power she enjoyed.

In the examples, most families provide ideal models of hierarchies based on imposed status. Children see parents as the two highest spheres of power in the family. The mother and father's status may change depending on the task; the children's status normally depends on birth order, and sometimes gender. Parents impose a new status with the older children at the time of the new child's birth, or with the younger children when the eldest leaves home. A child's sense of internal power may change radically; this is especially true after the birth of a new child. In this case, each child attempts to preserve external perceptions of power and status to other children in the family. These roles may be different depending on family dynamics, but status related to birth order is very common.

As we have seen, hierarchical systems do not encourage individuals to believe in their own power to advance. Instead, it often teaches us to manipulate the power of others to gain perceived power. Thus we feel a gained sense of power when we subvert or undermine the power of others and alter the perception of our power. Consider our current system of politics. We often elect the candidate with the least amount of "mud" instead of the most qualified. In political races, candidates often try to deflect scrutiny by pointing out supposed failings of their opponents.

We can find this mudslinging tactic in many segments of society. A childhood form of mudslinging is namecalling. Our society tends to focus on dichotomies or two-sided splits between good and bad, right and wrong, strong and weak, winning and losing, and we often favor the individual who is less bad, less wrong, or less weak.

Figure 2.2 shows how a person may attempt to climb the hierarchy by usurping or "jumping over" someone above them. We could think

Figure 2.2   Attempts to Gain Power through Undermining and Usurping Others

of it like a race wherein we must overtake someone ahead of us in order to move up in the standings. We base our culture on preserving external perceptions of status power (while internal perceptions may vary depending on the situation). Most people realize that they can affect the power of others very easily. At some level, most of us are aware that if we keep pushing someone's buttons, we will get the reaction we want. We see that others can manipulate our power and so we know it is possible to do the same to them. Yes, you read it correctly; people manipulate your power and you allow it. Sometimes it is almost impossible to avoid our emotional reactions. With this realization, relinquishing power becomes a choice; it is a voluntary act.

Figure 2.3 illustrates an example of subverting or undermining someone's power. Let's say that we have a mutual friend named Fred. Let's also say that you are much closer friends with Fred than I am, but I want to improve my friendship with Fred. So, I invite Fred to come and play cards with me and a few other friends. I feel somewhat rejected when he tells me that he already has plans to eat dinner at your house. This leads me to feel unpopular and that I need more friends. How might I try to gain Fred as my good friend? The first order of business is to lead him to prefer spending time with me to spending it with you. I could choose several ways to set about subverting your power. I might tell Fred that you talk about him behind his back or that you make fun

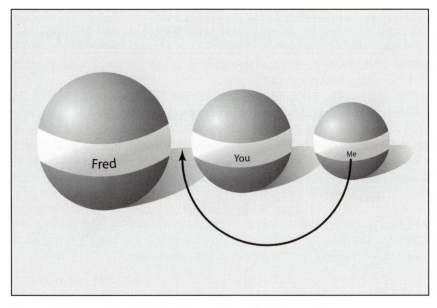

Figure 2.3 Example of Gaining Power through Undermining

of him. In doing so, I might spawn some mistrust toward you and incite him to avoid associating with you. As an added bonus, I could offer to rally to his aid, present myself as his ally, and portray you as a common enemy. In addition, I might do favors for him or otherwise try to make it seem more advantageous to him to be my friend than yours. In doing these things, I try to reduce your power and clear the way to create a situation that makes the odds more favorable for me to have a better friendship with Fred.

I did not gain any personal power in either approach. On the surface, it may seem that if I am successful in my efforts that I increased my power, but I did not. I simply tried to decrease the influence you had with Fred so I could exploit the weakening of his relationship with you and thereby increase my chances of bolstering my friendship with him. In short, I do not need to try to increase my power; I only need to undermine yours. Aside from directing all of my efforts at Fred, I could also approach you and lead you to believe that Fred speaks ill of you or that he may not be a very true friend to you.

The sample hierarchy in the illustration reflects my perceptions, since in the example, I view myself as being disadvantaged, and we are focusing on my vantage point right now. In a sense, it does not matter what you or Fred perceive in this situation, because my reality comes from my perceptions. The success of my scheme depends upon you and

Fred not speaking to each other about what I said. If you and Fred discuss my assertions, you'll likely find that I behave as a manipulative liar, and both of you will probably avoid me. However, due to fear, shame, and possible rejection, you and Fred may not speak to each other and thereby allow my plan to work.

On a brief note, in a hierarchical system, we may sometimes gain power by maintaining the lowest amount of power. A person (or group) may take the role of "victim," in anticipation of being "rescued" or given power by others. I will discuss this point in greater depth later in the book. The key issue to understand for now is that power is an illusion, and there are many ways to manipulate it. In this example with Fred, you, and me, if you catch me at my plan to manipulate, I can play innocent and pretend that I knew nothing about the situation. In doing so, I can make it look as though you were simply trying to make me look bad. Therefore, I look like the weaker party and may "win" Fred's friendship by appearing more honorable than you.

MULTIPLE HIERARCHIES

A person in one hierarchical system may belong to many others as well. The primary hierarchy exists within the family; many people are striving, throughout their lives, to outgrow their perceived status in the family. Hierarchies exist in schools and even in different class subjects at school. A student's place in this hierarchy depends on all the students' perceived abilities in each subject. However, many other aspects enter into the equation. These things include peers, sports, religions and churches, income, level of education, political affiliation and even status within the party, job, or club . . . and the list goes on. Some argue that individuals within a hierarchy struggle to attain power and status to gain recognition and a sense of control.

It seems that most individuals will identify most closely with the hierarchy where they sense the most power or feel the safest, especially if they doubt their abilities to make decisions for themselves. Many times, as children mature and want to express more power, conflict increases between parents and children. At this time, primarily when their children are in their early teens, parents often fear that their child may make unwise choices, and they seek to gain more control over their child. As parents seek more control, their children continue to seek more power. When a child feels that his/her power is ignored in the home, they may steer their energy toward their peer group. Within this group, they feel more powerful, and/or the differences in power in the hierarchy are not as pronounced. Many teens are also able to pool their power together against the common foe, the parents, especially if the parents appear to be abusing their power. In this manner, the child plays the victim role with their peers and describes the parent as being the oppressor. In a peer group, teens can justify their victimization by their parents and defiance of them to each other, and feel understood by their peers. Similar scenarios exist in school and job settings. There are many groups and organizations with hierarchies and sub-hierarchies where the same situations can occur.

We now have a basic understanding of power hierarchies and sub-hierarchies. It may seem that the answer to solving conflict involves eliminating sub-hierarchies and seeking to maintain one hierarchy. First, seeking control of this type often stems from fear of lack of control and fear of losing power or status. Additionally, striving for this type of control will always meet with frustration and resistance; it is within the will of the individual to maximize their personal power.[2]

FEARING THE POWERFUL

In a hierarchical system, sometimes the individual with the highest status power stands to feel the most threatened. Others in the group may fear that the "strongest" group member may abuse their power. Because people fear the strongest person's potential for abuse of power, the group may feel that they have to remain on guard and cut down the power of the highest. A perfect example of this scenario is what happens with the president of the United States. Politics aside, many view the president of the United States as the world's most powerful person. Although a system of checks and balances in our government limits the power of the president, there is still a great deal of fear and mistrust of what he could do. As we all know, fear and mistrust are emotions. We understand this element of human behavior that seeks to maximize personal power, based on a hierarchical power model, and we have seen abuses of power by past world leaders. This combination may cause a sense of fear and mistrust toward political leaders. Additionally, a common perception of politicians is that they hide their true agendas from the public.

We know of many past presidential scandals. Was a leader guilty of wrongdoing? We often do not know; the media and others make assertions and allegations that can include various and sundry proposed and actual illegal actions. The public, however, does not know the whole story. Whether involved in wrongdoing or not, many attempts have been made to disempower these individuals through bringing up their "questionable" actions.

For example, Bill Clinton was the focal point of many scandals during his tenure as president. Was he involved in Whitewater? Did he and

Monica Lewinsky have an affair? His accusers said he avoided the draft and committed several other illegal acts. Regardless of the truth or extent of his involvement in these events, some of his political opponents attempted to disempower him by publicizing these actions.

Some comedians earn a living by making fun of political leaders' flaws and human frailties. We often hold these leaders up to inhuman standards of reproach. This type of humor humanizes and disempowers our leaders. When a leader's credibility is undermined, we lose faith in their vision and guidance. Does the current state of our society deter the most qualified candidates? Many believe that the most qualified presidential candidates will not run; it is felt that they avoid the emotional turmoil associated with the role of being the most powerful. We will look more closely at the power and emotional implications later.

Who benefits if the person at the top of the hierarchy is disempowered? If the "top dog" falls from power, the person in the next position may gain more perceived power. In the earlier example, we looked at why the president must often defend himself from media attacks. The vice president's power may survive the controversy unharmed, if he has kept his political distance. This permits him to be in place to run for the presidency when the president's term is complete. In families, a similar scenario occurs when the parent who asserts more control is the subject of conflict. This situation could allow the other parent to quietly direct and guide. A wise but manipulative individual in this second position could detect this tendency and may use it to his or her advantage. These actions may or may not be in the best interest of those involved; however, the outcome depends upon the situation and their actions.

People often want to become the most powerful person in a hierarchical structure. I ask children, whom I counsel and teach, which position of power they would choose. In their own way, even children want to have the most power. They often feel that they wish no one could tell them what to do. For many of these children, growing up does not change this underlying belief that it is best to be the most powerful. These beliefs commonly become sublimated (placed within the subconscious) but are acted out in people's personal and professional lives.

Many feel that the desire to become powerful feeds the success of capitalism. If we look more closely, such a belief system often promotes abuse of power, corruption and lying. The belief system becomes, "Win at any cost." The belief that the end justifies the means is dangerous to a society. Many empires throughout history fell because of this arrogant attitude, and it may prove to be the downfall of our society, as we know it, if the belief does not change. Although there are many who wish to change their view, they do not feel that there are options. Furthermore, the fear behind changing the belief system is, "If I am not still competing to keep ahead, then I will fall behind, and I cannot afford to fall behind."

LEARNED HELPLESSNESS

What happens if someone feels that he cannot compete or succeed? We looked at a scenario where others may sacrifice their power to gain favor with others. For those, however, who feel stuck at the bottom of the ranks, they may flounder emotionally at the bottom of the hierarchies and can feel like the proverbial whipping boy. These people feel a lack of direction, or fear of change, underlying depression, and often both a fear of failure and a fear of success. These people feel that they will never reach their highest aspirations because the system, by design, will beat them. We call this behavior "learned helplessness."

In the research lab, we can show learned helplessness by repeatedly shocking an animal that has no means of escape. After the animal realizes that it cannot avoid the shock, it gives up and takes the shock, in spite of the pain. Additionally, when the animal can escape (the door to the cage is open), it will not do so. The dog will still lie in its cage and take the shock. This animal does not "play" the victim. The dog does not anticipate outside help and does not believe that it can do anything to rescue itself. Therefore, the dog just gives up.

People in all factions of our society are stuck in a similar learned-helplessness belief system, which limits their learning and growth. It is true we are limited in what we can truly change in our lives. However, if we are a passive captain on a ship sailing nowhere, then we must hold ourselves responsible when our ship remains lost at sea.

An interesting aspect of a hierarchical model of power lies in the fact that there is often much conflict between the two bottom positions. There are two lines of thinking for people in these positions. One is that of trying to gain more power to avoid being last. The other is trying to remain disempowered and remain the victim. When these two groups are struggling with each other, it often allows those higher in the hierarchy to remain unthreatened.

As do most conspiracy theories, this one makes sense as it attempts to divert the attention of the masses away from those with higher levels of status power. Regardless of the truth, which we may never know, it behooves each individual to believe in their own sense of power; only then can we make choices that are in our best interest. While conspiracies do exist, when we surrender energy to them, they can affect our lives more profoundly. Fabricating conspiracy theories often serves a purpose. Inventing such a theory allows the creator to assert his power in a passive-aggressive manner. Fear of losing power or status is often a strong motivating factor for these people. Some in government positions may fabricate conspiracy theories or commit other abuses of power to serve a questionable agenda. However, there are many others whose purpose is to serve the public interest and who behave in a very conscientious and responsible manner.

SUMMARY

You may have surmised from this discussion that I do not believe that a hierarchical model is in the best interest of all; this system often breeds conflict since it implies inequity. If we continue to accept a belief system marked by differing levels of power and status, we fall into playing the power game. This system distracts a person from finding understanding within our world and us. It is in our best interest to question why we are here and what we want from our lives, as well as what life is trying to offer us.

The survival of the hierarchical model of power depends, in part, in belief in scarcity. Yes, many things in our world exist in limited supply. However, it is often not in our best interest to indulge ourselves in possessions. Two reasons people overindulge are to mask their insecurities and/or to assert importance and value.

Often the fear of relinquishing this hierarchical model is due to the fear of anarchy and that those who gain power will abuse it. It is true that if someone has been held in shackles for much of their lives, they may make some unwise choices once released from their chains. The question is, where did the shackles come from?

Yes, by virtue of being human, we will make mistakes, some larger than others. However, it may serve us well to guide and support people in the wake of their mistakes. We should learn from mistakes, rather than withdraw our affection and punish those who make mistakes. After all, what does a child learn when he is spanked for hitting someone else? I believe that he learns that anger and force cause fear in the people it is directed toward and gives power to the person who delivers it. He also learns that someone bigger and older has the power to hit, so when he gets older, he can hit too.

QUESTIONS

1. Can you think of instances when someone abused their power over you? Can you identify some cases where you abused your power over other people? In your journal, jot down your ideas on the reasons why others may have manipulated you with their

power, and the reasons you may have chosen to manipulate others with your power.

2. Have there been times you can identify when you played the role of a victim or gave away your power to gain power from someone else?

3. Can you think of instances in your life when you (and others) would benefit if we all could treat each other as equals instead of vying for more power?

Think about your responses and jot them down in your journal.

3

Equity Power Systems and How They Remove Conflict

By law of nature, all men are equal.
—Domitius Ulpian (170?–228)

TEACHING OBJECTIVES

- Explain equity model of power
- Provide support for value of equity model in reducing conflict
- Discuss the concept of balance in life
- Compare and contrast hierarchical and equity models of power

Without trying too hard, we could probably think of some historical documents that promote the idea of equality for all. Consider the Bible and the Declaration of Independence; both of these documents center on respecting other people. However, people commonly manipulate the words and use them as a source of power.

Wouldn't it be wonderful if we all believed in mutual equality and value? Most people believe that equality is a myth. It would take generations to replace our current power structure with something else. In a hierarchical structure, we must depend upon those with higher levels of status power to make changes in the system; they are the sources that determine laws, norms, and mores; but the desire for change may start at a lower, grassroots level. There are, however, many likely sources to overpower such a rebellion since those in power will not sit by and allow themselves to become disempowered. We can find examples of such uprisings in the civil rights movements of the 1960s, U.S. college student demonstrations against the Vietnam War in the late 1960s and early 1970s, and Tiananmen Square in China in the 1980s.

Changing the power structure poses a challenge. Those with status do not want to surrender it and often fear losing power. But what do they fear? They may not trust the abilities of the people who assume power or they may feel arrogant in their own ability to use power. Some may simply feel that they have a God-given right to power and refuse to relinquish their status. Those at the top of the power system are likely to feel that the system is working in their favor and feel content to keep things as they are; these are only a few of the obstacles. It does not mean, however, that such a change is impossible; it is often wise to point out barriers to success so one can enter into their life change with their eyes open. So if we were to change the structure of the world, how would we do it, and what would we change it to? Anarchy is not the answer. There is a need for organization and structure. If we are to all believe in our strengths and equity, the place to start is within ourselves.

EQUITY SYSTEM OF POWER

The equity system (see Figure 3.1) asserts that from the moment of birth, or before, everyone is equal in power. It goes on to state that people may be equal in power, but we have different particular strengths and weaknesses. In this model, we are not implying that everyone is the same, but that our different abilities, strengths and weaknesses result in balance. If we were to pool all of our abilities together under this model, we would be able to accomplish almost anything that the collective set their intentions and energy toward. In this model, there is room for everyone and all have equitable opportunities to influence the group. I want to acknowledge, here, that some of these ideas parallel some tenets of communism, but I do not mean to assert that a political communism is the answer to our societal power issues.

In the equity system, there are those with the strength of leadership and those who take direction well. There are those who enjoy cleaning up messes and those who are gifted creators, thinkers, and dreamers. Each of these individuals has a valuable place in the world. Believing in our power is a two-way street. First, we must recognize what we have to offer to others and ourselves and be willing to accept what others can offer us. If we look at an example using the blind, we may understand a little more about this model of strengths and weaknesses. If the sense of sight is lost or greatly diminished, the other senses, such as hearing, may become more acute. The increased performance of other senses helps to bring balance for the loss of sight. These enhanced senses enable the blind to appreciate things in this world that those with sight overlook.

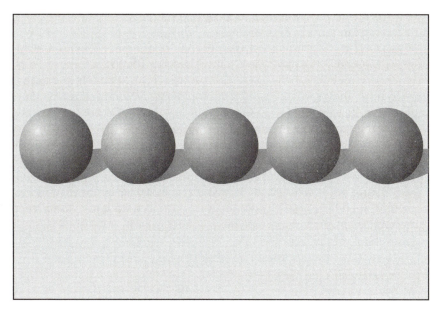

Figure 3.1 Equity System of Power

What does this model say about us as individuals and as a group? We are equal in power, but we must respect the territory or talents of others to maintain the balance of the system. Boundaries must be respected and we must treat people as we want to be treated. For an equity system to exist, each individual must have a sense of self-respect and respect for others. The attitude behind the equity system could be summed up as follows: "I treat people as I want to be treated, because it is in my best interest, and therefore serves the best interest of all." The team grows as its members grow and become self-actualized. Self-actualization is a psychological term that simply means a person (or group) has reached its full potential and has become all that it can be. Within the group, it is important that the members exchange knowledge and ideas and learn from each other. The support of the team is an important resource. As a team member, we come to understand that we do not have to be all things to all people. We may best use our talents and, in turn, learn new skills and abilities from our fellow teammates. We do not focus on failure, but instead, we concentrate on what we can learn from any experience. Additionally, if we believe that our power is equal to that of others, then we are not going to feel the need to usurp or undermine their power; therefore, conflict is decreased.

The theory of an equitable system lends itself to the growth of its members. In this system, there is an understanding of balance in everything. Life events, therefore, are taken from a different point of view. If we believe that our experiences help us grow, then we are less likely to see life as good or bad. Instead, we may see challenges as opportunities that are helping us to see where we need to learn more.

Earlier we looked at examples that involved a fear of failure. Failure is an emotion that tells us that it is time to learn. With this belief system there is less avoidance, because we are less likely to fear the outcome if failure is not bad or wrong. We are not concerned about how others may think of us, because our perception of ourselves rests upon our own interpretation. If we stop worrying about how others view us, we can see the lessons life has to offer without feeling shame, guilt, or inadequacy. When we seek to respect others—and ourselves—we minimize the likelihood of harming others by our actions. If our actions have upset someone, that person will be more likely to express their feelings because they do not fear that we will dislike them for being honest. By sharing their feelings with us, they help us to continue to learn from our experiences.

At this point in the reading, some readers may have doubts, or may think of reasons why such an equity model cannot work. In the face of these new ideas, please try to keep an open mind. It is natural to feel doubtful about new ideas, but do not let this doubt prevent you from giving due consideration to these thoughts. The theory, as it is presented, is an ideal: a purely equitable society. As I mentioned earlier, it would take many years to implement such a system. It is a process of change and growth, of raising children, and changing beliefs from the inside out. In our culture as it is now, purely equitable hierarchies do not exist. While some groups in our society promote hierarchical power models, others promote equality. It should be clear, however, that those groups who promote hierarchical power structures overshadow those who promote equity.

The equitable power system forms the basis for many religions. When we think of notable figures in history, Jesus, Buddha, and Confucius are a few of those that quickly come to mind. The basic teachings of these men involve moderation, balance and order in our lives. To see an example of the equity model, let's think about the criteria for decisions you would need to consider if you were a part of a team of twenty people chosen to start a colony on Mars. This colony would have to function as a self-sustaining society. Obviously, it would not be convenient or feasible to ferry people between the space station and Mars. Therefore, the members of this team would need to have the skills and talents necessary to accomplish all the needed functions. For this colony to survive, what kinds of skills would be required of its members? Certainly there would be a need for a doctor, someone skilled at cultivating food, engineers, a chemist, other scientists . . . and more.

These candidates would also need to be young men and women capable of producing children to perpetuate the colony. In this situation, it may be easier to see that each role is crucial. Although an expert in space horticulture may only have a four-year degree and a doctor has at least eight years of college, there is no need for a doctor, or anyone else, if there is no food to eat—so we cannot say that the doctor is more important than the person responsible for growing food. Likewise, we cannot say that the chemist is more important than the engineer. All of these individuals must accept the fact that they are all crucial. They must also recognize that if they refuse to work as a team and they begin to compete with each other and create conflict, they will all likely die. It is in their best interest to learn from each other and respect the fact that they all have roles that are crucial to the function of this society.

COMPARISONS OF HIERARCHICAL AND EQUITY POWER MODELS

We now have a basic understanding of the two models. Let's look more closely at their similarities and differences. As you read these comparisons, try to relate the ideas to events in your life.

A hierarchical model tends to cause people to fear those with higher levels of power. Fearing power and respecting it have little to do with respecting the person who holds it. By this, I mean that we know, for example, that we are supposed to respect our boss, yet we often try to look for flaws that undermine his/her human qualities. By noticing these flaws, we may feel that we have reduced their power, but are still supposed to respect his status as boss. In an equity system, individuals learn to respect themselves and in turn, they will respect others. There is no need to look for flaws in others, because there is no need to demean them.

"Seek fame, seek recognition and be noticed; these things create power. . . . If everyone notices me, I must be powerful. Therefore, I work harder and harder to seek attention, at any cost. Since I may believe that nothing lasts forever, I have to get what I can when I can get it." This situation helps to create the belief that power is obtained from outside sources, and only outside sources can recognize our power. These types of beliefs and behaviors often lie at the heart of the hierarchical model.

In an equity system, each person gives and takes, proportionally. We may view giving and taking in different ways. For our purposes, let's think of this mutual sharing as a form of cooperation wherein each person has certain skills and knowledge and shares his talents with the others. By teaching and learning, each member of the group gains self-power while increasing the power of the group.

Hierarchical models do not breed trust or respect. The hierarchical system, instead, causes people to feel the need to watch their back to protect their power. In an equity system, each member can trust the others because they share common goals and seek to help and receive help from each other.

People who live in a hierarchical model must struggle to maintain power and live with the fear that a higher-ranking member will attempt to sap power from them. In an equitable model, we do not see others as a source of threat; we see them as a source of strength, learning and support. In this respect, in a hierarchical model, we are more likely to believe that things happen to harm us; in an equity model, we are more likely to believe that things happen in order to teach us.

What about competition? A hierarchical model holds that there can only be one winner and the winner deserves all the power. Therefore, we feel pushed to seek the rewards of winning. Consider the saying, "Winning isn't everything, it's the only thing," and similar expressions that pertain to the importance of winning. Besides team recognition for winning, individual athletes may translate being the best into earning more money.

An equity system, in contrast, promotes the success of the individual and embodies the belief that it is in our best interest to be the best we can become. The motive for growth and excelling is internal, and others who outperform us set our standards. They may become markers for us from the standpoint of teaching us or by letting us see the rewards of practice, commitment, and persistence. Even in an equity model, it is important for members to recognize the achievements of others, but it is most important for each individual to recognize their own achievements, regardless of whether they "win" or "lose."

There has been a movement in children's sports to stop keeping score during games. The idea holds that focusing on personal skills and enjoying the game are far more important than worrying about the outcome of the contest. If the child feels good about playing, learns to function as a team player, makes new friends, gets exercise, improves physical skills and coordination, the child is winning, regardless of which team scores the most points.

It's important that we learn to separate feelings of power and success from the enjoyment of competition. If we associate success only with winning and failure with losing, we deny the experience and learning that take place while playing. A healthy perspective on this matter pertains to the idea that nothing is about failure—it's about success. As long as we find ways to learn and grow, then we succeed.

In regard to financial wealth, a hierarchical system places barriers and obstacles to prevent lower and middle classes from becoming wealthy. In keeping the poor from becoming rich, the fortunes of the powerful remain protected. With an equity model of wealth, all have an equal chance to gain wealth, if they are willing to work for it.

SUMMARY

I often make a distinction between the "golden rules" of each model. The golden rule of the equity model is one that we may have grown up with and probably know well through religious education. It is, "Do unto others as you would have them do unto you." I am sure that most of us have heard this from early ages. Although many of us learned this rule, how many of us actually live it? The "golden rule" of the hierarchical model is, "He who has the gold, makes the rules." While this may seem humorous, it is actually quite a tragedy in our society. Parents, teachers, politicians, countries, and other entities model this rule cross-culturally. We must recognize the truth of the rules. What does our culture want for its future generations? Instead of denying what we indirectly learned over the past millennia of human existence, when will we admit that the destruction and carnage that litter our past are simply not an option for the future?

QUESTIONS

1. Can you identify situations wherein you honestly felt you did your best but somehow failed, or that your good intentions led to an unfavorable outcome? Have you found yourself avoiding tasks or pursuits because you were afraid you might fail?
2. Do you feel that most of your relationships and the systems of power in your life are equitable? Why or why not?
3. Do you feel that it is more important to attain power or to adhere to your standards of morality and ethics?

Take a few moments to note your thoughts and responses to these questions.

4

The Problem with All-or-Nothing Situations

If mankind minus one were of one opinion, and only one person were of the contrary opinion, mankind would be no more justified in silencing that one person than he, if he had the power, would be justified in silencing mankind.

—*John Stuart Mill (1806–1873)*

TEACHING OBJECTIVES

- Provide an understanding of the dichotomous beliefs present in our culture
- Discuss the need in our culture to be good, strong, and right
- Provide exercises to instruct the reader about dichotomies
- Discuss childhood development issues in relation to internalization of societal dichotomies

We've seen the connection between power, emotion, and conflict. Let's look at some other issues that help outline our views on emotions as they pertain to conflict. Throughout our lives, we learn that structure and order make life easier for us. As we try to simplify our lives, we often do this without even thinking about it. For example, if I asked someone to tell me all the words they can think of when I say the word *cat*, they will likely recite a predictable list of nouns or adjectives. In the sample of words that they give me, there are logical relationships to the word cat. Our brain seems to help us out by relating or grouping things. These bonds form as we continue to experience life and make connections between various things. This type of list is what researchers call a spreading activation model of memory. Similar to this example, we tend to relate one emotional or logical association to another. We form these relationships in ways that depend upon how we think about our emotions, how we express them, and our experiences.

To understand the topic of this chapter, we must understand the meaning of the word *dichotomy*. A dichotomy is what we might call a situation when there are only two possible and opposing answers. So, it follows that a dichotomous system affords only two possible choices: true–false, right–wrong, win–lose, good–bad, strong–weak, etc. If a situation is simple and there is a clear "right" or "wrong" answer, dichotomous structures are adequate. How many things in real life are obviously right or wrong? In our lives, others may try to force us to categorize a thought, word, emotion, or deed, or try to make the decision for us. Sometimes it seems that we have no choice but to follow their direction. This chapter covers four major dichotomous structures: Good vs. Bad, Right vs. Wrong, Strong vs. Weak, and Win vs. Lose.

GOOD VERSUS BAD

When we're kids, adults often tell us that we are "good" or "bad." The intention of these words is to indicate approval or disapproval of our behavior at that moment. We come to learn that when our behavior is acceptable, we are good, and when it's not, we're bad; this is one way we begin to categorize feelings as good versus bad.

We miss many chances to teach our children about their emotions. Whether a child is happy, helpful, respectful or obedient, we simply say they are "being good." Although many kids know the differences between emotions, they may not know how to express them. To prove that we describe a child's behavior or feelings as simply good or bad, just ask children. When being punished, kids will often say, "I did a bad thing," or "I was bad." Even if you press to know exactly what they are feeling, they will often repeat, "I feel bad," but it's likely that they feel sad, guilty and/or angry. As they continue to develop, they begin to understand the words for the emotions they feel. We need to remember, however, that even as adults, we often say, "I feel bad" or "depressed," instead of being specific and saying we are feeling sad, fatigued, failure, shame. . . . We seldom take the time to think about the emotions that make up good, bad, or depressed.

Here is a brief exercise to follow:

1. On a piece of paper, make a list of emotions just to see how many different emotions you can generate.

2. Now, after making your list, mark the emotions you would identify as bad. Count the emotions marked as good and those marked
   as bad.
3. Turn to the Appendix in the back of the book and look at the list
   of emotions.
   a. Compare the total number of emotions you wrote down with
      the number of emotions on the list. How many more emotions
      were on the book's list than on your list? (There are 259 emo-
      tions listed in the Appendix of the book.)
   b. Now look through the book's list and count the number of
      emotions you would label as bad.
   c. Subtract the number of "bad" emotions from the total number
      of emotions in the list to figure out the number of emotions you
      would label as good.

QUESTIONS

1. How many more emotions did you label as bad than good?
2. Now think about the times that you may have looked happy or
   laughed when you were getting in trouble. Think about when you
   felt love for someone who did not love you back, or felt proud of
   the artwork you drew on the wall when you were a child and your
   parent did not share your feeling of pride. For each emotion you
   listed as good, you may be able to remember a time that others
   thought it was bad to show it.

When you think of emotions that fall under the heading of "Good"
or "Bad," what comes to mind? Under Good, the list may include:
happy, love, confident, proud, strong, responsible, brave, and humorous. But even in this list, sometimes there are "bad times" to be happy,
confident, proud . . . therefore, these emotions may also be listed under
"Bad." Under Bad, one may list: sad, fear, terror, guilt, shame, doubt,
frustration, failure, confusion, stupid, misunderstood, jealous, envious,
threatened, judged, unloved, inferior, manipulated. . . . Notice that the
list of good feelings is a short list, and most of them could also be seen
as bad, depending upon the situation.

Let's think of all these emotions as different colors. Imagine two
buckets, one labeled "Good," another labeled "Bad." Now we will pour
each emotion (or color) into either bucket, depending on the list you
created, and stir each bucket. When we mix all the colors of the spectrum together, they blend to form black. We wind up with a bucket of
drippy, black emotions with a label that says "Bad." Beside it, we have
a small bucket of "Good" emotions that's virtually empty. While think-

..

 : .

ing about this example, it's easy to see why it is not a good habit to be vague and arbitrary when we think of this colorful assortment of emotions. After all, what is a world without rainbows?

STRONG VERSUS WEAK

Now, let's think about "strong" and "weak." This dichotomy directly relates to our feeling and expression of power. We seldom tell others that we feel strong or weak, but the process normally happens at a subconscious level. As we've already established, our culture is one that believes in being good, strong, and right. We feel that being strong or powerful is good and being weak or powerless is bad. Because of this, it is unavoidable that we evaluate our own perceptions of our emotions, and that of our society, in terms of strong versus weak.

We seldom think about our emotions on a conscious level. We're more likely to muddle through our day without really expressing ourselves to those around us. Behaving this way happens at the direction of our subconscious and learned belief systems. Is the process of self-analyzing our emotions an unnecessary act? Maybe, maybe not. It seems that those who are afraid to examine their emotions in a conscious manner may feel threatened, at some level, by what they may find. We can only run from our emotions for so long. Eventually they find us. So why not accept them with openness and understanding rather than elude, manipulate, and punish them and ourselves?

EXERCISE

1. Before we get too far into this discussion, I would like you to refer back to the Appendix and review the list of emotions. This time, make a list of all the emotions you feel are strong or powerful when others display them toward you. In other words, how powerful does someone look to you when they show, for example, sadness, anger, fear, guilt?
2. Count the emotions and subtract them from the total number of emotions (259). The remaining emotions should be those you would call weak.

We know what we feel is strong or weak in terms of emotions, but the basis for the categories depend upon what society thinks. It is common for a person to discard personal perceptions when conflict arises. We normally push our thoughts aside in favor of what we feel society prefers. This often happens because we sense the power associated with emotion, and we feel that others will judge us. It's important to understand this situation and why it happens. In a situation that involves conflict, we seem to abandon our belief system and revert to one that we feel suits the expectations of those around us. Once again, one part of us has a set of goals and values, but we may resort to a response set that surprises us when we feel threatened or pressed.

There is a logical side to the expression of emotions. That is, if I experience or express emotions, will I appear "good," "bad," "strong," or "weak"? If there is a good chance that I will look bad or weak, I may avoid expressing my emotions. We can think of this as a game of odds. If we feel the odds favor us looking strong, brave or good for the feelings we share, we'll share them. If the odds are against us, we're apt to keep our thoughts to ourselves. This probability approach is appealing to those who take a logical or rational approach to life.

Think about this model. It shows the connection between potential conflict, emotions, and power. If we use this model, maybe we can find an explanation for why men tend to withhold emotions. Most cultures instill the idea in their young men that they are the more powerful of the two sexes. If they grow up believing that they have power because they are male, they may avoid displays of emotions that could appear weak or cost them some power. Most cultures accept—and even expect—women to behave more emotionally than men do.

What about emotions when we're at work? Bosses normally don't like to see displays of emotion in the workplace, unless it's enthusiasm. Our boss may say it is "unprofessional" or "improper" to display emotions at work. However, why are we really supposed to avoid emotional expressions at work? There could be many answers. It is often true that strong emotional reactions damage decision-making skills. It follows that employees who make decisions based upon emotion will use improper reasoning to make decisions; this is bad for the business. Think of how we feel if we go into a bank and the teller has just had a fight with her husband and is rude in her dealings with the public. Even worse, what if a police officer has a tiff with his wife before going to work and decides to vent his anger on the first speeder he catches that day? In these cases, people will likely suffer the wrath of undeserved or misplaced anger.

Logic does not involve feeling. There are emotions that we use to defend ourselves that don't appear to involve feeling. The purpose of these emotions is, in part, to help us preserve our sense of power. Some of these emotions include flippancy and defiance, and several others. We'll spend more time on these emotions later.

RIGHT VERSUS WRONG

People often fight over the notion of being right. We must ask ourselves what "right" means, and why I must feel like I'm right. Many times the answer is, "Because I don't want to feel wrong." When involved in an argument, admitting fault means admitting to being wrong. Admitting to being wrong arouses the fear of losing power. Just as we are reluctant to admit to being wrong, we also avoid admitting our rival is right. Seeing our opponent's point of view may make us feel wrong, stupid, or weak. At this point, the dispute becomes more about saving face (or similarly, power) and less about objectivity.

In the course of growing up, the struggle over right versus wrong happens many times between parents and children. I believe that we begin to learn our perceptions about right and wrong through these conflicts. In many of the conflicts between parent and child, the parent is not willing to listen to the child's point of view. Even if the child has a valid point, the parent will commonly dismiss the point for fear of losing face. Therefore, as we saw earlier, we find that the conflict turns into an issue of maintaining power instead of what is right or wrong.

Once again, we may want to look to cultural teaching about our use of language. Think about the most common words used to judge a child's actions. The words "right" and "wrong" likely overshadow all others. When our parents said, "That was wrong," it led us to feel certain emotions. When they said, "You're right!" we felt happy, intelligent, confident, and powerful. When they said, "You're wrong!" we felt sad, stupid, disappointed and a sense of failure.

Since we learn from our experiences, hearing that we are wrong often deters us from taking chances in the future. If we feel punished by negative evaluations, we become less likely to take chances. Why don't many students like to raise their hands during class when the teacher asks a question? The association between "wrong" and punishment causes an individual to want to feel "right." Simply put, this belief system says, "'Right' is good and 'wrong' is bad. So as long as I'm right, there's no need to feel those negative emotions that come with being wrong." When people feel evaluated or judged they often feel fear, stupidity, worthlessness, shame, and failure, which often shuts down a person's creativity. This principle harks back to the old adage, "It's better to keep your mouth shut and have people think you're a fool than to open your mouth and prove them right."

People usually develop one of two major approaches in response to feeling that they are wrong. The first approach is what I call "I'd rather not play the game at all than play the game and lose." The other approach is "I'm going play the game until I win or until no one wants to play with me." Some of these traits may be genetic as well as learned—to what extent is unclear. But we know there are many ways that the environment reinforces these types of behaviors. The first statement may come from a person who feels weak and feels powerless, and has experienced a state of learned helplessness. The second statement is typical of a person who comes across as powerful or even arrogant, but internally feels weak and misunderstood. The difference in these two people lies in how they want society to view them. Their outward attitudes may be different, but their feeling about themselves is likely to be similar. When interacting with each individual, there are different ways to communicate with him or her to reach a mutually beneficial outcome.

When lecturing to groups, I like to ask, "How many ways can a person clean dishes?" The audience will come up with the answers you'd expect: hot soapy water in the sink or with a dishwasher. Some people even suggest avoiding the whole matter by throwing the dirty dishes away or using paper plates. However, there are many other ways to wash dishes, such as in a lake, hosing them off in the yard, in the shower, or out in the rain. In generating a list of ideas for many things in life, we often do not explore all of our options. We sense a "right way" of doing dishes, and that's that. Washing dishes in a lake may sound silly if you're at home. If, however, you're camping, it may be the most logical option. Furthermore, the best way to approach a task or problem may depend upon the situation.

By thinking about how many ways you can wash your dishes, I hope you realize that the way we normally do it is only one way. It's true, we are creatures of habit. Therefore, we often do the same things, the same way, without exploring other solutions to problems. We want to pass our "right" ways along to our children so they may benefit from our learning. In doing this, however, though we may have the best intentions at heart, we eliminate all the other ways to go about doing something and discount them as not being "right." Children may want to do things differently than their parents do. In this case, a child may feel that his parents ignore his power because he tried to do things differently. The child may seek other ways to express power, especially toward his parents. This is the core of various continual conflicts between parent and child.

Many people fight many battles over being right or wrong. These battles often boil down to "survival of the fittest." We hear this phrase and take it to mean that only the strong survive, and being "right" helps us appear strong and powerful. We've all heard children having a dispute; the object is to outlast the opponent. The logic is that if Billy can say, "It is too," more times than Joe can say, "Is not," then Billy is right and wins the argument. In the end, whether we won the conflict or only outlasted our opponent, no one's mind has changed. The argument dies, and both parties walk away feeling frustrated and irritated.

It seems that we don't know how to resolve disagreements when both parties are claiming to be right. So, we resort to fighting because we don't know how else to settle the matter. If we prove we are correct, we protect emotions such as ignorance, guilt, shame, failure and stupidity. When such a conflict occurs, it may be in our best interest to ask ourselves, "What am I protecting?" In most conflicts, both sides offer smatterings of truth in what they express. However, both parties refuse to see the other's side of things. This refusal takes us back to the win-lose aspect of conflict. In other words, you aren't right unless I say you're right and you don't win unless I say you win. And if one combatant allows the other to win, by default, he loses.

If we remove the need for winning or losing in our dealings with other people, we may find that these aspects aren't important. It is far more important to ask ourselves what we want from our communication. Most people don't search for an argument, yelling match, or physical conflict. Why, then, does this happen so often? As I mentioned earlier, we are probably trying to force our viewpoint onto someone else. Remember, though, that failure to agree and failure to understand are not the same things.

Let's return to our example of the "best way" to wash dishes. Remember, we said that the "best" way of doing something may depend upon the situation. We can try to do what is in our best interest, and that of those around us. On the other hand, we can continue to worry about doing things the right or wrong way. What sounds more reasonable?

Consider the following example as it pertains to rituals and traditions that we never stop to rationalize. Greg and Marion get married and, shortly thereafter, she decides to make a nice meal that includes baked ham. Greg stands in the kitchen, chatting with her as she cuts both ends off the ham, puts the ham in a pan and then slides it into the oven. Greg asks why she cut the ends off the ham. Marion tells him that her grandmother always does this, and her grandmother is the best cook she knows. He tells her he's never seen that done before, but she assures him that it's common practice.

Nevertheless, she becomes curious and decides to call her grandmother and ask her. Her grandmother tells her she always cut the ends off the ham because the hams she bought were always too big for her baking pan. In this little story, as you see, we introduce the notion of adults influencing children (or grandchildren) into blindly doing things without knowing why and defending the things they do without even knowing why they do them. How do we act in our best interest? We serve our best interest by adapting our ways of doing things to the situation at hand. Do you remember the lists of "rights" and "wrongs" we made earlier? That list is what we often try to use to determine our behavior. But we often find ourselves confronted with a situation with no clear answer.

Let us use an extreme example. We learn not to kill other people. If we think of this in terms of a dichotomy, killing is wrong and, therefore, not right. Does this still hold true if the person in question points a gun at you and seems to be ready to pull the trigger? Should you wait for them to pull the trigger if a means of protection exists? If we protect ourselves, however, with any means possible, the other person may die. Still, we learned that killing another person is wrong. Logic and learning do not fit together in this situation. There is likely no right way to resolve this scenario. Sadly, there are many different kill-or-be-killed situations that we could debate on many moral, instinctive, logical, and practical levels. However, that would require another book.

If we think of what is in our best interest and the best interest of others, we can see many different options. Answers may vary, depending upon the context. Sometimes, our best choice serves our best interest. Other times, our best choice may involve what's best for someone else, and sometimes we may find a solution that benefits both. This best interest approach to problem solving allows us to draw upon our learning and combine it with a given situation, thereby allowing us to determine what to do. In our example, we are staring down the barrel of a gun and have the means to protect ourselves. What do we do? If we remember that killing is wrong and fear making the wrong choice, we may allow them to shoot. If we want to live, we may try to run or elude them in some manner. But what if this person has vowed to kill my entire family whether I survive or not? I have to consider not only my survival but also the survival of those whom I love. This complicates the scenario, and there are many social, religious, and political issues to consider; however, when someone is pointing a gun at you, there's no time to mull through all of these issues. When confronted with surviving, killing the assailant may save more lives than the one it cost.

Now I would like you to imagine the scenario if the gunman's only intent was to try to kill you, not your family. Would your answer change? Some people may say yes; perhaps because they fear living with the guilt afterward. However, what is the value of your life to you? It may be wise to consider your view of your personal power. Regardless of the choice you felt you would make in this scenario, we would likely never know unless the situation arose.

The point of the discussion was to think of other ways to approach a difficult problem instead of using our learned sense of right and wrong. Right versus wrong is not always clear-cut and does not teach us how to solve problems. Parents should ask themselves, "Do I want to give my children all the answers in life? Or do I want them to learn how to find them?" If you want to give them the answers, you are likely teaching them to depend on others for guidance and not trust themselves. If you want to teach them how to find the answers, you are likely teaching them to listen within and know when to ask for help.

WIN VERSUS LOSE

The dichotomy of win versus lose is perhaps the way that we look to measure the sum total of our life's success. It is the ultimate dichotomy in that we evaluate the outcome of our life experiences as to whether we feel like a winner or a loser. The other three dichotomies are employed to gauge our response, but win/lose is used to measure the outcome. Remember that if we look good, strong and right, we win! We often feel pressure, directly and indirectly, to win, and it permeates our culture, especially, though not only, in sports and politics. Who are the individuals and teams remembered by posterity? The winners. Think of political races. Even when a candidate is being soundly defeated in a race, it is undesirable to admit defeat. Those around us may teach us to do anything to win. "Win at any cost," "winner takes all," "may the best man win" and "second place is first loser" are just a few phrases that point to our emphasis on winning.

It seems that we measure the success of our life by totaling our perceived wins and losses. Since no one wants to appear or feel like a loser, we may color our perception of an event so that it fits with what we want to see. Even if a child received a beating in a fistfight, they will often mention the one punch they got in rather than admit a loss. Losing means failing and weakness, and we all know that others see this as bad, wrong, and weak. It's a matter of wanting to avoid looking like a loser instead of creating the perception that we're a winner, in this case. In the world of dichotomies, however, we are one or the other.

What does it mean to win? Is it having the most points at the end of the game, the most votes at the end of the election, the most land at the end of the war, making the most biting comments during an argument? What have we gained from this? Recognition? Power? Respect? What if we cheated to win? Is that a matter of feeling proud about our success and accomplishments, or are we looking to others to give us power? Who judges or decides who the winners are? Parents? Teachers? Referees? Judges? In most situations, other people decide who wins. In our culture, winning has less to do with how we feel about ourselves, and more to do with what other people think of us. We learn to gain recognition by winning, even at an early age. We are noticed when we do things well. Family members cheer for our success whether we make a goal or make an "A," and we don't get this positive attention when we don't win. It just continues to grow from there. Think of the widespread cheating that goes on in our education system.

The purpose of an education is to gain knowledge that prepares us for life. The more prepared we are in life, then the better chance we have to win in life. However, in many ways, our education system focuses on grades instead of educating. Grades are supposed to be an indication of what we have learned in school. If that is the case, however, consider why there seems to be a need for classes specifically aimed at helping students achieve higher scores on standardized tests. There are classes to prepare students for the ACT, SAT, GRE, LSAT, GMAT, and so on. It's a bit like studying for an I.Q. test and then professing to be more intelligent after receiving a higher score than when you previously took it. The intent of these tests is to gain a measure of aptitude and general knowledge. That aspect, however, has been lost and these assessments of skills are flawed. Getting higher grades through any means possible is how you win the game in school. I know countless stories of parents doing their child's homework or science projects to help the child get a better grade. The pressure for many is that, if I don't do well in this effort, then I will be left behind. Whether the goal is to win or not lose, this dangerous pattern continues to spiral out of control.

The next issue to address in our cultural view of winning is that people cannot admit to cheating because that looks bad, wrong and weak. Even if caught in the act of some misdeed, they have to provide excuses for their behaviors so that they can at least try to look good, and with enough justification and manipulation, they may appear to be right. Why do lawyers make so much money? Fear. Fear of looking bad, fear of appearing weak, or fear of being called a loser. We pay good money to purchase an ally, one who will present us as a good and right person who is not at fault in a legal matter.

How we look at winning affects the way we look at life. Consider the many times I play games with my child clients. I often play checkers (and I hate to lose . . . I grew up in this culture, after all). Those kids know that I am playing my best every time. So, if they win, they know that they beat me at my best. But if I won, they know that they lost to my best. Regardless of whether they get upset (and there are many who will get upset and pout, cry, or show anger), we talk about the process. Did they learn something? Did they make a mistake? Did they have fun playing? Did they feel like they had to cheat to win? In this process, I feel that it is more important to learn from losing than it is to win.

How many more times in our life do we lose (by society's definition) than win? Any time we commit to try something, we take the chance that we may not succeed. If we feel that we will not succeed, or win, then that may affect the effort we invest. How many times have you avoided trying your hardest at something because you didn't want to feel that you tried your hardest and still failed? Self-sabotage is common in our culture, and we do this to avoid the emotion. Thus, even if we don't win, we know we didn't try our best, so we can give ourselves a break. As was stated before, a life approach I see, as I call it, is that I'd rather not play the game at all than play the game and lose. If we don't try, then we don't fail and we don't lose. But how much do we miss out in life because we fear the loss? Our act of not trying is more about the emotions we are afraid to feel (shame, failure, insecurity, worthlessness) than about our ability.

I would hope to promote the idea that winning is a process, not an outcome. Winning relates to how we carry ourselves through an experience; it is in what we learn, and how we grow from an event. As individuals, I hope that we decide to consider how we see ourselves as winners or losers, and not allow others to hang such labels on us. We decide to feel like a winner or loser.

SUMMARY

In this chapter, we explored four major dichotomies that strongly influence our lives and the lives of others in our culture. I hope that this discussion enables you to see the issues that affect us every day. When we see these issues, we can begin to make conscious decisions as to how we want to live our lives. Each dichotomy aids in understanding our world and our development of a social view. However, any viewpoint, if taken to the extreme, becomes meaningless.

QUESTIONS

1. Which dichotomy do you feel most strongly motivates you, overall?
2. Can you think of situations where your most influential dichotomy varies, depending upon the situation?
3. Can you see how various dichotomies influence other people?

5

The Players

When you prevent me from doing anything I want to do, that is persecution; but when I prevent you from doing anything you want to do, that is law, order, and morals.

—*George Bernard Shaw*

LEARNING OBJECTIVES

- Provide a framework for understanding Victim, Persecutor, Rescuer and Instigator
- Explain the nature of each role
- Provide examples of how each role is played
- Illustrate the changing role of Instigator

I remember first reading about the victim, persecutor, and rescuer (I use the abbreviation: "V-P-R") in *Born to Win*.[3] This was a best-selling book from the sixties, and I read it in the eighties as I began my major in psychology. This book gave me a flavor of self-help books and of the field of psychology. Just as with many other things I read, I put this knowledge aside, and it became one piece of data that I mixed in with all of the subsequent learning through my undergraduate and graduate education. As I continued to evolve as a clinician and to practice in my field, I began to formulate the theories presented on conflict and power. These theories developed and solidified, and I remembered the information presented by *Born to Win* on this commonly occurring, yet seldom-recognized triad. I also realized the importance of this triad in helping people to understand the roles that they often played in terms of power and the factors that contribute to and maintain conflict. In addition, as I looked at power issues and the dynamics of conflict, I realized the importance and prevalence of the fourth role that I added to this discussion: Instigator (or the "I" in this group). The dynamics of these four roles are crucial in understanding facets of the hierarchical model of power. My brief exposure to the V-P-R triad, years ago, reminded me that sometimes it takes a while for the pieces of the puzzle to fit together.

In this chapter, I will define each role in this V-P-R-I "quadrad" and the features that characterize each role. I will also provide a more detailed discussion of each role and provide examples of each. Regarding the instigator, this role has not been discussed in depth to my knowledge. Therefore, it is important to discuss fully how the instigator can play the victim, persecutor, or rescuer while they are also playing their respective role. The most important fact to remember through this discussion is that in our lives, we all have played each of these roles, whether we realize it or not.

As we enter into this discussion, please understand that I want to look at all sides of each issue. Some of these issues can create emotional reactions when we see others or ourselves in those roles. Emotions often flare when talking about sensitive issues such as victims and who is responsible for their actions.[4] We are supposed to feel sorry for the victim and we do not want to do anything to harm them further. We have to consider how our society views these roles relative to a deeper truth. The underlying goal of this discussion is for each person to look at ways they can take responsibility for their actions and see what part they played in the process, no matter how minor. While painful things can happen in our lives, feeling like a victim is a state of mind, not a reality.

Figure 5.1 is a visual representation of the roles in the V-P-R-I quadrad. Notice that we can view them in a hierarchical model. These will become clearer as you read on, so please refer back to this often. As you may realize, the victim would have the least amount of perceived power and therefore would be the smallest circle. The persecutor would be any circle larger than the victim would, but the rescuer has to have more perceived power than the persecutor; otherwise, they would not be able to rescue the victim from the persecutor. The instigator could play any role, as you will see.

VICTIM

The victim is the person in the quadrad who feels harmed or negatively affected by another person. They may feel controlled, manipu-

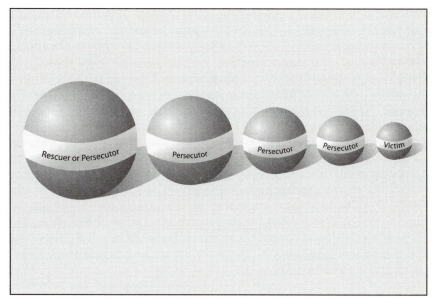

Note: Instigator can play any role.

Figure 5.1 Levels of Power for Victim, Persecutor, and Rescuer

lated, cheated, physically or emotionally hurt, abandoned, slighted or any other emotion that they feel disempowers them. There are a series of steps to consider when someone feels like or plays the victim.

- In order to play the victim, they have to believe that something negative, that was beyond their control, happened to them.
- If they could not control their circumstance, then they do not have to feel responsible, guilt, shame, blame, or failure, because they were faultless in the matter.
- If they did something to cause their circumstance, then they can no longer be a victim.
- If they feel many of these emotions, then they feel that they are off the hook for having to change anything. It is the person who caused the pain who has to change.

The important feature of the victim role is that in order to play the victim, they have to surrender their power.[5] It is because of this surrendering of power that they do not have to feel responsible. It is also important for the victim to feel that they did nothing bad or wrong (who would want to rescue someone who was not innocent?). Instead, they choose to feel weaker in some way than the person who caused the harm, whether they recognize it or not.

Undoubtedly, many people fall prey to our hierarchical world. People's lives are affected every day by unscrupulous, cruel, and even careless or thoughtless people, and those affected (the victims) had nothing to do with the events other than being in the wrong place at the wrong time. Victimization does not discriminate with regard to age, gender, race, or religion. Ironically, sometimes the person playing the victim also preys upon those trying to help. I've read about a scam wherein a person parks their car on the side of the road and pretends to have car trouble. When a good Samaritan shows up to help, this stranded motorist attacks and/or robs the person who tried to help.

The idea that I want to present is that by labeling people as victims, we are interpreting them in a way that can potentially affect the way they act and can impact whether or not they heal from this experience and how they experience the rest of their lives. Feeling labeled as the victim by others sometimes leads a person to continue to hold onto that label because they feel empowered by receiving care from others. This power can become very addictive, but is it productive?

Labeling a person as a victim can also negatively affect a person's life, such as a parent who received abuse as a child. I will make an example of a woman whom I will call Peggy. During her abusive childhood, the state protective services took Peggy into custody. Peggy heard people say she was a victim because of her abusive parents. Because of that labeling, people tended to ignore her disruptive actions and behaviors. Peggy came to expect that whenever life got tough, someone would come take care of her and fix everything as nothing was her fault. As Peggy got older, she found relationship after relationship where a person would take care of her, but when Peggy did not get what she wanted, she would feel angry, sometimes even violent, and blame the other person. When she was a young adult, Peggy had a child, expecting this child to fill the empty space inside her that was there because of the lack of love she experienced as a child. As Peggy's daughter grew older, she misbehaved. Peggy's inability to know how to parent productively fueled her daughter's bad behavior.

When Peggy's daughter misbehaved, Peggy blamed her and called her horrible names. Eventually, Peggy felt so helpless that she resorted to violence to control her child. Peggy's daughter came to feel very angry and started taking her anger out on others. Peggy spoke of her "devil child" to friends and family, and the family often replied that her daughter just needed a good whipping. They never asked how Peggy might have contributed to the problem, and Peggy even played the victim to her daughter's behavior. When the daughter went to school one day, the teacher saw bruises on her, and reported that her mother had inflicted these. State authorities took her daughter into custody and labeled her the victim. They arrested Peggy, but she blamed the child. The police, the court, and most others saw Peggy as a horrible person who refused to take responsibility for her actions. The pattern started all over again.

Remember the dichotomies (good/bad, right/wrong . . .)? We need to consider how the victim needs to be seen by others to continue to play the role. Would a victim more likely want others to see them as good or bad, right or wrong, strong or weak? We already know that the victim feels weak or presents themselves as weak, which is why they choose the role of victim. They would not want others to see them as bad, because few people want to take care of a bad person; therefore, it is important for them to appear good. In addition, they would not want to appear wrong, because others generally do not want to support a person or cause that they view as wrong. Therefore, they have to be right. If they were wrong, then they would have to accept responsibility. In order to find protection or rescue, the victim has to appear good and right, but weak. These characteristics have to be maintained throughout the period that the person is seen as the victim, and often the victim will do whatever they can to maintain these dynamics, including lying, cheating and manipulating.

In this discussion, remember that we are not often looking at the truth of the situation as we define the victim; we must look at the perception of the person who plays the victim role. Think of Bobby, who comes to his father crying and saying that Jeff, his big brother, pushed him down. When the father asks Bobby if he did anything to cause it, Bobby says that he was just riding his bike when Jeff came up and pushed him down for no reason. At this point, Bobby has surrendered his power to Jeff. He did this by portraying himself as helpless to stop the attack that he did nothing to cause. Additionally, the attack was committed by someone older, bigger, and stronger than he is. At this point, Bobby has chosen to go to someone with more authority, their father, in hopes that he will fight this battle for him. In the unraveling of the story, their father finds out from Jeff and his friends that the "victim" had been riding his bike through the middle of Jeff's basketball game. When they asked Bobby to stop, he would not. Additionally, Bobby tried to run over Jeff, and Jeff had pushed him to avoid being hit by Bobby's bike.

The point of the example is that the person claiming to be the victim was not as innocent as he portrayed himself to be, and he left out some important information to avoid blame and thereby avoid feeling guilt, shame, responsibility, and failure. Bobby did not want to appear bad or wrong in his father's eyes, so he did not tell the whole story. Still, why did Bobby do what he did? It is likely that he was trying to challenge his brother's power; he may have felt excluded from the basketball game, or he may have wanted to undermine his brother's power in front of others.

If we look at our culture, it is apparent that we almost encourage victims. Victims are supposed to get pity and attention. Someone is supposed to take care of them and rescue them or bail them out. What rewards do we get when we rescue a victim? What rewards does the victim receive from playing the role?

Lawyers' commercials often seek out victims. They sell the point that victims can seek compensation for something unjust that happened to them. Beyond that, there is often an underlying message that victims who take legal action may quickly become rich. In reality, however, these lawyers often stand to gain as much or more compensation than the victim, if it turns out that a settlement occurs. In this sense, the lawyer claiming to be an ally to the victim may actually re-victimize the client. In my work, I find that many people hold onto an incredible amount of anger, hatred, and rage toward those whom they feel harmed them. I believe this happens because their power is still surrendered to this person. In many situations, I see parents portray their children as victims of the school system, of their peers, and of their disorders. Issues such as A.D.D., learning disabilities, and/or physical or mental handi-caps are often convenient claims to justify a child's problems in school. Children often notice this label and continue to try to play this role throughout their life. Whether it is the school system, a parent, a peer, a boss, a spouse or even their child, someone who consistently plays a victim will always find someone to blame so they can justify their actions and seek someone to care for them.

What happens when someone justifiably feels victimized? He or she likely feels many "negative" feelings. At this point, the victim has a few choices of how to respond. The degree to which they feel victimized depends upon whether or not they feel that they can fight back. If someone feels like they cannot get even with the person who harmed them, or get them to take responsibility for their actions, then that inequity often contributes to a feeling of victimization.

For an example on the dynamics of victimization, let's consider Jane. Jane said she visited a large corporate chain that sold food. Jane went on to say that she bought some food and took a bite. Jane then realized that there were cockroaches in her food and that she may have swal-lowed some of them. Obviously, Jane was disgusted by this situation and felt sickened by the very thought of what she had just eaten. She notified the manager, but he did not seem to want to help her, and she felt rebuffed. After this episode, Jane said that she had a hard time eating because she felt nauseated and gagged whenever she tried to eat. By her account, she seemed to feel that the ill effects of this event continued to worsen and disrupted her ability to eat. Therefore, Jane contacted a large law firm and they took on the case. She told me that this case could have financial implications amounting to millions of dollars.

There are many areas to address in this example.

Variable 1: I cannot say whether there was a bug in her food. If there was, I have no way of knowing whether there was one or "many," as she said. Victims often exaggerate their situation to try to get more help or support. This also helps them to continue to play the victim role, since the victim comes to believe these exaggerations, and it can become part of their memory. I think that we have all done this at some time or another. It is possible that there were more than one or two bugs in the food, but she may have added a few bugs to the story.

Variable 2: Another variable was her reaction to the experience. In some countries, people think nothing of eating a few bugs, but because she did not expect this little surprise ingredient in her food, and Jane does not view bugs as appetizing, she felt that this was a very negative experience. In this variable, we must remember that how a person interprets the event will determine whether they feel victimized.

Variable 3: Another important variable is how others responded to the incident. Since she felt that the manager offered no help or support, she felt disrespected and possibly humiliated. The manager may have tried to be very helpful to her, but if she wanted to play the victim to reap the rewards, she would not want his help. If the manager refused to take an interest in her problem, then Jane did not feel safe or supported. It is likely that the legal matter was pointless and avoidable through better customer service. In our culture, lawyers often tell people never to apologize or accept responsibility for things that may happen because that could be harmful if a case goes to court. However, these matters are often avoidable if people accept responsibility at the time.

Variable 4: Jane's history of feeling victimized. As we have discussed, people tend to carry their past with them. Their past can influence how they interpret the present. It is unlikely that someone purposely caught some bugs and put them in her food. It follows that it's even less likely that someone targeted her for this buggy food. However, if she feels that she has a history of falling victim to other people, or that she's a pushover, then it is likely that her pent-up anger and rage may have come out in this situation. Therefore, she would not admit this because it might compromise her case. Often a victim will minimize past experiences that may contribute to their current sense of victimization. Why? Because they cannot feel that they have influenced the situation; that would dilute their ability to play the role. Remember, they did not do anything to cause the situation—it happened *to* them.

Variable 5: Other people's interpretation of the event is crucial to playing the role of a victim. Sometimes, people do not feel like a victim until other people tell them that they should. Think about a little kid who falls down. After he falls, he looks around to see how others react. If his parents rush over to pick him up, he learns that something horrible happened and plays to the concern that he receives. In the same circumstance, if no one notices the fall, or if they are unconcerned, he will likely get up and go play again. It is possible that Jane went home after this event and felt mildly upset, but when she talked to friends and family, they indicated that she should feel horrified, and that the business should pay for their negligence. Furthermore, her lawyer more than likely fed into this belief system.

Variable 6: What is the payoff for the victim? At the time that this person came to my office, a woman was suing McDonald's for an outrageous amount of money after she spilled hot coffee in her lap while driving. The victim often has to hang on to their victimization, until they get their payoff. When I talked to Jane, I asked her what would happen if we were able to help her feel better before the trial. In many situations such as hers, when we work on these issues related to a specific event, there can be a quick recovery. If she did recover, no matter what had really happened, it is likely that a judge or jury would not see her as seriously wounded from this event, which would affect what they might award her. When I asked this question, I encountered resistance from Jane; she became a bit defiant, and did not return for another session. In her mind, I believe she had to maintain her role as the victim until she got her payoff. Even after this, sometimes people feel guilty about getting a payoff and maintain their perceptions, symptoms, pains long after the supposed resolution of the event.

Variable 7: Many victims want the person that hurt them to pay dearly for what they did. The feeling of the victim may be, "The longer I experience the pain of being the victim, the more that person should be punished." This belief can also result in resistance to healing. In physically abused people, I often see this resistance to healing, because many times, they feel that their abuser got away with what they did, and they want their abuser to hurt as much as they did. They often miss the fact that it is likely that the person who abused them was also abused at some time. If Jane wanted these people to pay for what they did and did not want them to forget it, then she might hold onto her symptoms for a long, long time.

Variable 8: How much do you love me? Many times a person not only feels victimized by the persecutor, but they feel victimized by the rescuer. In our example, the lawyer and legal system become Jane's rescuer. Let's also suppose that Jane never felt very important in her past and constantly questions how much people love or support her. As a result, she tests the people around her to see how much they love her and will protect her. Depending on the outcome of the trial, she may feel rejected by the judge and/or jury, as well as by her lawyer, if she feels that they did not take care of her (to the tune of a few million dollars). This can result in a "revictimization" if she feels that those charged with her care failed her. This revictimization can sometimes feel more severe than the initial event, because they feel that no one really loves them or wants them. I see this circumstance happening in rape and abuse cases when a rapist or abuser is found not guilty or let go due to a lack of evidence. The scars of this can run deep in a victim. This sometimes explains why people may not pursue a trial in these cases.

Variable 9: Who is the victim? In this example, some may perceive Jane as the victim after she ate this food with cockroaches in it. Some may say the business being sued for millions is the victim; some may even say that the judicial system getting bogged down with such cases is the victim. In some cases, businesses do not keep their kitchens clean and such negligence can harm their customers, and the customers, as a group, can become the victims.

In our hierarchical society, we see much evidence that money talks. However, let's entertain the idea that Jane is not being honest. Jane wants to make money in the same way others got rich from spilling a hot cup of coffee and getting burned. It is possible that she took a bite of her cake, planted a few bugs in it and then cried wolf. She then finds any number of lawyers willing to represent her and gains their support. She finds someone (a doctor) who will support her pain and advance her case so that she can get rich quickly. If we view the situation in this way, the large corporation becomes a victim. Additionally, the victims are the consumers who pay higher prices, the duped legal system, the jurors who lost time from their work and families, and the list goes on. We often cannot quantify the victims, nor should we.

I do not know the outcome of this trial, and it is not important. When I was asked to provide my observations about Jane, I gave my impressions in a letter, and was not contacted again. As I said before, many people heinously cause harm to people, and they should take responsibility for their actions. Our disciplinary systems are in place to assist this. My hope is for the victim to realize that it is a choice for them to feel what they feel and to choose to find their power again.

PERSECUTOR

The persecutor is the person who negatively affects the victim's power. The persecutor's action can be as small as humming a tune which annoys someone else, or something as large as murder. The persecutor's goal is often to decrease the power of or take the power away from someone else (the victim). In almost all situations, the only reason that the persecutor wants to affect the victim's power is that, at some level, they feel a sense of powerlessness within themselves. Therefore, it is likely that the persecutor has felt like a victim at some point in their life, and more often than not, they have felt like a victim many times. However, they become the persecutor because they feel shame about feeling weakness and hide this weakness in their ability to push others around.

Persecutors can come in many forms. They can be the bully on the playground, older siblings, a neighbor, teacher, spouse, boss, co-worker. . . . Almost anyone anywhere can become a persecutor. As I have said, all of us have been persecutors at some time or another. The key feature is that, for some reason, we tried to affect someone else's power in a negative way. These actions still constitute persecution even if our actions represent retaliation for some misdeed that befell us. Often, when siblings snipe back at each other, the conflict grows to the point that one or both get hurt. Both may feel like victims, but both are behaving like persecutors.

There is an interesting twist in the issue of retaliation when a "victim" fights back at a "persecutor." Like a cornered animal, people tend to fight back when they feel that there is no other way out, and they do not want to hand over their power to a rescuer. When they do fight back, they could be perceived by others as a persecutor (remember Jeff in the initial example in the chapter). I call the retaliating victim a "Justified Persecutor." Justified persecutors may see themselves as victims. However, if they are blamed or implicated, they will usually blame the other person for starting the conflict and will claim that they were only protecting themselves or getting even.

Because they are able to fall back on the victim role and justify their retaliation, they believe that they do not have to accept blame, guilt, or shame. Consider the child whom a father sees taking a swing at one of his playmates. The father may jump in and admonish the child that they shouldn't hit other people. The child may respond: "But she hit me first!" as if this is just cause to strike the other child. The difficulty occurs when both (or sometimes all) parties in the conflict are playing the justified persecutor, as in a case when the first child may say, "I hit him because he threw sand in my face." When someone such as a parent, teacher, or judge has the task of resolving the conflict, the problem is in knowing whom to believe. Often, one or both seek to manipulate the person in the judging or rescuing role. This is because the justified persecutor wants this power or support. The belief, according to the hierarchical model, is that if I do not have the support of someone with greater power, then I will lose. Taken further, others will not see me as good or right in using my strength to protect myself. Therefore, I have to get support from those who are in a more powerful, judging position. This is why our legal system survives and thrives.

In addition, persecutors may not realize that others view them as such. For example, in the situation with the justified persecutor, often both people feel that the other has victimized them. The person playing the victim identifies a person as the persecutor, whether "the persecutor" deserves it or not. I see this happening many times with parents and children. The parent is often trying to do their best to help their child succeed, and when they push their child to do their best, the child often feels the pressure to be perfect. In this situation, the child feels persecuted by the parent's demands and the parent can't figure out why the child withdraws and will not communicate. Since the parents intend to help their child, they have a difficult time seeing their child's viewpoint. Often, the parent can become angry and more controlling, which furthers the child's perception of victimization. Furthermore, situations arise wherein the parents do not hear themselves when they are talking to their child. If they listen to themselves and the tone they use, they would probably see the situation more accurately. As you may have heard before, "Denial ain't just a river in Egypt."

What happens when people feel threatened by others? As we have seen throughout the examples in this book, people will react to threats by trying to protect themselves and their interests. Many times, we do not consciously think about reacting; it just happens. Therefore, we do not take the time to be aware of how we are affecting others. Additionally, we find it difficult to see our own actions without bias. Depending on our assessment of the situation and our personal issues, we will gauge our reaction. Often our reaction is not based entirely upon what that person did to us at that moment, but also past incidences. First, the person whom we feel threatened by (our persecutor) may not have intended for us to feel threatened. Second, as you know from reading this book, if they were trying to threaten us, their need to scare us is more about them and their emotions. Regardless, most of us do not like to stay in the victim role. Therefore, we retaliate to try to regain our power. It is at that point that we have become the persecutor, justified or not. If we look closely, however, we are reacting against our emotions and our perceptions, not the other person. This is often true when we hear someone say, "It's the principle of the thing," when they seem to make a big deal out of something small. Remember that the emotions are there for a reason, and often they help us to figure out what is going on in our present environment. Also, remember, however, that since our emotions are often stuck in the past, our reactions come from more than just the present.

RESCUER

The rescuer is the person who takes care of the victim or "rescues" them from their circumstance. The rescuer may not always know when they are playing that role. Some people seek out occasions to be the rescuer because they feel a sense of gain from playing the role; they get power in some way. The rescuer often feels a sense of recognition and appreciation from the victim. In extreme situations, some rescuers also believe that the victim should feel indebted to them for what they have done.[6]

Rescuers, as shown in the diagram at the beginning of the chapter, have to have more power than the persecutor; otherwise, they would not be able to rescue the victim. Another situation may be similar to a revolution or mutiny, when victims (who have become justified persecutors) collectively pool their power together to become more powerful than the persecutor(s) and "overthrow" them, effectively rescuing each other from their circumstance.

A "rescuer" may not know that a victim sees them as their rescuer. This can happen when a child comes to the parent to tell on a sibling, when a co-worker talks to a fellow employee or boss about a problem with a co-worker or family member, or when a person is in a relationship with someone with a difficult past. Sometimes we have to look very carefully at the dynamics of a situation to see what role we are playing. One problem with receiving the role of rescuer, especially when we do not know that we have this role, is that the victim is often looking to us to take care of them, which can feel very draining, yet at the same time, intoxicating.

As for the rescuer who seeks that role, they may find themselves in positions of status: psychologist, parent, caseworker, teacher, foster parent, minister, politician. Many people who continuously find themselves in the rescuer role may seek situations where they can help the disadvantaged. By rescuing others, they may feel a sense of value or importance (their power goes up). In this manner, they seek their power from others, and in many ways want accolades from those they rescue. This is a somewhat direct way of putting it, but nonetheless, there is truth to it. *Worship* is a term commonly reserved for religion. Therefore, if we see someone who appears to want to be worshipped or idolized, we might see that person as bad and wrong, but strong. Think about the implications of that. When I have made comments to clients about wanting to be worshipped, they often immediately have a negative reaction, because it evokes feelings of shame and guilt. Being a rescuer feeds our ego. In my field, we call this a "God Complex," hence the term "worship." It is important to realize that when a person chooses to be a rescuer, it is likely because they do not believe in their own power at some level. So, they seek power and recognition of their status from others. As a result, the rescuer is looking for acknowledgment and/or appreciation from those that they rescue.

When the rescuer does not feel acknowledged or worshipped and/or feels victimized by the person(s) that they have rescued, they feel betrayed and resentful and take the martyr role. The martyr, as I see it, is a victimized rescuer. In other words, they feel that they have been taken advantage of in some way when their intention was to help. A martyr may ask, "What have you done for me lately?" However, this type of sentiment can lead the victim to feel that unfair demands or conditions were placed upon them, resulting in their feeling victimized by the rescuer. It is crucial to understand this dynamic since the victim seeks a rescuer and the victim feels that the rescuer has turned on them; the rescuer then becomes a persecutor. The victim then has to look for another rescuer. If this continues to happen with the same person feeling like the victim, then there is a risk of creating what I call a chronic victim. This will be addressed, shortly.

This martyr issue often occurs in adoptive families and foster families. The parents take in a formerly abused or neglected child. The parents' goal is to help the child feel loved, safe, and protected, and in many ways hope that the child will leave their past behind and realize how much they are loved in their new home. However, these children often carry scars from their past into these situations. The children project their past onto the present and start behaving in unproductive ways. In short, for whatever reason, but likely due to their past, the child turns their foster parents into the persecutor and the parent sees the child as their persecutor. The parents cannot understand why these children would treat them so badly after they took them into their home, and feel that these children are ungrateful and uncaring. The behaviors of the child and the parents can then spiral out of control (they both become justified persecutors) and everybody loses.

Finally, we cannot discount the situation where the rescuer is actually exploiting or persecuting those people that they are supposed to be supporting, guiding or protecting. This wolf in rescuer's clothing is often looking to engender trust in those that they appear to be rescuing. As they are able to build this level of trust, they may subtly or obviously exploit or abuse their victims. This situation can happen in the family (abusive parent), community (exploitive priest), national level (manipulative politician), and even internationally. A manipulative rescuer can do serious damage to the level of trust in others; the fear is, if I cannot trust the person who is supposed to care for me, then whom can I trust?

THE CHRONICALLY CHALLENGED AND
THE GAMES THEY PLAY

Before we move on to the instigator, I would like to address an issue related to a side effect of playing these roles and the unproductive habits that can result. As I stated earlier, whether a person plays victim, persecutor, or rescuer, each role has its benefits in regards to perceptions of power and its apparent rewards. As an individual may become accustomed to playing a role, they can develop a habitual pattern and revert to this role to try to gain a sense of power. These roles continue to feed the conflicts we have in our lives, but often we resort to the patterns that we know best. As people play these roles repeatedly, I refer to these as chronic behavior patterns, and apply the labels: chronic victim, chronic persecutor, and chronic rescuer (and yes, there are also chronic instigators).

As I see it, each chronic role comes with its own game that people play. The victim is often looking to be rescued, and their game is "How much do you love me?" The persecutor is looking to prove their power by inflicting force over others, and their game is "How much do you fear me?" The rescuer is looking to gain power by saving and protecting others, and their game is "How much do you worship me?" The instigator, as will be discussed, is looking to gain power by seeing how they can impact others, without necessarily affecting themselves. Their game could be called "Let's see how big a splash I can make." As you can see, each game has its rewards, but also involves the manipulation of the power of others, thereby contributing to further conflict. Because each game has its rewards in terms of perceived increases in power, it is difficult to stop the chronic games because often those playing the games do not know other ways to regain power. Furthermore, increases in power are short-lived; therefore, each person must continue to play their game to continue to feed their internal lack of perceived power.

As was discussed before, a chronic victim is usually looking for someone to rescue them, and almost never wants to take responsibility for their own behaviors. What can happen is that when a victim is rescued, the rescuer may make demands on the victim that the victim feels are unfair. The victim may then feel persecuted by the rescuer, and therefore turn the rescuer into their persecutor. After that, the victim needs to seek out another rescuer. Remember that when a person plays the victim, they surrender their power, so they are not at fault for anything. I see this happen repeatedly.

Chronic rescuers are almost always looking for recognition, and their issues most likely started in early childhood when they felt that they did not get the attention that they needed. They are people who find themselves in positions ranging from leadership and management, to politics, and teaching. Not everyone who holds these positions is a chronic rescuer, but there is likely a large overlap.

Chronic persecutors are more difficult to recognize because often there is a great deal of shame behind recognizing the fact that they bully their way through life. They may often be those people who physically, mentally, or sexually abuse others, but they often hide these behaviors from many others. In situations when they feel judged by those whom they feel have more power, they may be able to act like angels. When cornered about their behaviors, they may always have an excuse or justification for their actions and have a difficult time taking responsibility for what they may do, because deep down inside, they feel like a victim, and have an insatiable need to hide their weakness.

INSTIGATOR

The role of the instigator does not appear in the discussion of V-P-R. Still, it is crucial to understand the role of the instigator. The instigator has the power to start the conflict. The person instigating the conflict always seeks power in some form. That is why they are starting the fight. The interesting fact about the instigator is that any person in the V-P-R triad can be the instigator. The instigator can also be someone altogether outside the conflict. I will discuss each condition separately.

SOLE INSTIGATOR

This is the situation when the person who starts the conflict does not seem to be a part of the conflict. An example of this is a child who tells two different kids that they are saying things about each other. This then starts a fight between the two kids, and the instigator gets to watch the fireworks. The instigator likes to feel the power of seeing the other two kids fight. In some cases, the instigator may want to redirect attention away from him- or herself and onto someone else.

This example of the child starting the fight between two other children sometimes happens with adults. In the example of you, Fred, and me (in Chapter 2), I acted as the sole instigator to disturb your friendship with Fred. However, I also had an ulterior motive of trying to gain a friendship with Fred. This process is called splitting and is self-explanatory. The instigator is trying to split the two people up and turn them against each other so that he or she can feel more powerful by creating an alliance with one or even with each of them. Splitting also commonly occurs when a child tries to split the parents in order to get their way. It is easy for an instigator to play this role when there is a lack of communication or trust in the environment. Regardless of the circumstance, the instigator derives their feeling of power by seeing the effect that they can have on others. This is similar to a child throwing a rock into a pond to see the big splash that it makes.

VICTIM AS THE INSTIGATOR

Can a victim be an instigator? How can a victim instigate when they are so weak? The victim has power, but the victim needs only to appear weak. They must look harmless to find a rescuer. A person who is accustomed to playing the victim needs reassurance that the rescuer will be there when they need them. Think of the fable, "The Boy Who Cried Wolf." This is a perfect example of the victim as the instigator. The boy had to make sure that the townspeople would come running if a wolf came. The problem was that the boy manipulated the townspeople until they no longer trusted him. As we all know, when the boy needed them, they were not there. The boy was deriving his power from the townspeople who came to rescue him. Can you see how this could be very dangerous? Think of false abuse claims to children's services, contrived legal suits, or false accusations of rape, and the list goes on.

People who play victim and instigator are often skillful at creating the circumstance to cover their tracks. Kids may learn to do this from early ages. They learn to put the emphasis on the supposed persecutor, who may just be reacting to the "victim's" attack. Even when the parent realizes what has happened, the older sibling is told, "You are older; you should know better." If they feel that in the end, even if they started the conflict, others will be blamed, then they may feel that they have nothing to lose. Therefore, the younger child figures that whenever they want to start something, nothing will happen to them. Thus, those around them behaviorally reinforce the child's pursuit of playing the victim role.

PERSECUTOR AS THE INSTIGATOR

This is probably the most common situation of the instigator that people think of when a conflict or fight starts. Remember "the bully"? This situation occurs when someone stronger starts picking on someone weaker. The persecutor is looking for someone smaller to reinforce their power so that the persecutor can avoid feeling powerless. Remember that there is a sense of weakness or vulnerability at the core of the persecutor. Because of their poor self-image, the persecutor wants reassurance that they are stronger than someone else is. In doing this, they continue to hide and protect themselves from their own fears of powerlessness. The persecutor wants to avoid detection by a potential rescuer who would then judge and likely punish the persecutor. As I mentioned earlier, when caught, they often play innocent, make an excuse, and/or try to play the victim.

The persecutor often feels disempowered by those with more power, so they seek power from someone who feels less powerful. This is not new; as I said earlier, the bigger circle seeks control of the smaller circles.

RESCUER AS THE INSTIGATOR

You may be wondering why the rescuer would start a conflict. We may ask how a rescuer gets his/her power. They get their power from the people that they rescue, whether the victim acknowledges their actions or not. Think of the person who likes to tell stories about all of the people that they have helped, whether the people knew it or not. If a person who plays rescuer needs reassurance of their power and status from others, they may look to instigate problems with others so they can ride in on their horse and come to the rescue of the damsel in distress.

The rescuer as instigator may be similar to the situation where there is a single instigator. When the rescuer plays instigator, they are not initially a direct part of the conflict. They have subtly contributed to the conflict, but are separate from the people engaged in the fighting. However, they share in the solution to gain recognition for their actions.

There are numerous examples of this scenario that span many smaller situations. Most of these are very subtle, but might become more obvious as you read this book. Consider a man who starts a house fire in order to rescue the people in the house and be the hero; this is one example. Another example would be a student who instigates a fight between two other kids only to report the fight to the teacher to gain praise.

At a global/political level, consider a situation where a government contributes to a conflict between countries or even within a country, and when conflict explodes, that government is there to aid one or both countries. Consider the insurgence of communism in Cuba, Vietnam, and Korea. A civil war could erupt and the government's military could justify its action to come to the rescue of the innocent civilians who were being controlled by the country's unscrupulous government. In this situation, the rescuing country can reinforce the necessity for itself to be in a position of power over others and justify itself as the caretaker.

SUMMARY

There is a great deal to consider regarding the roles we play and why. This has provided a more in-depth discussion, but, in many ways, it is merely an introduction to the issue. I think that if you look more carefully at the V-P-R-I dynamics throughout our culture, you will see that the desire for power lies at the root of the issue and the manner in which we get our power feeds the dynamic. I do not think that you can separate the two.

As a society, I feel that we need to look at the way we contribute to a culture of victimization. In addition, we should consider why so few people take responsibility for their actions. As was indicated, the fear is that if I take some of the blame, I take all of it; so I will try to take none of it. It is critical to see that our children see this pattern and learn to use it to their advantage. I hope you are able to look at these issues closely in your life to see how to step out of the roles. Whether or not we realize it when we do it, it is a choice, at some level, to play these games in life. I cannot tell you how many times I have had to help my clients to see how they play each of these roles, and furthermore, how many times I have caught myself. People do not always like to hear me point this out, but when they are able to listen, their lives often improve dramatically. Don't shoot the messenger, just hear the message.

QUESTIONS

1. Can you think of different situations where, at different times, you played each of the four roles mentioned in this chapter?
2. Which of these four roles do you feel that you most commonly play in everyday life?
3. Do you feel that others see you in the same role as you see yourself?

6

The Role of Emotion

Emotion has taught mankind to reason.
—*Marquis de Vauvenargues (1715–1747)*

TEACHING OBJECTIVES

- Provide a framework for understanding the purpose of emotions
- Discuss the concept of emotional aspects and how they affect each of us
- Provide a developmental model for emotions, beliefs, and attitudes

I've devoted a lot of time to laying groundwork in order to get to this point in the book. We've spent time on power structures and how they lead to conflict, on communication patterns, on historical perspectives of conflict, and on how emotion influences outcomes. We've looked at dichotomies that often result in an unfounded and often unproductive exchange of emotions, and at various roles people play in conflicts. Do you believe that there are any unneeded emotions? If it helps, return to the list of emotions and create your own list of emotions that you feel aren't necessary.

Have you ever asked yourself, "Why am I feeling what I am feeling? What possible purpose could this feeling have?" We often forget to ask, "What can I learn from this feeling?" Instead, we often try to hide the emotion or to run from it. Emotions play a fundamental role in life.[7] What do emotions do for our lives? They help us to form relationships, experience growth, and evaluate our performance. Besides that, they prompt us to learn and sometimes prompt us to quit, fight, cry, lie, and/or to hide.

A REASON FOR FEELING

Did you ever wonder how long a person would live if they could not feel fear? Why would someone want to apologize if guilt was not present? Why would someone miss the company of others if they could not feel loneliness or sadness? We couldn't appreciate life if these emotions disappeared. Unfortunately, many times, we feel unable to pick and choose the emotions we feel; even so, we try to select how we display them. As I said early on, everyone feels all of the same emotions; it is what we do with them that makes us different. In the dichotomy of strong versus weak, we learned to perceive these emotions differently, and depending on how we perceive them, we will show them differently to others.

Are we a society of manipulators? We favor rational thought instead of expressing emotion. We must consider emotions as they pertain to dealing with life issues, but logic is an integral part of that process. In addition, when emotion enters into the process, it is important to make sure we balance these emotions with logic. Often people try to use logic, or they become carried away with emotion, but they do not seek the balance in understanding that emotion can be a healthy part of an interaction. Most emotions have a logical place, depending on the situation. If we can consider what the emotions are trying to tell us, then they can often help us to understand how to address the issue. Thus, instead of responding in a reactive manner, we need to learn how to respond in a proactive manner.

We often speak with logic instead of feeling; we believe that we are not vulnerable if we are not feeling. Through logic, we believe we can mask emotions and defend ourselves from threat. This type of logic-based, emotionally avoidant communication occurs with children and world leaders alike, and at all levels in between. As such, communication has become a cat and mouse game, sometimes with deadly results. We often mistake arrogance for pride, and believe in the nobility of martyrs. If we look at these martyrs more closely, we may see that many died of fear of expressing their true feelings. At first glance, it seems that emotions and logic do not mesh well. Although you may not want to do so, it may be in your best interest to consider the notion that there could be a logical purpose for each emotion.

Many of my clients often feel that fear, shame, sadness, and guilt are worthless feelings. They feel that if these emotions did not exist, they would be much better off. Upon further discussion, they often find that they cannot do without these emotions. Instead, they realize that they chose to deal with the emotions in an undesirable manner throughout their lives, which contributed to many of their problems.

If we think about each emotion without clouding our judgment *with* emotions, we would see that all our feelings have a purpose. There are two major viewpoints regarding the development of the human race: creationism and evolution. Creationism centers on the belief that a Creator made us as we are. Evolutionism asserts that over a long period, we have adapted to our surroundings and became the humans of today. Perhaps we should think of the development of emotions from these same vantage points. If we believe in creationism, then we more easily accept the idea that all emotions are God-given and serve a purpose. We could then say that our challenge is to understand each emotion and master their meanings. If we believe in the concept of evolution and/or do not wish to consider a divine purpose for our emotions, we may consider that our emotions have evolved, and they have enabled us to survive. In this case, it makes sense to try to understand the roles they play in our life and thereby see how they may contribute to further growth and evolution.

EMOTIONAL MASTERY VERSUS CONTROL

You may have observed my use of the word *master* in reference to emotion. I distinguish between the terms *master* and *control*. According to *Webster's New World Dictionary*, Control is defined as:

> (Verb usage) "4. to exercise authority over; direct; command 5. to hold back; curb; restrain." (Noun usage) "1. The act or fact of controlling; power to direct or regulate; ability to use effectively 2. the condition of being directed or restrained." The most appropriate definition of the term *Master* is given as: (Verb usage) "3. to become an expert in."

I noticed that several of the definitions for the word "master" contain the word "control." However, the aspect that makes these words different is what we will examine. The act of becoming an expert indicates several things. Words like understanding, appreciation and management seem to lend themselves to the notion of mastery.

In contrast, "control" may cause us to think of a time, place or situation, but it doesn't seem to imply understanding or appreciation. It is likely that you know of two types of managers in the business world or in social dealings. One type of manager directs people through mastery of the task at hand and understands the goal; this manager knows and appreciates the talents of the employees he or she manages. The other type of manager controls or commands and orders his or her employees to do tasks that they may not be skilled at performing.

Businesses want their employees to be happy and productive and, above all, to work as a team; management, through mastery, often accomplishes these objectives.

The need for control comes from the desire to avoid experiencing fear. There is a simple logic behind having control. If I can control everything around me, I can control which emotions I will feel, and I may avoid feeling fear or any emotions connected to fear. To master our emotions, we must do a few things. We must understand, appreciate and manage the perception and expression of emotions in a manner that is respectful to us and to others.

If we can accept the idea that each emotion exists for a reason, then we can find the value that each emotion provides to us. Finding this value may allow us to understand our feelings and express them in more adaptive ways. The expression of anger does not have to involve yelling or violence, sadness does not have to involve crying, fear does not have to involve hiding or avoiding.

If we listen to our emotions, and understand what our emotions mean, we can respect them and their intensity often fades. But if we ignore what our emotions tell us, our feelings build up and may result in a display of negative behavior. People sometimes resort to shouting and physical violence if they cannot get their point across. Likewise, our emotions may incite the same types of behaviors in us if we ignore them.

Is it possible to express true feelings without extreme behavior? If we understand our feelings, we can express them in a rational manner but still convey what we feel. It is important to understand that we can express true emotion without shouting or the threat of violence. We may associate strong emotion with aggressive words or acts, but don't confuse these behaviors with the actual emotions. Similarly, simply because a person can state their feelings in a calm manner, it does not mean they are insincere.

NEWBORN FEELINGS

We will look at my theory of emotional development before further discussion of the purposes for our feelings. Newborn babies feel emotions, and some would agree that babies feel emotions before birth. In short, we can feel and express emotions at the time of birth. Babies may not understand their emotions, but they quickly learn that certain behaviors evoke certain responses from others.

Do infants know the differences between emotions? They probably develop this knowledge but cannot use words to express these differences. Babies—and everyone else, for that matter—want to feel loved and accepted. If someone loves and accepts a baby, they help to assure the baby's survival. However, even before we can seek love and acceptance, we must survive. This implies that, sometimes, a baby's need for survival can overwhelm the need for acceptance. The baby has no means of expressing these survival needs, except by crying or yelling. The people around the baby may not respond to its cries with love and acceptance, but will likely feed or change them. Depending on the feedback the baby receives, the baby may experience confusion, frustration, and other emotions without understanding them; but it gets what it needs to survive: food. Let's assume that, at the moment of birth, a newborn is fully aware of all emotions, but cannot understand or express them. As the infant continues to experience life, the emotions and experiences contribute to the development of the conscious mind and unconscious or subconscious mind.

There is no single definition for the unconscious and/or subconscious in literature. I will use these terms interchangeably in this text, but some authors differentiate between them. For our discussion, I will use a definition for unconscious from *Webster's New World Dictionary*, which is, "the sum of all thoughts, memories, impulses, desires, feelings of which the individual is not conscious, but which influence his emotions and behavior." As the conscious and unconscious develop, a child receives feedback from his environment in many ways, which affects the development of the conscious and unconscious. They learn the relationship between actions that gain rewards and those that evoke punishment.

If we want to feel loved and accepted, then we might learn to try to hide or reject parts of our self that do not help us attain these things. As we mature, we may experience many memories, thoughts, attitudes, emotions and beliefs that our conscious mind cannot store; in this case, we need to place some events and experiences out of our conscious awareness. So, the subconscious develops out of a need for storage for our experiences and emotions. We tend to repress events and emotions that we wish to forget, did not receive love or acceptance from, or couldn't understand. As I see it, we begin to create an internal hierarchy of emotions and experiences to influence our daily lives, whether we know it or not. This hierarchy of emotions often become an ingrained part of our subconscious.

In Figure 6.1, human awareness is represented as a large sphere of energy. Each emotional experience, and each developing attitude or belief, becomes a deposit of energy or aspect of self that we may use or store. The smaller "spheres of influence" in the unconscious indicate these aspects. The varying size of each sphere shows the relative power or importance of each sphere as we may judge them. If a person wants to keep an experience or emotion out of the conscious mind, he must

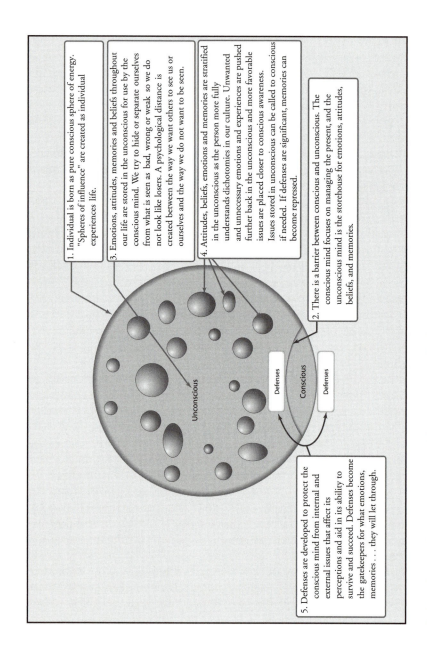

1. Individual is born as pure conscious sphere of energy. "Spheres of influence" are created as individual experiences life.

3. Emotions, attitudes, memories and beliefs throughout our life are stored in the unconscious for use by the conscious mind. We try to hide or separate ourselves from what is seen as bad, wrong or weak so we do not look like losers. A psychological distance is created between the way we want others to see us or ourselves and the way we do not want to be seen.

4. Attitudes, beliefs, emotions and memories are stratified in the unconscious as the person more fully understands dichotomies in our culture. Unwanted and unnecessary emotions and experiences are pushed further back in the unconscious and more favorable issues are placed closer to conscious awareness. Issues stored in unconscious can be called to conscious if needed. If defenses are significant, memories can become repressed.

2. There is a barrier between conscious and unconscious. The conscious mind focuses on managing the present, and the unconscious mind is the storehouse for emotions, attitudes, beliefs, and memories.

5. Defenses are developed to protect the conscious mind from internal and external issues that affect its perceptions and aid in its ability to survive and succeed. Defenses become the gatekeepers for what emotions, memories . . . they will let through.

Unconscious

Defenses

Conscious

Defenses

Figure 6.1 Development of Conscious and Unconscious Mind

expend energy to keep it away. For us to accomplish this, the need for defenses arises.

Commonly, we use one of two ways to defend emotions and experiences that we want to protect. We can use emotions to intimidate other people or other aspects of ourselves. That is where the term "sphere of influence" comes into play. The other means of defense involves a logical approach that might seek to outwit other emotions and individuals, and in a sense, we talk ourselves out of unwanted situations or perceptions.

We use defenses to guard emotions and to fend off certain experiences. We also use these defenses to protect us from external attacks. Depending on how the subconscious perceives a threat, it may call on defenses to protect aspects of itself from threats to the conscious and unconscious. Defense tactics will differ from person to person.

As stated earlier, through life events, a person may learn that emotions are bad, wrong, and/or weak. Over the years, our conscious mind learns to rely upon logic as a medium for processing experiences. If the conscious mind only needs reason, in theory, life should be easier to figure out and deal with.

Emotions may become taboo to the conscious mind, because of the numerous times in life when emotions only seemed to make things worse. Although the conscious mind may seek to block emotions, it never fully succeeds. This situation is similar to a person standing on the other side of a fence calling you names. You hear what they say and, although you cannot see the source of these insults, the words still hurt. You may try to distance yourself from the fence, but you can only go so far, because the fence surrounds you. In other words, we cannot escape our emotions and memories, but we can make every effort to avoid them. It is usually only a matter of time before we have to deal with them, in some capacity.

Let us continue this fence metaphor. Imagine that the individual calling you names felt a strong need to let you know he was there; he may have a difficult time knowing whether you can hear him because he cannot see your reaction. He may decide to try to tear down the fence. If that does not work, he may dig a hole under the fence, or set the fence on fire (if he feels desperate enough). Besides these things, he may try to find more people to make noise to get our attention. In relating this to a person, considering mind-body connections, it makes sense that people who do not deal with emotions often have health issues such as heart problems, cancer, immune deficiencies, etc. The relationship between these health factors and repressed emotions is too high to ignore. We can view this situation as our emotions' way of telling our logic-based conscious mind that it is time to listen. It is clear, however, that people fail to listen to these emotions and solely blame their health problems on things like diet, smoking or genetics. My experience with hypnosis has proved to me time and again that unresolved emotional issues contribute to many physical problems. The biggest issue beyond that is that many people do not want to take the time and expense to work through those issues to full resolution.

In order to consider the cause of disease, we need to look at theories about what causes disease. One important theory is the diathesis-stress model of disease. This theory asserts that people contract a disease when they are predisposed *and* experience an amount of stress that activates the disease. Without these stressors, or if the strategic group of stressors never occurs, it is less likely that the person will develop the disease. The diathesis-stress model is similar to finding the weakest link in the chain. It does not matter how strong all of the other links of the chain are; if there is a single weak link, the chain will break. The weakest link goes unnoticed, unless we stress the chain.

Regarding the impact of emotions on ourselves, whether we realize it or not, we often use our emotions to manipulate perceptions of others and possibly more often of ourselves. We may use anger to invoke fear, sadness to receive pity, and guilt to gain control. In this manner, some-times our unconscious may try to influence our conscious mind through these same tactics.

If you focus on the expression of these emotions, there is *always* some experience of a weakly perceived emotion shortly before the conflict. As such, we see that a protective emotion always appears in the wake of a weaker emotion. We need to understand the main purpose of these protective emotions; this information may help us to resolve conflicts. Taken further, there are unique features to each emotion that are import-ant to discuss.

CONCEPT OF EMOTIONAL ASPECTS

We often "hear" many different voices or opinions within us at any one time. We should not confuse these internal voices with those of schizophrenics or "multiple personalities." The degree to which these internal voices affect us, as well as the verbal content of the voices, may cover a range of expressions. At the point where these voices interfere with our thoughts or suggest harmful behaviors, they become patho-logical.

I have developed a theoretical perspective that we all exist within the range of having a single identity to having many aspects or spheres of influence. If we only contained one identity, then we could expect to respond the same way in similar situations, much as a computer pro-gram operates. We do not respond the same way every time; there are many times that we may do something and wonder why. In such cases, we may feel as if someone else took over and acted in our place. This model is difficult to prove through research.

Since we all are different and may have several aspects, no two people will respond the same way in a research setting. It is likely you have seen books on the "inner child" and other similar concepts. In addition to inner children, so, too, could there be adolescents and other aspects. This theory can be used as a model to aid in understanding why we do the things we do, since the logic from a single identity model often fails of explanation.

Do most adults have more than one aspect? If so, why? Most likely it is because, throughout our lives, we repress emotion and experiences. Adults often have many different points of view. The extent to which an individual represses or isolates their emotions and memories will depend on their experiences, attitudes, and beliefs. The more someone tries to repress or forget their past and build walls or defenses around these experiences (most often because of the pain and trauma from those experiences), the more they might create other identities or personalities beyond what I would refer to as an aspect of our personality. When people who have experienced severe and/or recurrent trauma from early ages create multiple personalities or identities, we call this condition dissociative identity disorder (DID).

Perhaps you have seen movies or books like *Three Faces of Eve* and *Sybil*. These provide examples of a person who has different personalities, and the "core personality" is most often not initially aware of the others. Such a situation is common for people with this condition. During the periods when an alternate personality assumes control, the person often blacks out and cannot recall what happened. Through therapy, the client may learn about the existence of these other identities and how they express themselves. DID creates some interesting psychological issues. Some clients with DID tend to form some identities that are psychologically adaptive and are very distinct from other identities. Since the personalities are independent, they do not influence each other, but they often have conflicts internally and their behaviors can cause problems for "everyone" when they are out on the surface.

SUMMARY

Looking back at Figure 6.1, consider the hierarchical structure of emotions and experiences within the subconscious mind. While there are implications to inner conflicts in regard to this, we will discuss internal power struggles in more depth in later chapters. A person's emotional hierarchy dictates which emotions a person expresses and which ones he/she hides. How do we form these emotional hierarchies? Often, our interactions with society and family influence these structures. You may find that, during a conflict, you cast aside your belief system in favor of one more commonly used in our society. When it comes to conflict, the two most important dichotomies become strong versus weak and win versus lose. To understand this, we may consider our emotional aspects and, in doing so, find that they add another dimension to our understanding of complex behavioral and emotional patterns. From this perspective, we will examine the interplay of emotion and its connection to conflict.

QUESTIONS

1. Can you think of some instances wherein "undesirable emotions" served their purpose to your benefit?
2. Do you recall situations that led you to make an effort to reject your feelings in favor of logic in order to maintain control of a situation?
3. We commonly realize that we have different facets to our personality. Does it sometimes seem that, at various times, different facets become more dominant? If so, how does it affect your attitude or actions?

7

Communicating Emotion

> If thought corrupts language, language can also corrupt thought.
> —*George Orwell*

TEACHING OBJECTIVES

- Discuss the nature of how what we say contributes to conflict
- Discuss the power of words and the effects of those words on conflict and emotion
- Provide examples of semantically inaccurate phraseology and suggested changes
- Increase self-awareness of conflict and semantics

People often use inaccurate words to express themselves to those around them. In most languages, people use slang words to make communication easier or to set them apart from other groups of people. Teenagers provide a good example of speech that sets them apart from others. Over the generations, teenagers have adopted their own words to mean certain things. Their terms and phrases separate them from adults and tend to unite them as a group.

SHORTCUTS

By simplifying language, we may cause confusion. Slang often detracts from the accuracy of a statement and can alter its meaning for those who are unfamiliar with this language usage. Have you ever spoken to a foreigner who received only a formal training—no casual experience—in English? If so, they probably did not understand many slang or idiomatic expressions that pop up in everyday conversations. Many foreigners speak and write English more properly than most Americans do, and they have not learned much of the slang and "lazy usage."

At this point, you might think it odd that I am talking about word usage and slang in a book about conflict and emotions. The reason is simple: It is very important to think clearly about how we express our emotions and feelings to others and how that contributes to conflict. What we intend to convey when we say a word is called "semantics." More accurately, Webster's *New World Dictionary* says that semantics is "the branch of linguistics concerned with the nature, structure and changes of the meanings of speech forms or contextual meanings of language." In other words, semantics helps us understand the precise use of our language. If we begin to pay attention to the literal meaning of what we say, we can begin to realize how sloppy our usage often is.

SAY WHAT YOU MEAN

It's important to use literal language around children who are learning to speak. Toddlers have no experience with language and can't tell subtle differences in word meanings. Young children take language very literally, which can lead to intense emotional displays. One example of their literal language style is in the type of jokes that they find amusing. A classic child's joke is, "What is black and white and red all over?" Common answers are a newspaper or a skunk with diaper rash. The reason they laugh at these sorts of jokes is that they are consistent with the child's cognitive development, which is more literal. They are laughing at the play on words.

The subconscious may be an important factor in how we communicate. Many believe that the subconscious is very literal in the way it translates language. When we speak to someone, the subconscious is also hearing our words. The subconscious may interpret the words in a way that can result in both internal and external reactions, which neither party may understand. The issue of the subconscious will be addressed more thoroughly in the next chapter.

Let's address the issue of the communication of emotion. What does it mean when someone says, "I am angry at you"? If we dissect this phrase, the words to consider are "am" and "at you." The word "am" is a form of the verb "to be," which means "to exist." What do we say when we introduce ourselves? "Hello, I *am* Erik Fisher." In this statement, I will always be Erik Fisher, all day, everyday. To the literal mind, when I say, "I am angry," it means all of me is always angry. In other words, anger becomes my identity. Let's consider that we want to explore literal meanings rather than common usage or implied meanings. Given this interpretation when we say, "I am" something, consider the literal meaning taken from saying "I'm angry *at you*." This "at you" implies "all of you," not part of you or your actions. To a child, this phrase can feel very intimidating and over-powering. The child tends to interpret the phrase to mean *they* were bad or wrong, not *what they did*.

What we mean to say when we communicate this thought is, "I feel anger with what you did." This phrase takes a few more words to state, but it's much more accurate. The most accurate way to express emotions is with the verb *feel*, not *be*. Feel anger, but don't "be" or "become" angry. We can "feel" more than one emotion at a time, but it is difficult to "be" more than one emotion at a time. We might see that the second part of the phrase, "with what you did," addresses the issue of the action of the person, not the person himself.

In teaching children and adults the language of emotion, I often tell children that their parents will always love them, but they may not like what they do. If we address the action of the individual (what they did), it points out what they can change. If we address the individual as the object of our anger (at you), it is difficult to know what to change. If we say, "I am angry (sad, afraid, stupid)," we only express the major emotion (anger), while we are almost always feeling other emotions. When we say, "I am angry at you," we probably feel many other things at the same time.

Why don't we express these other emotions? Most likely, it's because we seldom take the time to think of *all* the emotions we feel.[8] Besides that, we might also fear that voicing the other emotions could give the impression that we *are* weak or vulnerable. It's important to consider what we teach children about emotions when we express things to them. They often cannot grasp the underlying elements of what we say; they take what we say at face value. They may learn from us to over-simplify their thoughts and emotions. If they feel we manipulate them through language, they will learn to manipulate from our example. If there's any question in your mind that a child learns to manipulate adults before even learning to speak, consider the two-year-old who bumps her head and waits until she knows someone is listening before crying.

If children oversimplify their emotions, they may never understand what other emotions trigger the main emotion they feel. Anger is an emotion that serves as a good example. Feelings of anger result when someone is at least feeling threatened, but it often goes beyond that. If someone tells a child that he must clean his room before going out to play, he may exhibit anger. Why? The anger comes from the threat to his sense of priority (to go and play) and resentment of the power that forces this new priority (to clean his room) that he wants to challenge. Not learning how to separate and address these different emotions can cause children to lump emotions together. If they cannot sort out the underlying emotions, they cannot understand or express these feelings. Children may expect others to react to emotions as they do. When someone tells a child, "I am angry at you," the child learns to take this as a cue to correct the situation. When they begin to try to play the "I am angry at you" game on others, they expect the same response. Unknowingly, many parents respond to these tactics, which makes it more likely that children are going to try this with others. But they will find that it doesn't always work, and may receive harsh reactions from some.

When adults are harsh with children over the child's attempts to evoke fear or guilt in others, the child begins to learn about status power. This motivates the child to wonder why someone else has the right to manipulate others' emotions, but the child doesn't. These types of situation continue to form a child's struggle for power and may help contribute to a lot of confusion.

Other things go with the comment "I'm angry at you." In one such example, a child may be asked to clean his room. When he expresses anger, his mother may say, "I am your mother and you will listen to me! I get so mad at you when you smart-mouth me. You will either do as I say, and do it right now, or you'll be grounded for a week." The child may resist by saying that he doesn't want to clean his room, or claim that it's clean enough, or he might even tell his mother to clean it herself. His mother responds by saying, "You have no right to talk to me like that. I am your mother." Just the day before, he wouldn't go to his room when told to do so, which prompted his mother to tell him, "You'd better listen to me when I tell you to do something, I'm very angry at you." In both incidents, the child cannot understand the differences between what he is allowed to express as compared to what his parent can express. The child only wants to get what he wants. The day before, the things his mother said resulted in his feeling guilt and shame that affected his behavior, and he only wanted to do the same to her. His mother's expression of anger results in his feeling confusion, misunderstood, and mistreated.

An example of the next type of vague emotional comment to examine is, "You are making me angry" (sad, confused . . .). When we make this statement, we tell the other person that we have given them the power to make us feel something. Why would we tell someone that they have the power to control our emotions? Perhaps we tell them this because it allows us to feel as though we are not responsible for our emotions. Additionally, it allows us to place blame and evoke a feeling of guilt, shame, or responsibility in others. By telling others they "make us feel" some emotion, we imply that we cannot help how we feel but only feel what they incite in us. By avoiding responsibility for our reactions, it is easier to play a victim role. If we react to them, we feel justified in stating that our reaction to their comment was only to protect ourselves. Our personal power benefits from accepting and taking responsibility for our emotions, feelings and actions.

FREEDOM TO CHOOSE

What I try to help others to recognize is that we have the power to choose to feel what we want to feel. Others can express their wishes and these comments may bring out feelings in us, but we always have the power to choose what we want to feel. It is in our best interest to recognize what we are feeling, so we can choose to react in a manner that is respectful of all. We must be the keepers of our ability to recognize that no one can take our power away from us, unless we choose to give it away. The ability to maintain our power is crucial to understanding and resolving conflict.

It is important to understand that people only try to take our power when they feel threatened in some way. We can exploit their vulnerability and exert our own sense of power, or we can understand what they are feeling and respond in a manner that is respectful of them and us. Sometimes, anger and rage are appropriate, but this is rare. You must use your power to choose to feel your own emotions wisely. We may rationalize and/or deny what people say to us and thereby avoid feeling anything. In order to change how we communicate, we must listen to what we say. It is very easy to rationalize and say, "It doesn't matter how I say things; people know what I mean." That statement is often hiding the fear that it is too hard to change, and expresses a fear of accepting the idea that people may feel hurt by what you have said. Many times this indicates that we feel guilt, shame, sadness and regret, as well as anger toward ourselves, but we have to hide it behind this rationalization.

Changing your language patterns is like changing a habit. Habits form over time and it takes time to develop new habits. It is in your best interest to allow yourself the freedom to make mistakes in order to see where you need to improve. When you realize the shortcomings in your speech, you may also realize the inaccuracies in your belief systems. Why? Because what we say reflects what we believe. You owe it to yourself to be aware of how your communication affects your emotions.

When I work with clients, I often help them to focus on the meanings of the words they use, and they notice that the words they use influence how they feel. While trying to change how they speak or behave, people often become easily irritated when they feel corrected or correct themselves. As such, they may react to their errors and the comments of others. Their reactions often stem from their feelings of failure, which they often project onto others to protect themselves.

SUMMARY

This chapter has presented a very brief overview of semantics in the communication of emotion. I will provide more of these issues and examples later in the book. At this point, I hope that you review your communication patterns and attempt to communicate with more accuracy. The process of communication is crucial to conflict. One word or phrase can help either to resolve a conflict or feed the flames.

QUESTIONS

1. Can you think of instances when a conflict erupted because someone misunderstood what you were trying to say? Have you been on the other side of such a misunderstanding?
2. Do you often find yourself not saying what you actually mean but instead talking in vague generalities?
3. Can you define what makes some people "easier to talk to" than others?

You may find it helpful to consider these questions and make a note of your thoughts in your journal for later reference.

8

Emotions Viewed as Strong or Powerful

There is nothing so powerful as truth—and often nothing so strange.
—*Daniel Webster (1782–1852)*

TEACHING OBJECTIVES

- Provide an understanding of what emotions are viewed as strong and why
- Explain how emotions viewed as strong may be used both in and out of conflict
- Explain the value of these emotions

We commonly view the emotions discussed in this chapter as the ones we see as strong or powerful. As you will see, the hidden purpose of many of them is self-protection, and these are often the emotions used in conflict. The list of emotions discussed is not exhaustive; it simply seeks to discuss the more prominent emotions we express. Why do we use protective emotions, and what do they hide? Most often, protective emotions protect and hide vulnerable emotions, those that denote weakness to us. We must remember that most people use these emotions when they feel threatened; they employ protective emotions, regardless of their intellectual skills or belief systems. If we feel a great sense of threat in a conflict, we often allow emotions, not our logic, to determine our responses.

ANGER

Anger's primary purpose is to protect us when we feel threatened. Our expression of anger may be external or internal. We react to anger based upon several factors. We consider the level of threat and gauge our perception of powerlessness. In addition, we consider the consequences of expressing our anger. Is our reaction justified? Depending upon what we conclude from these factors, we express our anger in a manner that we feel may accomplish our goal. When we feel threatened, we often display anger as a way to control the person causing the threat by inciting fear. When successful, the opposing force backs down and behaves as we wish. However, when we concede to anger, we reinforce that anger is a viable mode of expression. This increases the chances of a person relying upon anger to have their way to get results.

Temper tantrums are very common in children; parents will often give in to these tantrums, especially if they occur in public places. Children learn to use temper tantrums to manipulate others by using anger. If we do not understand this situation and correct it, these patterns can continue to create problems well into adulthood. When you encounter a person expressing anger, try to understand that the person displaying anger feels threatened. What is beneath the anger? What is this person trying to protect? Since children often lack the words to express emotion, they, and some adults, resort to tantrums to gain notice.

RAGE

The purpose of rage is to protect us when we feel in fear of our life, or when our integrity feels threatened. Rage is an expression of aggression beyond anger and often takes on the form of physical violence. Rage often occurs after anger does not receive the response it was seeking and a perceived threat still exists. We may describe rage by saying that a person is "out of control." Rage may incite us to kill the opposing force in order to survive. Because of this kill-or-be-killed aspect of rage, it serves to protect or ensure our survival. In my work, I have seen many individuals who suppress and repress their rage. Sometimes these clients express rage reactions to experiences that they do not recall or consciously remember. By the time suppressed emotion reaches this level, there are many other issues to deal with in therapy as well. Regardless of whether we express rage or suppress it, its purpose is to protect us.

During a conflict, sometimes one person provokes rage in their opponent simply to get a sense of his or her own strength or weakness, goodness or badness, or rightness or wrongness. Sometimes it can feel very powerful to see the reaction we can evoke from others. Children and spouses occasionally try to get a rise out of their parent or spouse in this manner. On the other hand, if a man often feels victimized, he may tend to try to evoke anger and rage in order to maintain his status as a victim. It may be of interest to note that we often call this type of psychological defense projective identification. This is only one example of projective identification and you may wish to look into this topic further. In regard to rage, if we feel safe, respected, and powerful, the need to express this powerful emotion is not likely to present itself. Still, rage serves the purpose of benefiting our survival.

Here is an example of an experience that shows the purpose of rage; this occurred with a client I will call Sarah, in therapy. Sarah had endured years of physical, sexual and verbal abuse and incest. One mode of treatment for Sarah was hypnotherapy; it was through hypnotherapy that we discovered that she had some dissociative identities. After the repeated use of trance, we discovered various identities that were stuck at different stages of Sarah's development, mainly reflecting her emotions at the times of her abuse. We saw that each of these identities strongly related to a certain emotion. The first identity we worked with was fear. From fear, we moved to sadness, guilt, shame and others. At certain points throughout the trance experiences, we encountered a black door with a lock and chains. Whenever we approached this door, the active identity, whichever it was, would shy away from the door and tell me not to go near it.

As therapy progressed over two to three months, there came a time when I asked to approach the door. The other identities allowed me to pass through the door, while they stayed outside (in trance, nearly anything is possible). When I went behind the door, the identity inside of Sarah said, "I want to kill, I want to destroy." We repeated this many times, and the identity was not very willing to talk or reason. This identity vowed to kill anyone, even me and the client, if it got out of the cage. I said, "You sound angry." Sarah then retorted, "I'm not angry, I'm rage." It was at this point that our work really began.

Through patience and reason, I came to understand that this identity, Rage, was there to protect the child when the abuse occurred. The child's identity of Fear saw the person abusing her as being rageful. This identity perceived this rage and this spawned Rage, reactively, inside her. The logic of the child was that if she expressed this Rage that came to protect her, she would become like her abuser. Her abuser was much larger and more powerful than she was. She feared unleashing this Rage because her abuser might destroy her if she attacked, and she not only feared that she couldn't destroy him, but also feared destroying the person responsible for her care. She then chose to lock her Rage inside from that point on.

Rage perceived that it came to help the child but received punishment for coming to her aid. As Rage remained locked inside for so long, it felt more and more resentment and hatred, as well as sadness and fear, because it seemed it would never gain its freedom (an important aspect to healing this patient focused on the concept of emotional identities experiencing emotions). This was the central point in helping to heal this client and many others. The main idea is that if rage can feel fear, for example, then it can feel any other emotion and therefore, be able to take the viewpoint of other emotions.

As I continued to understand Rage, I also helped it to understand why the other emotions locked it inside its cage. Rage, while it showed so much strength and contempt, also felt sadness, hurt, mistrust, and other emotions about being locked up. At the point when Rage was able to admit to its own feelings of weakness and understand the perceptions of the other emotions, Rage agreed not to hurt anyone, or itself, and the identities outside the cage agreed to open the cage. When the door opened and Rage walked out, the client pointed, while in trance. I asked what she was pointing at. The week before, we worked with Shame, simply described as a dirty little girl that no one wanted. Rage then stated, "I'll take the little one," and Rage walked over to Shame, picked her up and became her caretaker. At that point, I told Rage, "I understand what you were looking for. You just wanted to love and be loved."

In a very soothing voice, Rage stated, "Yes." Just as some of the other emotions adopted other names when they healed, Rage took a different name, given to it by Shame. After that particular two-hour session, the client's feelings of Rage were changed, and the "transformed" Rage became a very powerful ally for all the other identities and aided in healing with other forthcoming identities. This single therapeutic experience, I believe, illustrates the true purpose of rage within us all, and I feel extremely thankful that I was a witness to this event.

SARCASM AND HUMOR

Sarcasm is an interesting emotion because of the way in which it protects us. The use of sarcasm is rampant in our culture, so common, in fact, that we rarely recognize it as sarcasm. The interesting fact of sarcasm is that people often use it for protection on two fronts. Sarcastic comments attempt to protect us by advising someone to "back off." In issuing this warning, sarcasm threatens another person's power as it hides an insult inside a joke or passive-aggressive comment. In light of this, the individual is subtly saying, "Leave me alone, or I will try to destroy you with my words." Often, people trade sarcastic comments and allow the conflict to build. Sometimes the conflict grows until one of the parties feels verbally defeated and resorts to physical violence to defend himself. In inner-city cultures, trading sarcastic put-downs is very common between children and teens but often, unfortunately, leads to violence.

The other front where sarcasm protects us is after the delivery of the comment. If the person chooses to take offense with the comment and tries to evoke guilt by showing hurt, we are able to protect ourselves by saying, "Can't you take a joke?" By asking this simple question, we place the burden of emotion on the recipient of the comment. If we place the burden of emotion upon the other person, we avoid the need to show or feel guilt or remorse, and we do not have to take responsibility for hurting someone. Also, if we were to show guilt or remorse, we may feel that the other individual may have the advantage. So we learn to deflect our emotion and avoid taking responsibility.

People in relationships may learn that sarcasm often places large barriers between them. It is common for intimate partners to resort to sarcasm when they argue. The damage caused by sarcasm is deceptive. Instead of expressing an honest feeling or thought, sarcasm comes across as an aggressive attempt to address issues that feel too sensitive to discuss openly. Sarcastic comments often affect trust, and such statements may even feel more harmful to the recipient than physical abuse. In most instances, sarcasm is needless but always serves as a protective mechanism.

We use humor to make light of a situation. Humor often helps us appreciate life and point out our human elements in a less threatening manner. When used properly, humor is an effective tool in helping us build relationships; people often like those who use humor appropriately. However, some people use humor as a protective emotion to hide painful thoughts; it may act as a means of defense, which is similar to denial. Many famous comedians use humor to hide their past and painful emotion. Still, many have resorted to drugs and sometimes suicide when they could no longer hide from their pain by using humor.

When used well, humor often receives a laugh and the person can help others "digest" the content of the humorous comment. Timing is often the most important part of humor. Humor is a very short-lived emotion, because it often only lasts as long as the laugh. After the laugh is over, the person using humor has to look for something else for themselves or others to laugh at.

Many people try to use humor to make friends, to get out of a difficult position, or to hide insecurities. Many times when this occurs, others who are present feel uncomfortable and/or the joke falls flat. The person who offered the comment often tries to diffuse the tension by trying to come up with another witty remark. But, since a feeling of embarrassment motivates the comment, it often lacks humor and the discomfort builds. Attempts at humor may continue to be made, which can result in a "train wreck" when one joke crashes into another and the casualties to that person's humiliation grow. At this point, the individual may choose to stop or withdraw, or he may try, in vain, to make yet another joke to recover.

In groups, those who have the status power often reserve the right to display humor. In such groups, those in power view attempts at humor by others as inappropriate. Certainly, we have all heard different people make the same joke or comment, and have seen a contrast in how others received it. Sometimes, the joke did not work because of a poor delivery. However, many times jokes do not work because of the status power held by the person who told the joke. The hidden undertone is that if we laugh at the comment, we are giving this individual power. If we deem ourselves at a higher status, we may feel threatened if they begin to believe in their power. Therefore, we fear ratifying their belief in newfound power by laughing since they could surpass our status if we support their skills at humor.

In many cases, there is a very fine line between humor and sarcasm. Commonly, a person that offers a joke poses a threat. This often provokes sarcasm intended to disempower the person making the joke. Also, there are occasions when someone tries to mask sarcastic comments with humor. This involves making a humorous remark that is tinged with "inside information" that others may not know. To illustrate this, let us consider an example. Mary and Jackie belong to a ladies club. Jackie knows that Mary ruined her living room carpet by spilling paint on it when she was redecorating. The incident embarrassed Mary and she did not tell the other women what happened. One day, a few of Mary and Jackie's friends discussed painting their houses. Jackie said, "I know some of us are wonderful with paint, isn't that right, Mary?" If Mary takes Jackie's words as a good-natured, humorous comment, then it serves its purpose. If Mary becomes angry or hostile, she may appear "overly sensitive" or "paranoid" unless she tells the others why the remark upset her. For this reason, the person receiving the comment may not respond for fear of the reaction of others, and the person making the comment needs not fear direct recourse.

We may see that sometimes conflict occurs when a remark meant to be humorous is overanalyzed. In either case, it is the choice of the receiving party to respond or choose to feel disrespected, hurt or attacked. Our first instinct may involve saving face, in cases like these. Such a response may lead to an unproductive exchange of words; you may also find that others see you as the offending agent.

Those with lower status power seem to endure more sarcasm and put-downs. I have pointed out that many people use humor and sarcasm to try to build relationships and gain status within groups. An unwritten code often dictates who receives the teasing. When entering into a group, a person must take care not to put down the wrong person or the results could be devastating to building relationships.

Depending on the power structure of the group, members often avoid putting down those in the group with the highest or lowest status. If someone attempts to insult the highest status member, this not only threatens that person, but all the other members, too. Likewise, the group members may see the lowest status members as weak and unable to defend themselves. In this situation, the others in the group may come to his/her rescue. We may sense this complex group dynamic, and often avoid humor or sarcasm until we feel safe and at ease with the members. People often see others who resort to humor or sarcasm as arrogant. When we view people as arrogant, we may feel the need to diminish their power. Why? People who come across as arrogant give an air of invulnerability; this impression may motivate us to defeat their sense of power.

ARROGANCE, PRIDE, AND CONFIDENCE

In terms of emotion, what is arrogance? I say that arrogance is a protective emotion used to defend a feeling of vulnerability. People normally display arrogance when they want to feel recognized for some talent or accomplishment viewed as strong, good, or right. The driving force behind arrogance comes from the belief that one talent or ability may overshadow all of the parts of one's life that feel bad, wrong or weak. Arrogance then becomes a defensive shield against our own shame, guilt, and inadequacy.

An arrogant person often appears unfazed by pain or hurt and may use sarcasm and humor to continue to maintain status. There are common traits often seen in arrogant people; they are quick to point out shortcomings in others while promoting themselves as experts in some area in order to obtain more status power. My clients who express arrogance often do so because of feelings of pain, sadness, and/or loneliness. Many times, they feel abused and manipulated by others. The purpose of using their arrogance is to assure them that no one can hurt them again. However, due to underlying feelings of hurt, anger and discontent, they may become the attacker or persecutor. In this case, they often rationalize away their aggression with their clouded sense of logic and justification.

Arrogance can take the form of withholding emotion. This follows the belief that some hold that expressed emotion shows weakness or vulnerability. Have you ever seen boxers giving each other "the eye" in the moments before a fight? This is an example of how athletes use arrogance in an attempt to intimidate their opponents. The art of using arrogance involves avoidance of showing others that their attacks or reprisals hurt. If the opponent sees any sign of weakness (humanness), they may seek to exploit it. An arrogant person may continue to attack as the behavior is reinforced by exposing the flaws of their victims— flaws the attacker may feel he has.

Similarly, this giving the eye is common in the animal world. Dogs, whether domesticated or wild, stare at each other to establish dominance. The dog that looks away first, or breaks the stare, expresses vulnerability and weakness.

Dennis Rodman was a professional basketball player who mastered the expression of arrogance. Rodman, often verbally, wore his opponents down to a point where they became frustrated and angry and committed fouls. He used sarcasm to evoke anger or frustration and when attacks came toward him, he played the innocent victim (remember the victim instigator). After a conflict, he would flash an arrogant smile that attempted to re-establish his status. While other players and even referees understood his tactics, he succeeded at nearly playing above the rules and he continued to draw other players in with his tactics.

There is, however, a problem with using arrogance. Often, it is difficult to let go of since we use it to protect our vulnerability. Because of this, many who use this emotion have difficulties in relationships. As time passes, arrogance often grows; this is because it seeks to hide more and more negative feelings and loneliness. If you will remember Dennis Rodman's actions and attempts to get attention off the court, I think it illustrates this point. Although some may see arrogance as a protective ally, it commonly becomes a serious detriment to their growth.

We often misunderstand pride in its purpose as an emotion. I would describe the purpose of pride as letting us know when we feel good about ourselves deep down inside. Let us not confuse pride with arrogance. We use arrogance to let others know when we have done something we want others to think is great. If we compare these two emotions, we see that pride is an emotion we experience inwardly, and arrogance is an emotion we express outwardly. Pride does not protect, it empowers. We often describe people who truly feel pride as humble, confident, reserved, and powerful. True pride may seem elusive, difficult to obtain. This is because it often does not come from actions of the individual; it comes from a belief in the self. Arrogance often comes from outward actions and attempts to hide internal beliefs.

Identifying pride as one of the seven deadly sins causes some problems. I would support substituting the emotion arrogance for pride on this list. I believe that pride has often been confused with arrogance and/or has been defined as the same emotion. If we consider a power model, pride expressed by those with lower levels of status can threaten those with higher levels of power in the hierarchy. Pride tends to decrease the need for dependency, direction, and guidance. This is because those who feel pride believe in their ability to care for themselves. Therefore, it would behoove those who wish to remain in power to find fault with, redirect, or put limits on positive emotions such as pride and self-confidence.

What have centuries of training and refocusing pride resulted in? We see a national and religious pride in addition to pride in our family and company. Often, however, we learn that people view pride in ourselves as bad or wrong. Pride is not always proper. We may encounter unfounded pride and try to educate people to help them see ways to manage their pride. In every place in this paragraph that I used the word *pride* it should likely be replaced with *arrogance*. How can we teach our children and others to manage their pride when we do not know how to manage our own? When other people feel pride, it can often bring up feelings of jealousy and envy in us, since we do not feel this. For these reasons, we often wish to find ways to take away their pride and power by finding fault with them. Suddenly, pride becomes a valuable commodity that we must protect and hide from others; this promotes the use of arrogance to protect our fear of having our pride taken away.

What helps you to feel confident? For most of us, confidence comes from feeling that we have a talent or ability for a task or group of tasks. There are times, however, we may feel proud of an achievement, but lack confidence in our ability to repeat our perceived success. After completing something positive, have you ever said, "I probably couldn't do that again in a million years?" We may also use arrogance along with our feelings of confidence. In addition, we may use arrogance to mask our lack of confidence. Very rarely do people feel confident in their whole self.

Confidence is often limited to certain abilities and may improve a person's view of himself or herself overall. People are, however, more likely to do things that accentuate areas where they feel confident. Why do we have this tendency? We often embrace things we feel we are good at in order to keep our status and to reduce the chance that others will see our weaknesses. For example, Michael Jordan probably would not attempt to become a comedian unless he had a reason to feel that he would be good at it. There are those who are skilled at athletics and their confidence is justified; still others may take stabs at them out of their own insecurity and feelings of inadequacy.

We may see that the interaction between arrogance, pride and confidence is ongoing. We still, however, tend to ignore how they affect us and how we react to our experience of these feelings and others. We must realize and take responsibility for our arrogance. Also, we should see that it is acceptable to feel pride and confidence. It is important to know that others often feel threatened when they see people who look confident or proud. If we feel proud and confident, people may try to alter our emotions in an attempt to try to decrease our sense of power or increase their own.

FLIPPANCY AND DEFIANCE

Figure 8.1 illustrates the use of flippancy as a first line of defense. We often overlook flippancy as a feeling. Flippancy is protective; it is often used as a shield of non-caring and is summed up by, "I don't care," or the contemporary "whatever." Flippancy comes out in children and teens toward their parents when their parents attempt to punish them. The intent of this phrase is to ward off efforts to try to diminish their power or try to overpower them. Thus, we may feel that if it looks like I don't care, then I don't feel pain. If I don't feel pain, then I do not hurt. If I do not hurt, then you cannot hurt me. If you cannot hurt me, then I cannot lose. If I cannot lose, then I must win. We do not necessarily consciously think this through, but we learn this through experience and observation.

The purpose of defiance is to help an individual hold on to the power they have obtained. A protective emotion is often the first line of de-

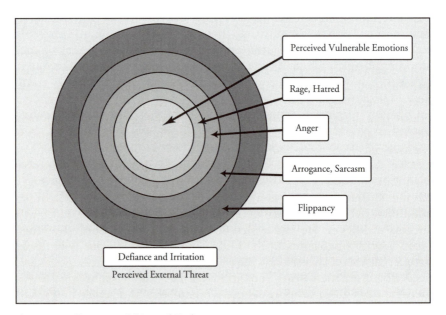

Figure 8.1 Emotional Line of Defenses

fense. The first stage in a conflict is to defend our point of view. If we feel that this does not ward off a threat, then we may resort to another protective emotion. People behave differently, and their emotions progress in various ways when they sense a conflict. Often the progression occurs in the following order: defiance ("You can't tell me what to do"), flippancy ("I don't care what you say"), sarcasm ("Sure, like you're so perfect"), arrogance ("At least I don't go around telling people what to do, like you do"), anger ("You're so stupid! Why don't you just leave me alone?"), and if anger does not work, then hatred ("I hate you! I wish you would die!") or rage ("I am going to kill you!"). We may now see that powerless feelings of weakness fuel these powerful outward displays of emotion. I tell people that there is an inverse relationship between the degree of strength being shown externally and the weakness felt inside. The purpose for the increase in defiant emotions is to keep others away from our feelings of pain and weakness, since we believe that our aggression may add to their hurt. With this understanding, it is necessary that both parties in the conflict see the sense of weakness in the opposing party to decrease their desire to counterattack.

HATRED AND FORGIVENESS

It should be easy to see that hatred is a very powerful protective emotion. People use hatred to condone every type of violence and injustice known to humankind. Hatred spawns wars, murders, beatings, bigotry and nearly every type of abuse that we can imagine. We can find so many saddening examples of hatred throughout our history. Hatred serves a protective purpose; it protects us from our own fears and vulnerabilities. Perhaps the most positive purpose of hatred is that it may teach us the value of love in a roundabout way. Remember the phrase that there is a fine line between love and hate. In these situations, hatred often protects us from feeling hurt when we feel that someone we love rejects or hurts us.

Why do some people find it so difficult to understand and resolve their hatred? Perhaps it is because people fear that doing so may mean having to confront their own guilt, shame or similar overwhelming emotions. Let's take a man we'll call Jacob as an example. Jacob is a successful lawyer. He has a nice home and drives a Corvette. When Jacob is with his friends at the health spa, he likes to put down poor people. Jacob tells his friends that winos and bums are freeloaders and need to get off their butts and find jobs. He gripes about how all the taxes he pays go to support people who are lazy and refuse to work.

Jacob, however, has a secret that he would never share with his friends. When he was young, his family received welfare because his father couldn't hold down a job; his father was an alcoholic, as was his mother. Jacob grew up feeling humiliation, shame, helplessness and disgrace because he had shabby clothes, lived in a bad neighborhood, and his parents were constantly fighting. He did not want to feel these things, but did not know what to do. He clawed his way through school, managed to get a scholarship and pursued his career. Over time, he developed hatred for poor people as he sought to distance himself from his past and the emotions he felt in his youth. As a man, Jacob shows hatred and contempt for poor people while hoping that no one will ever suspect that he was once one of them. In this manner, he uses hatred as protection from himself and his past.

Several things often surround hatred. We might think of ignorance, judgment, misinformation, and inaccurate logic, just to name a few of these things. We may feel the need to justify hatred, and we do so with logical defenses such as rationalization, denial, and projection. We use such strong defenses to justify our hatred; it is often very difficult to help people to change the belief systems surrounding their hatred. We may feel that by letting go of hatred, we are giving away power. Additionally, if someone decided to let go of their hatred, they might have to accept the idea that their hatred was wrong, and this might create renewed feelings of guilt, shame, weakness, etc. We discussed our society's feelings toward emotions that many think of as weak. We can therefore see that people may resist letting go of hatred to avoid showing weak emotions.

At first, we may see forgiveness as a weaker emotion, since it can involve giving in to others. But it takes a great deal of courage to find forgiveness inside ourselves because we must accept our own misperceptions. If we look closely at forgiveness, we can see that it teaches us about love. When we forgive, we experience the giving aspect of love. When we receive forgiveness, we learn to accept love. By either giving or receiving forgiveness, we can learn both sides of offering and accepting love. I believe that there are two reasons we have trouble forgiving. One reason may stem from having to accept the idea that we misjudged someone's intentions, which can lead to guilt. The other reason may involve having to decide that a change in the person has removed his or her ability to harm us.

We often hear the phrase, "Forgive and forget." For many who have suffered abuse, this phrase expresses something they do not desire. It is common that victims of abuse do not wish to forget what happened because they are afraid it may happen again. Forgiveness does not condone this behavior, nor does it mean that it was okay for someone to harm us. Forgiveness, instead, requires that we see that the person who harmed us was human, as are we; as such, we need to recognize that our hatred often continues to harm us by keeping the emotional wounds festering and open. As we keep it bottled up inside, our hatred can eat us alive from the inside out. While it may be the most challenging emotion to find, forgiveness can often be the key to our own healing and freedom. It is often our own fear that keeps us from forgiveness.

HAPPINESS AND LOVE

The purpose of happiness is to let us know when life or life events are going well. Happiness helps us enjoy what life has to offer; however, it is unrealistic to expect to feel happy all the time. Many times when I talk with parents, they tell me that they only want their child to *be* happy, but they feel no desire to try to address their own unhappiness. Eastern philosophy says that a search for happiness denotes an absence of happiness. On one front, happiness can appear to be a very powerful emotion. Yet, our society tends to view people whom are happy all the time as being ignorant, naïve, or simple-minded, which implies a weaker quality.

There are those in our culture who have a tendency to want to spoil happiness for others who are experiencing it. People will often ask, "What are you so happy about?" Feelings such as envy, jealousy and failure often inspire these types of questions or comments. We might identify this type of attitude as one we refer to as sour grapes. The result of those comments conveys the idea that we should avoid feeling happy or that we should hide it. In some situations, we use the illusion of happiness as a defense. Similar to denial, some use happiness as a defense to hide their true feelings, and avoid dealing with their unhappiness. We may call this "sweet lemons." There is danger in this because, while the person is using this façade of happiness, aspects of their life may be crumbling around them. Often, by the time they accept the truth in their life, a great deal of damage is present, and suffering through it is painful. This often reinforces attempts to deny reality.

In regard to our happiness, we have a right to find happiness in a wide range of things in life; from the simplest things to succeeding at the most difficult challenges. It is in our best interest to feel true happiness, as with all emotions, in balance with other emotions.

Some believe that a feeling of love permeates through all emotions and all interactions in our life. Along these same lines, some believe that we learn about love from each of life's experiences and from all of our emotions. The purpose of love is to help us know when we feel a connection with another person, our self or something else. Love is a very misunderstood emotion. There are many different theories of love, and each idea has its own unique qualities. We may feel love for our parents, our friends, our brothers and sisters, our husband or wife, our pets, among still other things.

DIFFERENT KINDS OF LOVE

Using the word *love* to indicate all the types of love we feel is vague and can cause confusion. If we look to various languages, especially the ancient derivations of languages, we see that there is more than one word used to describe different kinds of love. Ancient Greek writings discuss three different types of love. Agape is the type of love we may feel for a human being, for a sunny day, for the earth, for our pets. . . . Eros is a romantic type of love between people who have "fallen in love." Intimate partners, such as husband and wife, feel this type of love. Philos is a brotherly type of love often felt between a parent and child or brothers and sisters, or between friends, and, to some degree, even for a pet.

A major part of having a lasting marriage involves not only eros attraction, but also philos and agape types of love. Research shows that there is a physical connection to the feeling of being in love that continues for about seven years in most humans. This indicates that likely all couples who experience eros may have periods of falling in and out of love. Therefore, philos and agape may often determine whether a relationship is one that will last. Couples' relationships may endure if they feel philos and agape toward each other to bind them together while eros waxes and wanes. However, there are couples that feel a philos and/or agape attraction for each other; but one or both never find the eros connection. This sensation can result in a great deal of frustration and pain for one or both parties. In other words, philos or eros alone is not likely to sustain a healthy intimate relationship. A big reason people stay in marriage when they do not have these emotionally loving connections is out of fear. The difficulties mount when the consequences and side effects impact both people's lives and even the lives of their children.

If we cannot learn to love ourselves with all our shortcomings and imperfection, then how can we truly learn to love others? True love means accepting others and ourselves as we/they are, without wanting us/them to change. This means being willing to understand others and ourselves in all of our humanness. Learning to love one's self means loving all those bad habits and emotions that we don't like. This is a difficult concept because of what we learn in our culture relative to punishment, consequences, and conditions of worth. In most cases, it is true that we must love and minister to our self before we can experience personal growth. Unfortunately, there are many times when the path to learning self-love comes at the expense of those who travel the path of life with us.

This concept of self-love is easily twisted, perverted, and reshaped into what it should not be. Therefore, when we don't feel love toward ourselves, we often direct our pain and confusion onto others and blame them for our problems, which can result in emotional difficulties for both parties in the relationship.

We considered the notion that we may see happiness as a weaker or more vulnerable emotion. Similarly, it could be argued that love is an equally or more vulnerable emotion. Love can make us feel very vulnerable. This is quite true when we think that our partner is abusing their power, taking advantage of it, or giving their love to someone else. Men are especially sensitive to protecting the more vulnerable side of love; it can evoke an intense feeling of foolishness or shame. This feeling of vulnerability is common because love is a very strong emotion.

We can make an example of Bob and his wife, Ann. One day, Bob decided to surprise Ann by showing up at her office to take her to lunch. A co-worker tells Bob that Ann and another co-worker named Paul have already gone to lunch and that she won't be back for an hour. Bob first feels hurt that she has gone to lunch with a male co-worker, although he knows Ann and Paul are friends. His heart sinks and pounds, but he simply thanks the woman who bore this upsetting news and returns to his car.

Bob met Paul at a company picnic given by Paul and Ann's employer. Although Bob liked Paul, he may now feel that Paul is his opponent that vies for Ann's attention. Therefore, Bob may feel threatened on many levels and in many areas. If Ann disliked Paul (at the very least), she would not volunteer to spend time with him. Bob feels fear as he wonders about the extent of her feelings for Paul. Are they having an affair? What if they are? What will happen to the marriage, his life, and their finances, and how will he deal with what might be, in his eyes, the ultimate betrayal? Bob begins to feel angry and foolish for trying to surprise his wife and do something nice for her, only to find that she's spending her time with another man.

As he drives back to his office, Bob's anger becomes sprinkled with another fear: what if he was unworthy of Ann's affection to begin with? Whom had he been fooling all this time, thinking he was good enough for her? He begins to think about all his shortcomings and senses that Ann probably could have found a man who is "better" than he is. We can see that Bob's initial feeling of vulnerability brought forth many other emotions. We may identify some of them as these: sadness, loneliness, abandonment, deception, fear, and/or unworthiness. Because these emotions feel so raw, individuals are prone to bring up anger, hatred, and rage to protect themselves from these emotions and others.

Bob felt hurt when he heard that Ann was eating with Paul. Still, he would not display this feeling because he, like many males, believes that he should avoid expressing these more vulnerable emotions. Our culture socializes boys to believe that they must act to convey strength and power, no matter what emotions they may feel. The result is that men are less willing to allow themselves to feel intense feelings of love in relationships. It is also common for a person to take a victim role when they feel that someone whom they care about does not seem to reciprocate their feelings of love.

Bob knows Ann loves him, but he may feel that his gesture of kindness backfired and that if Ann loved him as much as he loves her, she would have been there when he showed up. This is not rational; she didn't know he would surprise her for lunch and, therefore, lunching with a co-worker has nothing to do with how she feels toward her husband. However, he uses her perceived abandonment to call himself and his value into question. In his mind, he is right to feel hurt and angry because she shouldn't have lunch with men, especially when the outing excludes him. It is important to remember that when we feel rejected by others, it is often our own feelings of inadequacy and hurt, from which we are attempting to hide.

There are many phrases, songs, teachings, and writings on love. As many ways as the lessons are taught, it is unfortunate that we are not able to truly learn and apply them. I do not believe that the object or purpose of our lives is to provide only love, but if we can learn the value and power that love can bring us, and those around us. We may then learn to use it with more wisdom and understanding.

Each parent must remember that young children often offer unconditional love to their parents. We may believe that their love is out of dependency or ignorance; but we can choose to see that our children came from our own flesh, they may be trying to help us see our virtues and to help us accept our flaws. Our own perceptions and beliefs prevent us from loving ourselves as we are. We may have been given other less productive messages earlier in life. However, we make a choice to continue to believe the more negative messages and deny our own truth.

RESPECT

Respect is a somewhat elusive emotion. It is not easy to define or put into words, but, as I see it, respect is the act of acknowledging someone's power and their right to that power. Do not confuse this with acknowledging status. We all want respect and strive for respect from others. We do not necessarily want to do the work required to receive the respect, and in a hierarchical world, we think that we should be respected based on our status. Wanting respect based on our status is not based on what we have done to earn respect, but what others should think about us and how they should treat us, based on the position that we hold. We want our children to respect their elders, regardless of how their elders treat them. We must ask whether we have modeled respect to them.

I look at respect differently from the perspective of its definition in a hierarchical model by framing it in an equity model of power. A hierarchically based respect is based in fear (does this sound familiar?). In other words, "I am supposed to respect and fear your status for fear of what you can do to me if I don't." This often translates into those people demanding the same thing when they move into higher levels of status. An equity-based respect is based in love. "I will respect you for who you are. Not because you are less than or greater than me, but because we all deserve to be respected, not only by others, but most importantly by ourselves." In this manner, I learn to respect everyone and am more likely to treat others as I have been treated. Isn't that what we really want to teach our kids?

Hierarchically based respect is more about being worshipped than it is about true respect. I cannot tell you how many times I have had to have this discussion with parents and teach them that their children want to feel respected as much as the parents do. Often, I found that the problems in the family subsided when the parents moved more toward an equity-based level of respect. Remember that we are all going to seek power from others in different ways if we never feel worthy within ourselves.

LOGIC

You may be asking, "What is logic doing in a discussion of emotion?" Logic is a central part of our perception of power since, in its true form, it involves an absence of emotion. Its major purpose is that it helps us to make sense of the world; however, many times we may use it to try to twist the logic of others or outwit them in order to enhance our own sense of power or get us out of a difficult situation.

Children often become fluent at using logic with their parents and are able to talk their way out of trouble. At this point, the use of logic becomes a defensive or self-serving effort that loses its quality and benefits no one. We may use logic in the development of lies and manipulations of the truth. How do we abuse logic? People are most likely to feel inclined to abuse logic when they want to deny, justify, rationalize, deceive or manipulate. The purpose of this abuse is to help us advance our cause to manipulate our sense of right, not only to others, but to ourselves.

The premise behind using logic when we sense a conflict involves the following sequence of thoughts: 1. If I use logic, then I am not feeling emotion. 2. If I am not feeling, then I do not hurt. 3. If I do not hurt, then you cannot hurt me. 4. If you cannot hurt me, then I will not feel pain or weakness. 5. If I do not feel pain or weakness, then I cannot lose. 6. If I cannot lose, then I will always win. 7. If the conflict continues, I will continue to use logic until I tire out my adversary. 8. If my adversary continues to reject my logic, then I will have to exert it more forcefully. 9. If my logic is ultimately not accepted by others, then I will figure out a way to bend my logic to find victory in my perception. . . . There is no defeat . . . defeat is unacceptable, since it denotes weakness, and I am strong. Due to socialization issues, males often use this approach to logic. However, I see that as society evolves toward being more competitive in both genders, females are adopting the same approach.

The logic illustrated is flawed because in order to acknowledge a conflict, both parties have to sense and respond to a feeling of threat. Neither party may admit to feeling threatened, since perceiving threat might show weakness. But, how many times can you remember someone stating that they had an argument, only to find the other party stating that it was not an argument; it was a discussion. Once again, this is Logic's way of manipulating reality to fit its perception.

Some people using logic during conflict do not want to admit to feeling emotion; but they still react out of fear or threat when sensing that they need to defend a point of view. During therapy, I try to help the client see that there is a logical side to each emotion. Additionally, they may find that using logic is not bad or wrong, but grew out of the need to protect themselves and find a sense of control.

For this next section, I will refer to logic as an aspect of self (we mentioned the concept of "emotional aspects" in Chapter 6). Logic is often the best friend of the "control freak." Logic seeks a sense of control and power and has a way of getting itself out of many jams. In such a case, emotions become the enemy, because Logic sees emotions as obstacles that cloud Judgment's view. These perceptions cause Logic to try to outwit the emotions so that they will feel that they cannot compete with Logic.

To clarify this concept, I will use an analogy that I often use with my clients. Let us suppose that Logic is just one sphere of influence in our life along with all other aspects (emotions, attitudes, beliefs, and defenses) and all command a different space within the sphere of our self. As has been discussed before, defining the positions of these aspects comes about through the formation of an internal power structure. If

Logic wants to assume control, then it wants to be able to direct where the sphere goes. In order to direct the sphere, Logic has to see where it is going. To see where it is going, Logic needs to be in front. If Logic is to always be in front, defining the direction of the self, then the sphere has to stop spinning. How can a sphere get where it is going if it cannot roll? Spinning or rolling is what a sphere does best. Instead, Logic has to figure out how to get the sphere to move in the direction it wants to go without rolling.

From this viewpoint, Logic must expend a lot of energy to control the sphere and keep it from rolling so it can remain in front. Logic seeks to stay in control and it can only do so by stopping any movement of the sphere; another aspect of our self may alter Logic's desired course if allowed to block the vision of Logic. By the nature of this analogy, we see that if one aspect of ourselves must always stay on top, another must always be on the bottom.

Clients who have a dominant aspect (emotion, logic or defense) often have a distorted outlook on the direction of their life; this may lead a person to develop negative mental attitudes and unbalanced priorities. Because of this, we need to allow all aspects to function as intended. This is only a brief version of the therapeutic model; it does not address many areas relative to each person.

BOREDOM

We may think of boredom as an interesting emotion. Most people do not generally view it as an emotion, let alone see it as strong or weak, and it does not arouse many strong reactions. I see boredom as a neutral emotion; it may serve to offer protection or cause us to seek out stimulation. Commonly, we may think of boredom as an absence of emotion, in which people seek to feel some sense of stimulation. What do you feel when someone says, "I feel bored"? You may feel the need to suggest or offer some form of entertainment. Otherwise, you may respond with a task, or feel frustration, confusion, and/or helplessness . . . etc. If a guest continues to feel bored when they are visiting you, you may feel fearful that if you fail to entertain them, the person feeling bored will go elsewhere to find excitement.

How is boredom a protective emotion? We may use boredom to avoid feeling unpleasant emotions. Children in therapy often express feelings of boredom when we discuss topics that may feel intimidating or painful to them. Children also tend to become easily distracted and fidgety when they begin to feel uncomfortable. I quickly realized that when they stated their boredom, they used it as a means to avoid feeling some emotion. The child's attempt was to encourage me to change the activity or topic, and allow them to avoid having to deal with the emotion.

Sometimes using boredom as a distraction happens consciously; but more commonly, we unconsciously use it as a defense tactic. Although many use boredom, hyperactivity, and distractibility to help avoid emotions or memories, we don't often realize when we are using it.

When we use boredom to help us pursue excitement or activity, it is hard to pinpoint any one emotional experience that we seek. Boredom just seems to prompt us to look elsewhere for something to do. In order to help us focus our boredom in positive ways, it is important to have some structure defined or to have a list of ideas for things to do. When they feel bored, many children and teens have a tendency to find things to do that can be negative or dangerous; this is why having structure to guide their activity is so important.

As we age, we often rely on habitual behaviors when we feel bored. Some time-honored favorite responses to boredom include: eating, sleeping, drinking, watching television, and other habits that may be positive or negative. I am not sure whether boredom and the habitual behaviors arise to help people avoid feeling unpleasant emotions. Think about how you and those around you handle it. Is it a diversion for other emotions?

SUMMARY

This chapter has provided an overview of emotions that appear strong, and it gives you a good perspective of the emotions and how and why we view them as strong. I am sure that if you look more deeply at the protective emotions, anger, rage, arrogance, defiance, flippancy, sarcasm, and hatred, you will see that they serve to protect a deeper weakness. However, keep in mind that how these emotions come across to others determines if they look strong or weak. I also hope that you are able to see the value of these emotions and that they serve a purpose in the grand scheme of things. Keep in mind that we all have the same emotions; however, what we do with them makes us different.

QUESTIONS

1. If you look back at different events in your life, can you see how you may have used emotions for protection?
2. After reading this chapter, can you see how logic fits into your life and interactions? If so, how?
3. How do you respond to boredom? Does it ever lead you to try new things?

9

Emotions Viewed as Weak or Less Powerful

The true mirror of our discourse is the course of our lives.
—*Michel de Montaigne (1533–1592)*

TEACHING OBJECTIVES

- Provide an understanding of what emotions are viewed as weak and why
- Explain why emotions viewed as weak are avoided during conflict
- Explain the value of these emotions

We will now turn our attention to emotions that are often viewed as being weak or vulnerable. We may feel reluctant to display these emotions for fear of how others may perceive us. In conflict, our society often chooses to express strong emotions instead of weak ones. When a conflict arises, we avoid emotions that express weakness unless we feel that they may work to our advantage. Take a look at the following example.

Consider the situation of Abby and Sheila. Abby is the office manager where Sheila works. Sheila has a habit of spending too much time on her lunch break. Abby has told her that she must watch the amount of time she spends at lunch because it is unfair to her co-workers.

One afternoon, Sheila returns from lunch fifteen minutes late and Abby confronts her. Sheila first defends herself and says she could not avoid being late because of traffic. Abby ignores the excuse and continues to counsel Sheila about her lateness. Sheila sees that her protective anger is not working and she begins to cry. When Sheila starts crying, Abby offers her a tissue and pauses while Sheila composes herself. In the process, Abby calms down, then wonders if she overreacted to the situation and ends the confrontation. In this case, a weaker emotion served Sheila's cause. If Sheila felt successful in her effort to protect herself with anger, she would not need to use the weaker emotion.

We will explore the impact of these emotions we often view as weak, and consider why they lead us to spend so much energy to keep them at bay. I hope that you will understand and share my thoughts on this topic and see that all emotions are powerful and essential to our mental, physical, and spiritual health.

SADNESS

Have you ever thought of depression and sadness as being different? Many people think that these two are the same, but they are not. From a technical standpoint, depression is a cluster of emotions, feelings, and belief systems; it is true, however, that sadness may be a large component of depression, and so may hopelessness. Many view sadness as a very heavy emotion that is painful to feel, and is often painful to see in others. When people see others who appear to feel sad, they may try to cheer that person up, ignore the sadness, or leave. We, as a society, do not handle sadness well. We commonly do not know what to do with sadness when we feel it, and even more, do not know what to do when others feel it. It may seem that, in a perfect world, sadness would disappear from the deepest recesses of our minds. But sadness serves a very valuable purpose.

Although it may be difficult to accept, sadness lets us know when we feel pain and often helps us to express and let go of the pain. Similar to our emotions, our nervous system assists us in sensing cold and hot, being touched and physical pain. Think of what would happen to our bodies if we did not experience physical sensations of pain. Without a sense of pain, we would probably cut or burn ourselves very seriously before we even knew it. We partly owe to our sense of touch the debt of our survival as a species.

Some survivors of abuse learn to deaden their sense of both emotional and physical pain. The blocking of pain served a purpose for these people at the time of their abuse. Repressed pain, however, can have radical effects on their physical bodies, mental health, and relationships. Many people who cannot feel pain also cannot form emotional ties.

If we think about what helps us form relationships, we can see that there is a balance of emotions shared in the relationship. One of these is sadness. In a relationship, sharing these emotions with each other helps both parties to feel that the other can empathize with them; this gives one a chance to care for the other when pain and sadness are present. Allowing others to care for us is not only important to us, but is very important to our partner. It is often the fear of our own pain that keeps us from feeling our sadness.

Many clients I have helped have wanted to put a limit on their sadness or tried to say that the time for them to feel sad should be up. This effort to limit the expression of our sadness and grief to a set amount of time is often a conscious and logical choice, not an emotional one. Yes, it is true that while we are feeling sadness, we still have to live in this world. As adults, we may have children to care for, a job, and many other responsibilities. But, if we do not give ourselves the chance to feel our emotions, we will likely pay the price at some time either with an emotional or physical breakdown.

Many people avoid feeling sadness because feeling sadness tends to lead us to feel weak and vulnerable. This, in turn, may cause us to feel fearful that others will hurt us. In each of our lives, we have experienced sadness and someone has either made fun of us, or tried to hurt us more. It doesn't take very many times to learn to protect ourselves when we already feel hurt. We also may remember times when parents told us to stop crying or said, "Stop crying, or I'll give you something to cry about." To a small child, these are very strong comments, especially coming from a parent whom the child depends upon for survival.

I feel very strongly that the parent's purpose in trying to stop their child from crying is because they, as a human, feel unable to comfort their child; the child is mirroring the parent's sadness to them. The parent's fear is, "If I feel sadness with my child, then who will be in control?" Interpreting sadness to mean weakness is a myth handed down through the ages. Yes, some times are better than others to feel sadness, but sadness is not a weak emotion. To those feeling sadness and grief, it can feel overwhelming and can drain a person's ability to feel like they can function. As I work with people, they often defiantly want to know what they are supposed to do with their sadness; I often tell them that there is no one way to deal with sadness.

We most often see tears in expressions of sadness, and chemically, there is a difference between tears of sadness and all other tears. It is also common to see sadness combined with anger and rage; this is probably to protect the vulnerable aspect of sadness. Some people have formed this tight connection between anger or rage and sadness. For these people, punching soft objects, exercise, chopping wood, and other safe types of physical activity help them release these emotions. For others, writing, meditating, and talking help with expressing or releasing emotions. In short, it is crucial to listen closely to our emotions and hear what they want to help us heal. Only then will our pain truly be resolved, rather than shoved under our unconscious carpet.

FEAR

Fear is a very misread feeling, since many see it as a useless emotion that hinders us from doing what we need to do in life. If we stop, however, and reflect on what fear does for us, we can see that fear keeps us from doing things that could harm us or others close to us. If we did not experience fear, we would likely not survive long. As we said of the sense of touch, we also owe fear a debt for our survival; it has kept us safe from trying to pet dangerous animals, thinking we could fly, or trying to grab fire with our bare hands. It is when we let our fear grow too powerful that it can become a liability. Fear also emerges when we are uneducated about situations, and seeks to avoid the unknown, since it does not know what to expect.

In many cases, we learn fear through watching other people and hearing what we are told about what things to fear. Think of the many times that you saw someone do something that caused him or her harm in some way and/or were told not to do it, and because of that, you avoided doing the same. How often do you see someone do something that did not injure them, but because it seemed risky or stupid, you did not attempt it? The old saying states that curiosity killed the cat. In this case, it is likely that the power of curiosity overcame the feeling of fear.

As you look at your life and realize how fear has affected you, it is important not to punish your fears; they were only trying to serve their purpose and preserve your life. In my opinion, it is best to take the time to understand the origin of your fears, rather than trying to control them. Many times, through therapy, I have observed that fear will try to express itself in other manners.

Some type of anxiety disorder affects at least 20 percent of our society. You have probably heard of many different anxiety disorders. You, or someone you know, may have one or some of these disorders that include phobias, obsessive-compulsive disorder, agoraphobia and/or panic disorder. The bases for these fears may come from some aspect of the conscious, but most likely from the subconscious. We often want to try to talk ourselves out of our fears or find ways to hide them; but somewhere within, an aspect in us feels the need to maintain that fear.

Many things can trigger fears and behavior patterns. We find that such things include life events, seasons of the year, birthdays, and even weather patterns. Why? Often this happens when Fear finds a cause and effect pattern in the things around us to alert Fear when it should try to protect itself. During therapy, it is not uncommon to see that when fears are exposed, they alter themselves into other fears and behavioral patterns.

I would like for you to ponder the following thought presented to me by a very wise teacher of mine, "Needs and fears are not so very different. For you, and so many others, the need creates the fear, and the fear creates the need."

FEAR-BASED EMOTIONS

Fear is a complex emotion and forms the basis for many other emotions. If we looked closely at various emotions, we would see that at the core of these emotions is a component of fear. If we see the fear component in emotions, it may aid in the understanding of each emotion. Threat, for example, is a fear that someone may harm me. Guilt is a fear that I have done something to someone that I feel I need to correct. Shame is a fear that I have done something to myself that I feel I need to correct. Embarrassment is a fear that I have done something stupid that others may think badly of. Doubt is a mild fear that something may not be possible. Worthlessness is a fear that I have no value. Insecurity is a fear that I do not deserve to get what I need from others or myself.

Since fear is a component of these emotions, fear is a driving force that helps us resolve the issues related to the feeling. We find that fear often moves us away from its source, and so we may feel prone to work toward solutions. Many people do not understand fear, and therefore often avoid the emotion and project it onto others. As we see the aspect of fear within some of our emotions, we become more able to accept an emotion in terms of growth and resolution.

People have many different fears. Some fears affect our lives in a very complex and tangled manner. Often these fears are not apparent until we make an effort to explore our feeling and/or therapy occurs. Since we view fear as a weak and negative emotion, it is necessary to mask these fears or hide them in other attitudes, behaviors, or belief systems. People commonly fear things we view as positive as well as things we want to avoid. That is to say, some people feel fear of failure, while others feel fear of success. Some people feel fearful toward being alone, while others fear being in a crowd. In either case, the feeling of fear comes from something inside us that needs to feel safe, loved and/or accepted. Additionally, it is very important to realize that the protective emotions (anger, rage, arrogance, defiance, flippancy, sarcasm, and hatred) are all fear-based because they are triggered to protect ourselves when we feel fear or threat.

Nelson Mandela said it in a moving manner when he stated, "We are often afraid of our greatness because of how it may make those around us feel. But who are we not to be great, talented, intelligent, powerful. . . ." Our fears only prevent us from becoming the person we could become. Then, we not only fear that we would have to live up to those standards, but we fear making others feel less than us. When looking at these fears, it is in our best interest to take the viewpoint that we have the power to create positives or negatives in our lives; this is true whether we are consciously aware of it or not. Since this is true, then we can take responsibility for everything in our life, and this further enables us to learn from these events in a proactive manner instead of merely avoiding them.

GUILT, SHAME, AND REGRET

I often describe Guilt and Shame as siblings, and in many ways, Regret is their parent (we will get to that later). A close relationship exists between these three feelings in a sense that they tell us that we did something that we should not do. Guilt lets us know when we do something to someone else that we should rectify. Shame lets us know when we do something toward ourselves that we should rectify. Regret lets us know when we did not do something we wanted to do, or wanted to do differently. While most of us would view guilt and shame as weak emotions that feel vulnerable, these emotions can feel overwhelming and paralyzing. Think of a child who is confronted by a parent and cannot look them in the eye or even speak because of the degree of shame and guilt they feel.

We can see that people often behave in a certain way when they feel guilt and shame. People feeling guilt or shame tend to avoid eye contact and may display behaviors that avoid the object of their guilt. Children feeling guilt or shame become more easily distracted and often become more hyperactive. Many people attempt to use humor and/or sarcasm to protect themselves from feeling guilt or shame; some may resort to anger or rage if feeling sufficiently threatened. People often misunderstand guilt and shame, and in many pockets of society, people avoid them at all costs. Many people feel that if they accept life events that they feel guilty or shameful about, then others will avoid or reject them. I believe that this avoidance of guilt and shame is why we live in a society full of "victims."

It is common for people to use guilt and shame as weapons from two perspectives or methods. The first method involves evoking guilt in someone when you want them to feel guilty. We may use this as a method of control. Parents often use this as a tactic when they want a child to stop engaging in a behavior. After parents use this tactic, many times the effect is lost. If we allow their resentment or anger to build, counterbalance, and protect them from feeling guilt and shame, the effect is lost. Rather than feeling guilt or shame, the child, instead, mistrusts and questions the manipulative nature of the parents' statements. When someone learns to defend their feelings of guilt and shame, it is very hard to get them to take responsibility for their actions.[9]

For example, let's look at Sally, a three-year-old, playing in her mother's garden. She pulls up flowers to make a necklace with them. Sally's mother walks outside to see what she is doing and finds her flowers uprooted and wrapped around her daughter's neck. In a stern voice, she says, "What did you do? What were you thinking? Look what you have done to my flowers! You have destroyed all of my plants." The intent of these comments was to have Sally think about what she did; but her mother took it further and the goal became to try to *make* Sally feel badly. If something similar was said to an older child who had had that done to them many times before, the child would have likely responded with, "I don't care. What are you going to do about it?" The effect of this flippant response is self-protection and not wanting to take responsibility for their actions to avoid feeling guilt and having their nose rubbed in it.

For an example of how older children respond to a similar situation, let us consider Susan and Donna. Susan is a teenager who has learned to protect her feelings of guilt and shame. Donna is Susan's mother and has had a strained relationship with her daughter for several years. For several months, Susan dated a boy named Tom, whom Donna liked very much. Donna found out that Susan started seeing another boy behind Tom's back. Donna told her daughter that she should be ashamed of herself and that she was disappointed in her behavior. She said that Susan should be honest with Tom if she no longer wanted to date him and that Tom deserved to know the truth. Susan told her mother to stop telling her what she should or should not do. She went on to say that the matter was none of Donna's business, that she did not know the whole story, and that she had no regrets for her actions. Even if Susan felt guilty inside, she might feel that Donna is trying to manipulate her and will not let Donna see her guilt because of her own fear. Through this example, we may see that this conflict could continue if neither party is willing to accept her role in the conflict. In this case, if Susan admits to feeling guilty, her mother may use that guilt against her, so she displays anger, denial and flippancy to protect herself.

The other method of using guilt as a weapon involves playing a guilty role to incite feelings of guilt in others. This is a more subtle use of control from a passive perspective. The first party may be seeking to play the role of a victim who needs a rescuer in order to displace their guilt. There are also those people who truly feel excess guilt about their actions and feel the need to make amends for their feelings of ineptness. For the other party, this creates discomfort in that they often question their own actions and feel their own emotions.

As an example, suppose Mary says something to Joe, who takes offense to her comment. Mary responds with a profuse apology and says that she always seems to say the wrong thing and should just stop talking to people. Joe, in turn, feels guilty for saying anything to Mary and tells her that he was too sensitive and what she said was okay; he was just having a bad day. At this point, both parties may feel awkward and conversation from this point may be somewhat stunted. Whether or not Mary felt consciously aware of what she was doing is debatable. Those who feel sensitive to this tactic may think that Mary was purposely trying to make Joe feel guilty. If Joe feels that Mary intentionally made him feel guilt, he may feel that Mary has a great deal of power to cause that emotion in him. It is important to remember that no one can make anyone feel anything, no matter how hard they try. We choose to feel what we feel at any point in time. We may not be aware of the degree to which we have the ability to choose what we feel. However, when we are able to master our feelings and understand how we give our power to feel emotion to others, we must accept our role in the exchange.

Shame is an emotion that many people never heal in their lifetime. Often, we bury shame in the quiet recesses of the subconscious, where it seems to surface at the "worst times" (in therapy, I would say it surfaces at the "best times" for us to heal it). The biggest fear regarding shame is that those from whom we most want acceptance will reject us. These fears of rejection often begin during childhood and remain in our subconscious throughout our lives. Remember that the fear of rejection seeks to protect us and prevent us from feeling rejected, isolated, and alone when we fear that we cannot care for ourselves. However, we often keep our secrets inside, and never find out that others have made similar choices and mistakes. If we let go of these fears, we find that we can be and feel accepted.

Those who do not accept others' faults or shortcomings are usually protecting their own issues. We commonly refuse to accept flaws in others because they mirror our own flaws. Seeing our faults in someone else evokes shame that we do not want to face. Since we feel fear toward recognizing our own shame, we often hide it behind anger, rage, hatred, humor, sarcasm, judgment, justification, projection, and rationalization. We all have the power to heal our shame and are worthy of our own forgiveness; we should use this power, rather than allowing others to influence our worthiness and deservedness of forgiveness.

I stated earlier that regret is the parent of guilt and shame; regret is a milder emotion that prompts us to look at what we could have done differently in our lives. This emotion does not cast blame, but urges us to take responsibility for our actions and learn from them. As I also stated earlier, we often use guilt, as well as shame, as a method of control. Guilt and shame commonly involve blame, fear, and failure when used as a weapon or tool of control. In this way, guilt and shame may be socialized emotions, whether learned or prompted. I am not disputing that these are valuable emotions because of their ability to help us learn; however, we also need to recognize how they may unproductively affect our and others' sense of power.

I owe this realization of regret versus guilt and shame to a client who brought these issues to light in the process of doing trance-work with her. Let's compare regret to guilt and shame and how they affect our sense of power; regret often gives a far less disempowering feeling. So, when we feel regret, we are less likely to avoid the emotion (to protect themselves from feeling manipulated) and may find it easier to learn from our action. When we learn from regret, the emotion is quicker to heal and we can learn and move on more quickly than if we feel weighted down by guilt and shame.

When thinking of regret, guilt, and shame, a major point to consider is the seriousness of the action that prompted it. It is likely that the more serious the act, the more likely we are to feel guilt and/or shame. However, if we are in a position of judgment, we may be more likely to believe that our child, spouse, subordinate . . . should be feeling and showing guilt, even if unwarranted. I often ask parents to refrain from trying to make a child feel guilt or shame. Instead, I advise them to observe the child's actions and see whether the child learns to avoid doing improper things in an effort to avoid self-imposed feelings of guilt and shame.

CONFUSED, MISUNDERSTOOD, DOUBTFUL, AND SKEPTICAL

Confused, misunderstood and doubt relate to each other in that they require more information before we can form conclusions. We think of these emotions as weak because if we admit that we don't know something, we may appear stupid. When feeling these emotions, we may also fear that others may take advantage of us. The problem is that when we do not try to resolve these emotions, we allow ourselves to remain ignorant.

We may see that confusion lets us know that we need more data about something before forming a conclusion. When you think of confusion, do you think of things like inadequacy, failure, and stupidity? Many people do, so it is common that they think of confusion as a weak emotion. Because of this, we give confusion a great deal of power to determine our attitudes toward ourselves. In today's hectic pace, we may see confusion as a waste of time as we try to figure something out.

When we feel misunderstood, we know we must give more information about what we are trying to express. If we continue to feel misunderstood, we may feel insecure or rejected. To illustrate this point, let's use two friends, Carl and Dan. They spend a lot of time at each other's homes and sometimes meet with other guys at a sports bar to watch ballgames. On several occasions, Dan has teased Carl about Carl's growing bald spot. Carl tried to play it off, wanting to appear as though he took the comments as friendly ribbing. After several of these remarks, Carl begins to feel betrayed by his friend and doesn't appreciate feeling that Dan is making fun of him. He decides to call Dan and try to let him know that his comments hurt. Dan becomes defensive and tells Carl that he should learn to either take a joke or just stay home. In light of Dan's attitude, he no longer feels comfortable meeting his friends for drinks and so he just stays home. Carl's feelings, first misunderstood and then a sense of apathy, led him to feel uncomfortable or rejected because of Dan's unwillingness or inability to understand his feelings.

We may feel doubt for a variety of reasons. In fact, the things that can lead us to feel doubtful are endless. Most often, we doubt our abilities to accomplish something or doubt the ability of others. Sometimes we doubt the existence or occurrence of events. A sense of doubt helps make us aware that someone may try to take advantage of us; also, it leads us to ask questions before forming an opinion. Doubt often protects us from feeling foolish or naïve. However, when doubt becomes too powerful an influence, it often prevents us from accepting truth or understanding and can keep us from growing as a person.

Excess doubt often stems from a lack of trust in the self and others. If I fail to trust my decision-making skills or doubt the honesty of others, then how can I feel confident in my decision? When we surround doubt with a feeling of hostility, defiance or anger, we may call it skepticism. Skepticism can be healthy in the face of someone who is trying to force their sense of truth on someone else. In this manner, skepticism seeks to ward off a threat. However, in the face of truth, skepticism can be pointless.

It should be easy to see that doubt and skepticism in moderation can be very positive emotions; opposition to these feelings in others likely prompted many scientific advancements. The need to prove things to people and to themselves prompted attempts to fly, to jump buses and cars on motorcycles, to seek a cure for cancer, and many things once thought impossible. It is often our own doubt that prompts us to try. Our doubt may occur in the face of others, but it is because we asked ourselves if we could accomplish something that pushed us to try.

At this point, I will return to the discussion of balance. Doubt and skepticism are helpful and needed feelings, when we balance them with other emotions and logic. Are you questioning or doubting some of what I stated in this book? I hope so. By wondering whether some of the things stated here are true, maybe you will experiment with some of these ideas in your life. When you can make this information personal to you and your life experience, it will have more meaning to you. In developing the theory and writing this book, I have felt doubt in many areas. Instead of listening to doubt and fear of failure, I asked more questions and sought answers, and I hope you will do the same.

FRUSTRATION, HOPELESSNESS, AND HELPLESSNESS

Frustration is often confused with anger. Why? It is because feeling a sense of frustration quickly spawns anger. Frustration plays an important role in our lives because it lets us know when we need to look more closely for answers. Frustration is often telling us when we are banging our head against a wall, and resort to anger to try to knock it down. It is only after we knocked down the wall that we realize that we cannot replace it. Frustration breeds the feelings hopeless and helplessness when it does not find what it wants. Since frustration often feels powerless, confused and helpless, but wants answers and/or results, it will resort to anger to try to force the outcome. Failure closely follows frustration when answers or successes are not at hand.

Hopelessness and helplessness are twins who seek help and answers from others because they feel powerless to effect change or growth. Many times, experiencing these emotions lets someone know when they are out of balance. Our society views these emotions as weak and useless. Therefore, a person feeling these things will often try to hide them until feeling very bewildered. By then, it may be too late to help them. They may also quickly resort to expressing these feelings when playing the victim and looking for someone to rescue them. Think of the chronic victim who is almost always looking for someone to take care of them.

Feelings of hopelessness and helplessness may vary in a person, depending on the outlook of the person. In addition, it matters whether or not they believe in their ability to perform a task. At first, we may not think of hopelessness and helplessness as powerful emotions, but they are. They are powerful motivators, and they help us to know when we need guidance from others.

FAILURE AND STUPIDITY

I hold failure to be one of the most important emotions that we feel. Unfortunately, our society treats a sense of failure as a bad or wrong emotion that often leads us to feel weakness. If we were to look closely at failure, we can see its importance lies in letting us know when we need to learn. Failure, in itself, is a very simple emotion. However, surrounding it with other emotions can make it very complex. We should feel lucky to have a personal reminder to let us know when we should learn something.

Take a moment to think how simple the purpose of failure is: to let us know when it is time to learn. Failure is not there to taunt us, kick us, or put us down; it is there to help teach us . . . to let us know when it is time to learn something valuable. When we continue to refuse to learn from our feeling of failure, it often grows more powerful, because *we* are feeding it through our avoidance. We may try so hard to deny feelings of failure that it can feel overpowering. As we mentioned earlier, the power structure in our society often causes others to focus on our perceived failures so that they may boost their own power.

I often tell the people I teach that failure is only an emotion, but it becomes a reality if we quit. It is our current societal belief systems that make failure seem real. We look at people's lives and our own and say, "This person was a failure; this experience was a failure. . . ." Then we wipe our collective brow and thank someone that it was not us. How many times do we avoid experiences because we think we may fail? What would other people say if they saw us fail?

Isn't it common to hide things that others may feel were failures? We all like others to feel that we are successful. When we continue to hide our true flaws, it becomes harder and harder to remember more and more lies so that we can keep our stories straight. What if we did not feel the need to hide our feelings of failure? We are likely making this thing we call failure into something much bigger than it is.

Using hypnotherapy often brings about many emotions in my clients as they review life events. I then try to help the client better understand the emotion. I often do this by asking the subconscious to give emotion an identity. Failure, similar to rage, is commonly a sort of monster. And like rage, this ugly-looking monster is something to avoid but for different reasons. Looking at it often brings up feelings of shame, guilt, stupidity, inadequacy, insecurity, fear, doubt, confusion, helplessness, or hopelessness. We create this monster out of our own internal attitudes, views and belief systems. If we choose to change these views and stop trying to avoid these emotions, they would cease to grow into such ugly, unwanted monsters in our minds. In many cases, it is the monster we avoid, not the reality. This is because our fear of failure deters us from trying. It is the choice of others to try to manipulate our feelings of failure; it is our choice to let them.

Stupidity and failure often go hand in hand. The logic: if someone failed, then they must be stupid. Once again, failure becomes an entity as well as stupidity. In truth, we may feel failure and stupidity, but we are always going to be human. The purpose of stupidity is usually a more intense reminder to help us learn; however, feeling stupid can prevent us from learning. If we feel stupid, we may not believe in our ability to learn.

We should see that stupidity becomes a very clouded and complex emotion. This is because we also shroud stupidity with a combination of feelings such as failure, shame, and guilt. At this point, feeling stupid becomes an overwhelming and often painful ordeal. It is needless, and not in our best interest, to complicate these emotional experiences. From this perspective, we see that children refer to experiences as good or bad, or shut down verbally when we press them to feel emotion.

It is important for us to use our capacity to think and comprehend to teach kids new and better ways to understand and manage emotion, especially failure and stupidity. When people believe they are stupid, they often quit, because they believe that they cannot change who they are, so why try.

INSECURITY AND THREAT

Feelings of insecurity and threat let us know when we feel unsafe or disadvantaged in some way. We may think of insecurity as a feeling that wants to hide. On the other hand, we have threat that wants to mobilize our defenses and protect us. These feelings are very important to our sense of self-protection. But, how we view the potential outcome often determines whether we wish to avoid the threat or to defend ourselves. Many people live their lives with feelings of insecurity that they hide from everyone else. These people expend a lot of energy trying to keep others from knowing about these feelings. They hide these feelings because they are often afraid of the insecurity itself.

People who feel insecure often use subtle defenses such as passive-aggression or disguised sarcasm to try to enhance their own status. They may also try to draw upon other people's power, or try to play the role of victim so that others may come to the rescue. We need to remember that feelings of insecurity are facts of life. Insecurity can be a springboard to help us know when we should have more faith in ourselves, or it can become an obstacle for us to hide behind. It is up to us to decide.

Yes, insecurity is ever-present, but we feel it most when we question our confidence. Threat, on the other hand, is a more proactive emotion and most generally pops up in situations that create a need for caution. A feeling of threat often activates the nervous system to secrete adrenaline in case a feeling of panic should arise.

Have you ever noticed how tired and washed-out you feel after an adrenaline surge or conflict? The tiredness is the result of all the energy our bodies use to prepare us for a physical reaction. People who live with a feeling of constant threat, such as those with post-traumatic stress disorder, often have very weak immune systems. This is likely a result of the constant drain put on the system. Many individuals have learned to desensitize themselves to stress; they may not be aware of the constant stress they feel. As with those who repress sadness, those who do not resolve their stress often suffer physical and/or emotional breakdowns.

TERROR AND PANIC

Terror and *panic* are terms that indicate states of extreme fear; however, while terror often feels helpless, panic looks for options and teams with the nervous system to trigger "fight or flight." Many think of terror and panic as weak emotions, since we feel fear and threat, but like many other emotions we view as weak, their effect on us is often overpowering.

Panic and terror are emotions that teach us to act out of avoidance. They often try to tell us to avoid doing something again because of fear of harm or injury. These feelings even lead people to avoid addressing these issues in therapy such as phobias to snakes, flying, public speaking. . . . It is important to separate the emotions panic and terror from the event that brought on the emotion. These emotions can serve a very valuable survival purpose, but only in certain circumstances. It is when they become overgeneralized or indirectly associated with other issues (sometimes due to unconscious motivations) that they can cause problems.

Adrenaline is a very powerful hormone that we secrete in moments of panic. It produces a feeling of power and extreme energy and strength. Most of us are aware of documented stories wherein people perform super-human acts, often to save a loved one when in a state of panic. At that time of the event, they felt caught up in the emotion and "adrenaline rush" and acted without thinking. It is likely that if the person took time to think about what they needed to do, they could not do it.

Some people seek out the adrenaline rush and learn to overcome the feeling of panic to enjoy the adrenaline. These people may seek out dangerous activities to provide this rush. To continue to get this rush, they must find more and more daring behaviors. I feel that people seek out these dangerous acts in order to feel a sense of power over a strong emotion (panic) and the desire to experience a hormonal surge. It is very likely that many of these people are hiding other emotions behind their actions. For many reasons, what feels more powerful than defying fear?

WORTHLESSNESS AND WORTHINESS

Worthlessness and worthiness help us to assign value to a number of issues of self, others, and objects. Some people think in terms of varying degrees of worth. If we think of the old question "Is the glass half empty or half full?" we see that some people may think in terms of varying degrees of worth or lack of worth. If we think about lacking worth, issues of worth relate to weakness and vulnerability. This is because of the perception that if you have to question your worth, then you must not feel worthy. Of the two emotions, worthlessness and worthiness, we are more likely to pay attention to feelings of worthlessness. We all have the power to question the value of anything in life. But, how often do we question the value of others so we can attempt to boost our own sense of value within ourselves?

Is there any true means of proving our worth to the world? Many people may try to quantify worth in terms of lives saved or dollars earned, but why does it never seem to be enough for most of us? The only person that we can truly prove our worth to is our self. None of the awards, "attaboys," and praise ever seems to be enough because Worthlessness may never feel valuable. We tend to strongly connect self-worth to insecurity and fear and this often comes from a hierarchically based model of scarcity.

Issues of worth often stem from childhood when our parents, often unknowingly, placed conditions on our acceptance. If we did certain things, then they rewarded us. If we didn't do these things, they ignored or punished us. Some parents are harsher than others are. Then we went to school and started to learn that if we got the grades, then people noticed us. We may have felt that we always had to do something to get something in return. This is often the way of the world, and our parents probably did the best they knew how. They also had their own issues of worthiness. The gift of these issues is that they keep us searching for our value, but to experience our worth, we have to find it within. Is it possible that we all have the same worth? What I am able to learn from others and their lives is invaluable to my growth and to me.

JEALOUSY AND ENVY

Some call jealousy "the green-eyed monster," and many think of envy as one of the "seven deadly sins." These two emotions are sometimes hard to understand and respect. Jealousy lets us know when someone has something that we want. We may see what they have (a toy, the love of someone, business holding, or position of status) as a thing of power and think that we would be more powerful if we had the object. Many see jealousy as a weak emotion because it involves a lack of something we desire; it is in indicator of worth. We often use anger, sarcasm, hatred, or other logical defenses to help us focus our jealousy, which then turns it into the green-eyed monster.

We must understand that feeling jealousy comes from feeling deprived or less powerful in some way. If we listen to the gift of jealousy, we know that it is likely time for us to look at and feel satisfied with our own sense of power or worth. Jealousy can prompt us to work harder to obtain our goals rather than take something that does not belong to us. When we stop and focus our jealousy on what the other person has that we want, we stay stuck. We then have to ask ourselves, "Is it in my best interest or theirs to try to take that from them?"

I describe envy as being the softer side of jealousy. Just as I stated earlier in the book that pride and arrogance are confused, I believe that jealousy and envy are, too. Jealousy often wants to take what someone else has, but envy respects what they have attained and would like to have the same thing.

Respect for the other person is a key aspect of envy. We can use envy as a driving force to help us attain similar goals or focus in other directions. Neither jealousy nor envy is a bad emotion, but some may use them in way that do not serve anyone's best interest. If we can talk to others without feeling fear of them judging us, we can often resolve issues with jealousy or envy. I have found that many people's feeling of jealousy stem from unresolved issues lodged deep in the subconscious. Feeling jealous and envious was the subconscious' ways of letting the person know that the issue was still present.

SUMMARY

This chapter presented you with a number of issues and emotions to ponder. In writing the last two chapters, I hope I met my goal of demonstrating that we need each emotion in our life and that value exists in all of them. It is important to seek balance in the manner in which we feel and express our emotions, as well as in how we live our life every day. While you may be questioning how to live in balance, you might want to seek guidance from within. My goal is that you begin to question within yourself to find answers before I let you know what I have learned.

If you have reviewed the list of emotions in the Appendix, then you know that the emotions presented in this chapter comprise a short list. I hope you will take some time to consider each emotion on the list on your own, take what you have learned about the emotions presented in the chapter, and find the value and gifts in the other emotions. Some of the emotions on the list may seem synonymous, but I would ask that you search for the unique quality in each emotion; try to discover what it can add to your appreciation of the emotion and your life experience.

At this point in the book, I have set up a great deal of theory. I presented you with much information, and you may likely question past learning and present beliefs and attitudes. This process of questioning is good, and I commend you on your efforts. If you feel confused, then you have more questions, and that's great! I hope your questions continue to find answers as you read on.

QUESTIONS

1. Do you avoid feeling or expressing certain emotions in an effort to appear stronger to others?
2. Do you feel that those around you influence your willingness or the manner in which you express these "weaker" emotions?
3. Can you see how these emotions, even the ones we tend to dislike, serve a purpose in our lives?

10

Conflict and Power Struggles within the Self

The tragedy of life is what dies inside a man while he lives.
                                        —*Albert Schweitzer*
The measure of a man is what he does with his power.
                                        —*Pittacus (650?–569? B.C.)*

TEACHING OBJECTIVES

- Provide a framework for understanding internal power struggles
- Explain further the concept of emotional aspects as they relate to internal power issues
- Discuss developmental aspects of the subconscious and conscious
- Increase awareness of seeking balance through observing life events

So far, we have examined a number of issues. I hope that many of them have prompted you to turn questions inward, to ask yourself about your level of responsibility for the issues affecting your life. I have observed many clients who experience higher levels of power when they learn to accept all life events as opportunities for growth and learning. I find that this is also true in my life. At the root of most conflicts in life, there is some form of internal power struggle.

In Chapters 7, 8, and 9, I covered emotional aspects. I hope that these chapters taught you about the various parts, attitudes, or belief systems of our being. In addition, I hope that you see how these various aspects seem to develop their own life viewpoints. As most people know, Sigmund Freud addressed the id, ego and superego; some hold to the belief in ego states (similar to emotional aspects).[10] More recent self-help books talk about the inner child. The following information I provide takes that all a bit further.

INTERNAL DIALOGUE

This book's advance readers had more trouble grasping the idea of people having many aspects than any other of the book's positions. In Chapters 7, 8, and 9, I talked about the distinction between the separation of identities in those with dissociative identity disorder, and the more subtle differences within the self of most others. For so many years, people have thought that people who hear voices in their head are crazy. Yes, there are some who do hear disturbing voices in their minds who are more extreme than the norm; but I cannot begin to count the number of clients who have come to my office thinking they were crazy because of the chatter of different thoughts.

It is normal to make internal comments. This chapter comes from the perspective that we all have many internal aspects or "spheres of influence," as I referred to them earlier, that may affect us. Some of these aspects are vying for power and battling for expression to the conscious, while others are seeking to stay hidden deep within our unconscious. Once again, it is in our best interest to understand this interplay so we can learn to accept and respect every part of our being. How do all these emotional influences affect our choices?

REFLECTIONS

I have touched on the idea of life being a mirror to us, but that idea needs more attention for full understanding. The idea of life being a mirror reflects the idea that everything that happens in and around our life happens for a reason. Often the reason is to teach and challenge us so that we can grow and learn. Many prominent mental health experts, Carl Jung being among the earliest, feel that there is a strong bond between events in people's lives and the purposes of these events. When we think of life as a mirror, we may see the numerous chances to discover aspects of ourselves that may otherwise escape our view. However, it is hard to see life as a mirror when playing a victim role. Remember, if you feel like a victim, you feel that life happens *to* you. If you feel that everything happens for a reason, then it is easier to believe that life happens *for* you and you become the victor in your life. We may consider that the difference between "to" and "for" makes a world of difference in our own perceptions of our personal power.

When we consider the idea that everything happens for a reason, a completely new world of possibilities opens to us. We can then start to see and understand our strengths and weaknesses better, as well as those of others around us. I work with clients of all ages, and I often use various puzzles and toys to teach about life issues. I have two optical illusion boxes that are similar in concept and in construction. I use these boxes as an analogy of people. There are mirrors inside the boxes that affect the way people see what is in the box. When helping them explore the concept, we look at the illusion box that also has a slot to hold money inside. The goal is to figure out how the box and the illusion work so that the person can get the top off and get the money out, hence, finding the value within.

UNRAVELING ILLUSIONS

Similar to figuring out the illusion box, we often interact with others and try to look inside and figure what makes them tick. In doing so, we hope to receive the value they have to offer us. However, unless we can understand what makes us tick, how can we understand others? Once we complete the exercise in the first illusion, and the client opens it up, I present the other illusion and ask them how to figure it out. Because the boxes are similar, the clients often use what they learned about the first illusion and apply it to the other illusion. At this point, I take the idea one step further to make it personal to them. I try to help them see the connection between themselves and the illusion. In making this connection, I believe they need to understand themselves, so they may understand others. In my experience, people will spend a lot more time and energy thinking and talking about other people's flaws than on their own flaws.

I would like to refer back to the figure that was discussed in Chapter 6, titled "The Role of Emotions." I have reproduced the figure here (as Figure 10.1) to aid in our discussion. You may want to refer back to Chapter 6 to review any aspects of the discussion that will now be re-addressed.

We may see why our behaviors vary if we consider certain factors. If we think about inner power struggles caused by emotional, logical, and defending aspects, we may see some forces that affect our actions. As you review the figure, you may recall that each circle depicts a unique aspect or "sphere of influence." Each circle takes on the form of an emotional feeling, attitude, belief, defense structure, logical point of view and/or life event. I believe these fragmented aspects may form when we feel that we or others do not choose to understand, accept, and/or respect our feelings and ideas when that life event occurs. When

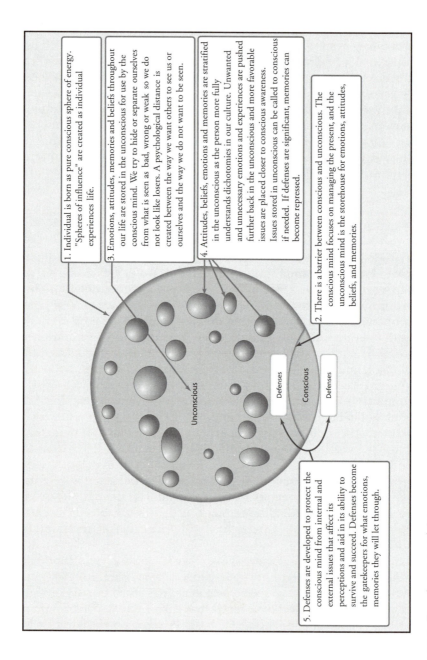

1. Individual is born as pure conscious sphere of energy. "Spheres of influence" are created as individual experiences life.

3. Emotions, attitudes, memories and beliefs throughout our life are stored in the unconscious for use by the conscious mind. We try to hide or separate ourselves from what is seen as bad, wrong or weak so we do not look like losers. A psychological distance is created between the way we want others to see us or ourselves and the way we do not want to be seen.

4. Attitudes, beliefs, emotions and memories are stratified in the unconscious as the person more fully understands dichotomies in our culture. Unwanted and unnecessary emotions and experiences are pushed further back in the unconscious and more favorable issues are placed closer to conscious awareness. Issues stored in unconscious can be called to conscious if needed. If defenses are significant, memories can become repressed.

2. There is a barrier between conscious and unconscious. The conscious mind focuses on managing the present, and the unconscious mind is the storehouse for emotions, attitudes, beliefs, and memories.

Unconscious

Defenses

Conscious

Defenses

5. Defenses are developed to protect the conscious mind from internal and external issues that affect its perceptions and aid in its ability to survive and succeed. Defenses become the gatekeepers for what emotions, memories they will let through.

Figure 10.1 Development of Conscious and Unconscious Mind

this happens, we may feed existing aspects or new ones may develop. Each aspect creates its own views and beliefs based on its life events and tries to function in a way that follows its beliefs.

Shame is a very powerful emotion that often impacts our attitudes and fosters the creation of aspects. We often try to hide events in our life or aspects of ourselves from the world, especially when we have felt shame in our life. We may want to continue to see how we feel about that event or aspect now. Remember the example of Jacob, the lawyer who wanted to reject his family, in Chapter 8. The events that evoked these feelings of shame occurred early in life, but affected the man throughout his life.

Let us return to the example of Sally, the young girl who made a necklace of flowers from her mother's garden; her mother responded in an effort to evoke guilt within the child. If Sally chose to feel guilt, she may also feel that she tried to do something good and screwed it up. This feeling may result in the creation of an emotional aspect that felt guilt, shame and/or worthlessness. After that experience, whenever she tried to do something good, Sally feared that she would screw it up. No matter how much praise she received from others throughout her life, Sally never believed it.

Sally faced an internal power struggle because she wanted to do something good, but she messed up and felt that she should not feel good. Does this mean that it is the mother's fault that her child internalized these feelings? No. But Sally's mother does share responsibility in the child's choice to create this aspect. The child had the choice, whether she realized it or not, to internalize her feelings but may not have known better.

Sally's mother behaved in a manner that put the child in this position to repress her feelings. Instead of shouting at the child, she could make Sally understand that she felt sad, frustrated, confused, angry and irritated to find her flowers pulled up. Her mother then could tell Sally that she did a wonderful job making the necklace, but that Sally should ask her which flowers she could use. In this manner, Sally understands her mother's reaction and can feel good about her necklace; however, Sally also learned that there is a different or better way to find the flowers to make necklaces in the future.

Many parents (mine included) have wondered, "Of all the great things I did for my child, are the negative events all they remember?" If we think about emotional aspects, we need to look at them in terms of ones that view life as "good" or "happy" and those that view life as bad or unhappy. We can easily see that happy feelings do not carry much stress with them and therefore do not require much resolution; we do not feel stuck when we feel happy. We may also see, however, that negative aspects often arise during stress and are often unresolved.

When these aspects remain unresolved, they retain their feelings of mistrust, anger, guilt and shame. The aspects try to protect their beliefs so that they can serve their purpose of protecting their existence and further protecting the individual from hurt or pain by maintaining their point of view.

HIDDEN PIECES

Rather than think about aspects that want to stay hidden, we often resort to the notion, out of sight, out of mind. This notion does not mean that the weaker or threatened aspect does not exist; but that it is not emotionally primed or is hiding until a situation arises that calls it forward. Children often learn that it is bad to show anger, sadness, and other feelings that we often are punished for or made fun of during childhood. As such, these feelings continue to build, as the person ages. Over time, they form stronger and stronger protective barriers and often use resentment, anger, and the other protective emotions to protect themselves.

Because parents often want to feel appreciated, they are not willing to look at their guilt and often use justification, rationalization, and denial to protect their more vulnerable emotions. The child and parent often end up feeling misunderstood, sad and uncared for, which often results in another fortification of the defenses and increases the resentment and defiance for both parties.

We may see a number of issues related to internal power struggles in this situation. It is in the parents' best interest to understand and heal their guilt, shame, and failure aspects. A parent may seem plagued by the interplay of these feelings and often try to find protection from it. On the other hand, the best interest of the child (of any age) lies in caring for their ailing emotional aspects in order to love and heal them so they can feel accepted. If this approach sounds sappy to you, then you may want to think about the emotional aspects that protect your desire to take care of and guard yourself.

PUTTING THE PIECES TOGETHER

In these examples of the child and parent issues, there is no need for both parties to work out their issues together. We need to look at our own inner aspects to know how they work before we can resolve the issues with the people in our past. If we want to resolve our conflicts, we need to remember that each aspect exists for a positive purpose, in its own view. In some way, each feeling exists to help us learn or grow; additionally, each aspect of us deserves understanding, respect, acceptance, and love. If we harbor anger toward anyone, we might realize that anger is trying to protect feelings that are more vulnerable. If anger is feeling the need to protect some weaker feelings, then it may not feel resolved until the other emotions find resolution.

If we try to control and manage our emotional issues or aspects, they will seek an outlet. Internal power struggles exist at many different levels of our existence. Therefore, unresolved aspects often present themselves in physical symptoms. Using trance work (hypnotherapy), clients and I learned to understand the nature of physical symptoms and patterns of behavior.

For example, a client I will call John had many problems with warts for some time. He had them surgically removed, but they would always return. In one session of hypnotherapy, we found that the warts were an expression of how he felt different from others and that he never "fit in." After we talked about this, I asked the aspect causing the warts if it was ready to heal, let the need to have the wart go away and let it fall off. While in trance, John said "yes" and within one week, the warts were gone; they have not returned. The main struggle with John was that he felt shame, sadness, humiliation, and worthlessness because he felt he did not fit in with his peers. John did not want to express these feelings to others. As a result, he needed to suppress and subsequently counter his feelings of shame, insecurity . . . which resulted in the development of arrogance, denial, and rationalization as defenses. As a result of the repression, the emotions needed to find a physical way to express themselves (the warts). This happened so that John would feel the emotions when he looked at the warts. When he acknowledged the emotions and their origin, in trance, they felt resolved, accepted, and respected and let go of the need to create the external symptoms (the warts).[11]

We can see an example of an unproductive behavior in a person we will call Marcia. Marcia had a phobia of paying bills and felt tense in even getting the mail from the mailbox. After a few sessions of trance work and cognitive-behavioral therapy, Marcia saw that her fear of paying bills came from childhood feelings of inadequacy. She also had a fear that she would never live up to her mother's expectations of her. As a child, Marcia feared that she could not handle the responsibilities that would come with adulthood. So, as she grew up, she hid her feelings of insecurity because she felt weak; she felt like a failure. After her marriage ended, she found herself forced to take charge of her own finances. This triggered her deeper fears, which sought expression. She repressed these fears until the emotional aspects could express themselves as a phobia of paying bills and worsened to the point of causing her to dread getting the mail.

The internal power struggle in this example stems from a lack of feeling accepted and from feelings of inadequacy. She then felt that she had to defend against this feeling, since it felt overpowering to her; Marcia's feeling of inadequacy fought with her attempts at denial. Over time, this conflict grew into an aspect of overwhelming emotions. We found that fear, shame, insecurity and failure battled with logic, denial, arrogance, and anger. When Marcia saw the link and grasped the logic of the child aspect versus the logic of the defenses, she accepted the feelings and resolved them. Her phobia faded away within six sessions. This conflict is simplistic, but it shows the complex feelings of some of our internalized aspects.

Not every client issue is as easy to solve as these examples; defense structures will vary between clients. Many people have problems in seeing why they may outwardly want to change their behaviors but just can't seem to do it. I find that most people have trouble changing due to the defensive walls that we put in place to protect us. The defense structures that lead to the internal conflicts result from their holding onto the power we gave them, and the conscious parts of us that are demanding change.

ACCEPTING EMOTIONS VERSUS EMOTIONAL INFIGHTING

What aspects of yourself would you like to change? Most people think of discarding unwanted emotions or habits. However, when people realize that their defenses prevent them from changing, they tend to want to usurp the power of the defenses; but this is often easier said than done. From the viewpoint of the emotional aspect, imagine a scenario where a gang attacked a town. This gang beat up some of the residents and took their belongings. The citizens felt unable to protect themselves and did not want to resort to violence. The townspeople decided that they needed help, and a couple of people came and agreed to protect the town from the gang. These people did a great job protecting the residents and restored peace.

After a while, the townspeople felt safe enough to meet with some of the gang members, and they talked about their differences. The protectors realized that if the citizens and the gang talked and worked out their differences, then they would serve no purpose because the townspeople will no longer need protection. So, the protectors began to lie to the townsfolk by reporting that the gang had waged another attack and that the protectors could continue to prevent these attacks, if allowed to. In reality, the gang did not attack the town for some time, because the protectors scared them away. At this point, the residents believe that they need the protectors to keep them safe, and the protectors need the residents for their jobs. Both sides fear change, but change is necessary for growth and evolution. This story sets the stage for the conflict between the conscious mind (townspeople), the defense structures (protectors) and the emotional aspects (gang).

The task, as I see it, is to help all "parties" (conscious mind, defense structures and emotional perspectives) to understand that they serve a purpose, but may have grown dependent upon each other even through their opposition. The idea of dependence on conflict seems ironic; however, let me give you an example. One of my very intelligent teenaged clients once said that the worst thing we could wish for is world peace, because so much of the world economy is tied to defense. If there were suddenly no more wars, the impact on the world economy would be devastating.

Related to our town example, although we may not need the defenses as much as they may want to be needed, they do not have to "leave town." Also, the conscious mind (townspeople) deserves the right to work through their issues with the emotional aspects in the inside world (the gang) so they do not have to live with their feelings of fear and animosity toward each other. Other "gangs" from the "outside world" could attack the "town," so we will still need protection. They may not have to work as hard to protect from attacks if they allow the feelings to learn to deal with some of the attacks and resolve the conflicts. The defenses, the emotions, and logic can work together to learn why each aspect reacts as it does so they can serve the purpose for which they were created. This becomes the manner in which we all can grasp our internal power struggles to seek resolution.

MAKING PEACE WITH OURSELVES

At this point, you may feel that this process of understanding and resolving internal power struggles is endless and possibly futile. The question may be, "Where do I begin?" Once again, think about the defenses that may prompt your feelings and attitudes. If you can get past feeling fearful of doing it wrong, your skills at resolving your emotions, when practiced often, become almost automatic, and life becomes much easier to deal with. Remember that we may be here to experience challenges to grow and learn from. If we are not willing to resolve our own issues, then we often end up airing our internal conflicts to the outside world, and the world starts reflecting our conflicts back to us. We can resist and possibly face more challenges, and/or we can look deeper into the challenges to see how we can grow. If similar conflicts continue to come up, then it may benefit us to continue to look deeper to see if we are missing something.[12]

SUMMARY

Perhaps one of the most enriching challenges in life is to find balance in our emotions, attitudes, and belief systems. Many meditative techniques, Eastern and religious philosophies, and therapeutic perspectives speak of finding balance in one's life. All of these different perspectives may have something here. Think of how difficult it would be to walk or run if we weren't able to balance ourselves. We also can have malnourished bodies if we do not eat a balanced diet. In our government's expenditures, we seek a balanced budget. The examples are endless. It may behoove us to ask ourselves, "What does emotional balance mean to me?" I will not provide the answer to this question. I want you to seek the answer, within.

QUESTIONS

1. What events in your life do you feel had the greatest impact on you and your perception of the world and your role in it?
2. Are there events in your life that you try to avoid or feel are too painful to think about or talk about? If so, consider what they are and what feelings you experience when you do think of these things.
3. Do you have a regular time set aside to collect your thoughts, meditate or reflect upon your life and the things that are important to you?

11

Power and the Family

The family you come from is not as important as the family you are going to have.

—Ring Lardner

The first half of our life is ruined by our parents and the second by our children.

—Clarence Darrow

TEACHING OBJECTIVES

- Discuss the nature of power struggles in families
- Explain power issues in different types of family settings
- Discuss belief systems that contribute to dysfunctional thoughts and behaviors in families
- Provide solutions and guidance to parents to find ways of resolving issues

The family is the most important relationship structure that most of us have in our lives. Yet, ironically, we receive little formal training on how to help the family succeed. We go to school to learn how to read and write; we go to church to learn about God and morality; we go to college to study topics related to our possible career interests; but no one teaches us how to live in a family. From another viewpoint, we have licenses to drive, to practice medicine and therapy, to operate machinery, but we are not required to have any training or credentials to become a parent. Being a parent is the most important job that a person will ever have, but few people take classes to learn parenting skills.

Parents are at the center of the family unit and are the guides, models and managing agents for the children they create. This chapter offers an introduction into family issues and sources of conflict, but is not exhaustive.

Parents often tend to adopt similar or opposite parenting styles to that of their parents, if there is no outside interference. When we think of our life experiences, we tend to either agree or disagree with the way we were treated. For example, if my parents hit me as a child, I will likely either strongly believe that I should hit or strongly believe I should not hit my child. I probably won't realize that other options exist, not unless I learned about these options from someone outside my family or read about them. My work experience has shown me examples of parents doing the same as or opposite of what their parents did to them.

I feel that many parents do not seek out parent training just because they feel fearful that their parenting views are not good; they fear being seen as a bad parent or just not good enough. Arrogance, rationalization and denial then defend and protect their desire to believe that they are good parents. It is true that there are many ways to raise a child, and each child is different. But children have a certain combination of genetic and innate traits, behavioral support patterns, and other factors that contribute to the uniqueness in each child. Once again, if we look at life as though it was a mirror, then the parent has a limitless amount of information to learn about himself or herself from this gift that their child has presented.

The family unit teaches children most of their behavioral patterns, and this is where power struggles begin. As we considered in the previous chapter, many of the internal power struggles we encounter later in life began in childhood. I don't know about you, but there is a significant emotional aspect within me that continues to try to prove its worth to father figures. I tend to have a difficult time with people telling me what to do because I want to prove to others that I already know everything. I believe I was born with some of this, but my family interaction reinforced it. The fact that I tried to seek approval is not good or bad; it just is. But, now it is my issue, not my family's. I also see many people at professional levels and elsewhere with the same issues. Most of us learn to mask it well, but others may still see it.

I believe that these issues often drive us onward to succeed at things we may not have otherwise attempted. Does it mean that there isn't a different or better way? No. However, so many times, parents will say, "My mom or dad did it to *me*, and *I* turned out okay. . . ." We may see that family members have little or no recourse to the actions of those with authority over them. Consider: how long would you remain at a job where your boss called you names and made you work overtime when you made a mistake? Is it likely that you would accept their power, doled out under the pretense of making you a better employee? This example is extreme, but it's worth considering that we often do things in our family that we would not think of doing with friends or co-workers.

We know that our culture includes an assortment of races, religions, income levels, previous marriages and stepchildren. As such, there are countless family arrangements that we could discuss. Due to the combinations of these factors and the number and the variety of issues a person may have, the scenarios become endless. We will discuss some common family issues that arise in our culture.

INTACT FAMILIES

When I say "intact family," I am referring to a family in which the genetic parents are both present in the home. This term does not refer to the quality of the relationship. Within any family, a chain of command or hierarchy usually develops. We live in what is still a largely male-dominated society; often the father is at the top of the hierarchy, followed by the mother and children, in order of birth. As we saw earlier in the book, hierarchical power structures tend to lead to conflict. This is due to the differences in each person's internal and external feelings of power. In families where there is a strict power model, there may be no signs of outward conflicts; but internally the members may show signs of emotional and physical issues because they feel greater levels of stress and internal conflict. They may not voice their feeling because they fear retaliation from those in higher positions of power. Some families do not face many conflicts, but such families often lack strict hierarchical boundaries. Overall, if you examine the structure of any family closely, you would likely find that, while sources of hierarchical power exist, there are interactions and relationships within the family that approximate the equity model. In this manner, most families find their balance or imbalance between hierarchical and equity models.

MEETING THE NEEDS OF ALL

What causes power struggles in the family? Many power struggles in the family center around vying for love, affection, notice and attention from one or both parents. These conflicts often involve two or more children acting out to get attention, and often involve one child trying to diminish the power of another sibling by getting them into trouble. Children are always watching and learning. Often before they can speak, children learn ways of getting noticed and manipulating behaviors. This goes back to the story of the toddler who fell down and then looked around to see if anyone was nearby before deciding whether he should cry. If he thinks no one will come running to comfort him, he probably will not cry. While they do not have the conscious ability to fathom the full meaning of their actions, they do see the cause and effect of their and other's actions.

Since parents hold the places at the top of the hierarchy and are primarily the caretakers, they are in high demand. It is impossible to give one child, let alone two or more, everything that they need, so there will be times when children's needs go unmet. The parent's biggest internal conflict arises when they feel guilt, shame, frustration, failure, and/or other emotions because they are not the perfect parent. Over time, when one or more of their children want attention or express a need, parents may begin to develop feelings of irritation, annoyance, anger, and possibly rage in order to guard their feelings of guilt, shame or failure. Their emotion is seldom about the child; instead, it is about their own views and feelings. The result is often that the parent vents their emotion toward the child in the form of a more powerful, protective emotion. The child responds with their emotion, and the parent may then feel guilt and other related feelings for treating the child as they did.

These emotional reactions feed a cycle that continues to ebb and flow. We will refer to this cycle as the guilt-resentment cycle. This cycle exists in all types of family situations and in many types of situations where there is a feeling of inequity. Through watching and listening, children learn that if they respond to their parents defiantly, for example, by stating, "You can't make me do that," sometimes the parent may not respond, so the child feels that this tactic has worked. The parent, however, often feels that the child's words attacked their status power and feel that this contempt calls for punishment. The parent also may feel afraid that their child will think that they can treat others in power the same way, which could cause problems for that child throughout their life. Because of the parent's emotional reaction, they punish the child. However, because of punishing the child, the parent may then feel guilt. Do you remember the phrase, "This hurts me more than it hurts you"? The parent will often turn to justification and rationalization as defenses to ward off these feelings of guilt.

Because of the guilt-resentment cycle, the guilt-ridden parent (in this example) feels the need to make amends for their actions. Many parents will try to buy their child's love back or may react inconsistently to their child's undesirable behaviors. They may feel fearful that they are being too hard on the child. These patterns of rewarding and punishing similar behaviors can send mixed signals to the child. This, in turn, often leads to confusion, frustration and very resistant behavior patterns in the child. As the parent makes requests of this child and the child does not follow through or complains about having to comply, the parent often feels resentful for all of the things that they have done for their child that they do not appreciate, while at the same time feeling the burden of being the parent.

SHARING

Conflicts between siblings often occur between two children close in age, since they are often competing for a higher place in the hierarchy. The subconscious feeling is often: the higher I can be in the hierarchy, then the closer I will be to my parents. This will mean they may love me more, and I will have more power. Young children often use their belongings to define their power; quality is rarely an issue. Children usually define their power by the number of toys, friends, baseball cards . . . ; possessions often equate to power to younger children because that is what they are taught by their parents and society.

Children do not normally understand the idea of things such as money, time, and other intangible concepts. They often require visual or tactile methods of defining value or mass. They find value in things such as toys, stickers, and other objects they can see and touch and which demonstrate their value. For example, if you give a child the option of keeping ten pennies or trading them for one quarter, they will keep the ten pennies. Sharing is also a hard concept to teach, because the child who wants all of the power does not understand the concept of sacrificing one thing to gain something else.

Sharing is too abstract for children to grasp. They often have to see the effect in their relationships. They need to make the connection that, "When I share, others will play more nicely with me." In order to learn to share, the child must see the cause and effect relationship and feel that they have something to gain. When children do not learn how to share without feeling that they have lost something, the issues often remain with that person throughout their life in one way or another. I think that we all have observed the materialistic nature of many people and the seeming me-first attitude. I believe that those behaviors are indications of unresolved issues related to sharing.

There are many sharing-related conflicts in families that occur between siblings. Sibling conflicts, however, often spread to parent-child and spousal conflicts. A dispute between siblings may start with problems sharing parents, toys and food, and can extend to problems sharing friends and other possessions. Parents may have difficulties sharing time with their children and their spouse, as well as other issues.

Sharing usually becomes an issue when there is a feeling of scarcity; children feel that there is not enough to go around for everyone. Feelings of fear and mistrust may encourage the idea of scarcity, even if there is an abundance of a certain item. "What if I do not get what I need? What if others take advantage of me? I have to look out for myself." These feelings of fear and concern often motivate stinginess or selfishness. When parents punish or scold their children for not sharing, it does not teach them to share; it only results in them feeling that the parents removed their power. Instead, it teaches them to avoid punishment for not sharing and can promote feelings of resentment of their siblings, peers and parents, and defiance of their parents' demands. While it may take more time, it is often more successful to explain the process of sharing and help them to see it in action.

COMPETITION

You may see that rivalry in families often comes from a notion of scarcity. We discussed competition in Chapter 3; but many issues people have with competition began in the family, so we should re-address it at this point. Many parents believe that fostering a desire to compete is an asset to their child. They feel that competition urges people to do better, and in many ways, that is true. The idea of scarcity enters into competition because there can only be one first, and the idea of competing is often to be the "best."

Whether it happens intentionally or unknowingly, parents often foster rivalry between their children. We do this by using good behavior, good grades, or athletic performance as grounds for approval. The goal may then become winning a contest for love and acceptance. There are cases where a parent may compete with their own children for attention and affection from the other parent. Such a parent may have issues, due to their own childhood, that are unresolved and repressed. These feelings often stem from issues with attention and affection they did or did not receive from their parents. Since the unresolved issues remain, they often continue to feel that love and affection are scarce items.

When the parent feels that their spouse's love is limited, they may feel that they need to stand in line with their children to receive love from their spouse. Sometimes, the parent will put his or her own needs last and feel lonely or rejected. Other times, the parent feels that their status entitles them to their spouse's attention ahead of the children. In either case, there may be feelings of resentment, fear, insecurity, and sometimes guilt. This interplay of emotions helps to continue the cycle of feelings. The cycles often worsen the conflict within the parent and within the family unit. This is just a single example of subtle rivalry that can foster mild, moderate and severe family conflicts.

Many children feel that the parents love their sibling(s) more than them, and sometimes this is true. The uniqueness of each child leads parents to love each child in slightly different ways. The child, however, may not see their uniqueness as special, and they sometimes focus instead on their own inadequacies. They fail to see the way in which their parent may love them as it pertains to who they are. However, as the child feels less love and support from their parents, they often feel that they have to battle with their siblings to try to win their parent's love and approval. This sometimes-cutthroat contest creates the often-cited sibling rivalry. We may see that if these issues remain unresolved and continue into adulthood, so do the sibling rivalries. In extreme instances, these can result in violence, and sometimes murder.

In many cases, sibling rivalries lead to academic and athletic successes in childhood. However, we may see that the unresolved desire to compete with others often crops up in the teen years and later in career and parenting issues. From the standpoint of parental successes, parents often look to their child's success to gauge their own feelings of success. Parents may then compare their children's wins to those of their sibling's children; this furthers sibling rivalry, even into adulthood.

Competition within the family in moderation can be healthy, but it is important to consider the drive behind the competition. As was stated in Chapter 3, our current concept of contests often involves a comparison with others. At some level, there is no way to prevent competition, and it does assist in growth and learning. Nevertheless, as parents and family members, we can discuss these contests with our families and try to help them see what they can learn about themselves. The family can then work toward resolution and growth. The rivalry is not, in itself, a problem; the problem comes when rivalry is misplaced and/or unresolved. Once again, in order for the family to resolve their issues with rivalry, the parents must be aware of their own issues.

Parents need to remember that kids do not know the parents' issues and often see them as perfect beings. It is only later in life, when the child's brain cognitively matures, that their attitudes change, and they can see their parents as imperfect humans.

Parents often unknowingly pass their issues along to their children through their behavioral and emotional, as well as genetic, patterns. This does not mean that the child's emotional issues are the parent's fault. This means that it is in the family's best interest for the parent to be aware of their issues and work to resolve them. So many parents love their children with all their heart and want to do the best for them; but they will not look closely at themselves to see how they could change.

Once again, fear, insecurity, guilt, failure, and shame are likely upholding the fear of self-exploration. The parents may protect themselves from feeling these emotions by using denial, arrogance, sarcasm, annoyance, anger, and/or rage to counter these emotions. The question becomes, "How many times will we allow our lives and the lives of others to be diminished by the emotional issues that we refuse to resolve?"

BIRTH ORDER

There has been a great deal of research done on the psychological implications of birth order, but it can be argued that there are no conclusive results. From the perspective of power, issues of status in hierarchical power systems contribute to some level of understanding of the effects of birth order.

As we mentioned, birth order in a family often determines some type of status level that aids in defining the power structure in a family. In the hierarchical structure, each child will often fight to hold onto the status that they gained by virtue of birth order. They may vie for higher levels of status, depending on the value of power and status within the family unit. The emphasis placed on status can lead to conflict in the family, since status can change, depending on many variables. Often, when status and birth order are not an issue, they are less likely to cause conflict between children. Issues of status invoked by parents can be subtle or obvious. However, usually, the children are sensitive to these issues.

Conflicts among siblings are going to occur and are a very important part of life. Through conflict, we learn how to express ourselves and communicate our wants and wishes. Parents serve the best interest of the family when they promote problem resolution and understanding, instead of trying either to avoid or to encourage conflict. If we look at the nature of many sibling conflicts, they often relate to issues of birth order and feelings of status. As children, we learn to handle problems, and what we learn often follows us into adulthood. Children who have lingering issues related to birth order and status tend to carry those issues with them as adults. These issues often play into the competition issue discussed previously.

A child's birth order definitely plays a role in influencing a person's behavior. Parents often depend upon the older child to help and take on more duties than their younger siblings. But, the older child may react by accepting or rebelling from the responsibility given.

When parents have their first child, they often want to be perfect parents and set very high hopes for their offspring. The first child often feels the pressure of these hopes. Depending on their self-esteem, perceived support system, outlook on life, and other factors, they may try to live up to these hopes or they may reject them. As parents have more children and learn many lessons, they alter their demands on subsequent children. The change in expectations can, however, lead to resentment and anger from the oldest child that they may vent on younger siblings. If the parents listen to their children's feelings and discuss their own experiences as children, they can often prevent building resentment and defiance.

When the older child receives more duties, the younger siblings may seek more duties from parents or interfere with the oldest child following through on tasks. These attempts by younger siblings may pose a threat to the power of the oldest child and can stir up conflict. We said earlier that children may play the role of the victim and give away their power when they want someone with more power to rescue them. Order of birth often decides whether a child will seek power through responsibility or seek power through victimization and seeking a rescuer.

Birth order can influence numerous reactions to events that may arise. Many believe that a vast array of personal issues influence behavior and beliefs. We may see that some of these issues include socioeconomics, parenting styles, and biology. Birth order may influence behavior patterns; however, the effects of these other factors are also very strong. I believe that it is important to explore all these factors when exploring behavioral trends.

THE ONLY CHILD

When a family only has one child, this child does not have to share any status power with other siblings and often gets most of the parents' attention. If there are no other siblings to challenge the child's power, the only child sometimes does not learn how to handle conflict well and may become stubborn and unyielding. This issue may carry on into adulthood. While some think of only children as selfish, spoiled, or self-centered, their behavior is often a matter of social learning and the formation of habits. Most of us would find it hard to feel that we must give up power we once had. Depending on the person, a child can respond in various ways to the demands of parents and the environment. When there is an only child, parents may want to make sure that their child interacts with other children often and that they teach their child the virtues of sharing and cooperation.

GENDER

Gender issues, as they relate to power in the families, tend to arise from parental beliefs and attitudes toward gender. Those who believe in male dominance will place a higher status on their sons, without respect to birth order. This can add to a sense of learned helplessness or resentment and hatred in the daughters. In these cases, it is common to see that parents often assign duties based on gender stereotypes.

If we assign tasks by gender, we may create needless conflict. Gender issues can cause resentment, anger, and conflict simply because there is no thought given to individual choice or actual strengths and weaknesses, even in children. Often, there is a steady demand for tasks like cooking and cleaning, while repair- and upkeep-type tasks may not require much effort or attention. We may avoid these conflicts by dividing tasks without regard for gender or the nature of the task. The result is a better-rounded child who realizes the demands of each task; each person can find where their interests and strengths lie.

Often, before parents have a child, they think about their preferences in the gender of their children. They then begin to develop expectations based on their hopes and dreams. Even when we think of birth order and gender, many parents would prefer to have a male, and then a female. But, what happens when the child they have is not the gender they wanted? Many parents will find the value and joy of their child, regardless of gender, but some parents have trouble accepting the child who is the "wrong" gender or was even unwanted. The result can be emotional distancing, anger and resentment, and even rejection or obvious favoritism for other siblings. These actions are often devastating to the child and have life-long implications.

How we act toward an unwanted or "wrong-gender" child has a powerful impact on how the child views him/herself and the world. From the beginning, their feelings of power suffer; they feel that they embody something bad or wrong, due to not being what their parents wanted. The problem begins when the parents project their own sense of failure or feelings of inability to have the child they wanted.

The parent, at this point, should consider again the idea of life being a mirror. They may then gain a sense of power and appreciate that this child came to them for a reason that they may not yet understand. For the child who, for some reason, feels that they were the wrong gender, born in the wrong order, or just unwanted, I would suggest that they consider the possibility that they came to their parents for a reason. They may find that these reasons include teaching their parents something of tremendous value, and learning something from the experience themselves. Parents sometimes do not seize the chance to learn the lessons in life presented to them. However, we all have the power to consider and learn our own lessons so that we can grow from them.

CROSSING THE FINE LINE OF DISCIPLINE

A common topic I often discuss with parents centers on the fine line between discipline and abuse. As long as parents feel that they are helping their child learn through discipline, they believe that they can justify almost any behavior as being in the best interest of their child. Many parents have strong feelings when it comes to discipline. This is particularly true when the topic comes up of how and to what extent they discipline their child. Many times, a parent feels defensive when we discuss these issues. In these situations, it seems that the parents harbor and protect feelings of guilt, shame, and remorse. In most cases, parents do not believe that their actions are abusive; they say they do what they do because they love their children. Their defensive reaction is understandable because, if they recognized their actions as abusive, they would feel guilty, bad and/or wrong, which would likely feel disempowering and cause them to question their true motivations as a parent.

Yelling, hitting, spanking, verbal abuse, and even physical defor-mation of the body are only a few of the things defended in the name of love. We will not criticize these methods. But, as a psychologist and a human being, I will ask parents who engage in any or all of these behaviors to consider carefully whether they believe that their child benefits from these actions. Ask yourself if you would enjoy dealing with what you do to your child. If when you were a child someone treated you this way, remember back and ask yourself how you felt when it happened. If you felt afraid, threatened, pained, or confused, then perhaps there are different and better ways to handle discipline.

Whether or not a person bases their beliefs in reality or rationality, many who abuse others have rationalized and justified their behaviors to the point where they feel correct in what they do. To understand the mind of an abusive person, we need to think about the defenses that this person builds around their belief systems. An abuser finds many defenses to protect them from feelings of wrongdoing. Abusive people often try to rationalize, deny and justify the things they do. The emo-tions that they try to fend off are guilt (that they hurt their child), shame (that they did something wrong), and sadness (related to the pain they feel about hurting their child). They may also try to avoid feeling helplessness (because they didn't know any other ways to teach their child), confusion (as to what their options were), failure (as a parent), as well as many of the negative emotions that they felt as a child when they felt abused.

Parents use many ideas and sayings to justify their actions. As men-tioned earlier, we may hear, "If it was good enough for me . . .," "Spare the rod and spoil the child" or similar ideas. Of course, there is the old favorite, "Do as I say, not as I do." If parents can accept the idea that we may be misusing our power toward our children in abusive ways, then we can often find the hidden issues that drive our actions. While most parents try to help their children, there are those who knowingly inflict abuse. In any regard, these issues of whether or not abuse is an intentional act often come down to repressed anger, hatred and rage. It is sad but true that the anger and other emotions often stem from feelings toward people in the past, not the family members that are the recipients of the abuse.

Let us consider the attitude of the abuser who suffered past abuse. The theory of these attitudes is based on clinical observations and experience with clients. When they felt abused, they may have felt forced to give up their power to their abuser, due to feelings of fear, helplessness and terror. (See Figures 11.1 and 11.2.) Remember that fear and terror keep us from doing things that could harm us and, in some abusive situations, it is not in our best interest to fight back. In order to hand over their power and prevent themselves from being hurt further, they likely had to repress their feelings of anger and rage (created instinctively to fight back and protect them from further harm). In turn, this resulted in feelings of shame, inadequacy, and failure in their ability to protect themselves. They cannot resolve these feelings of rage and

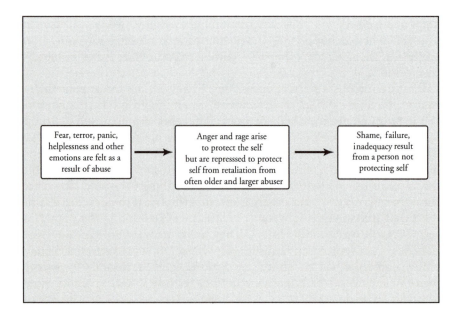

Figure 11.1 Chain of Emotion during Periods of Abuse

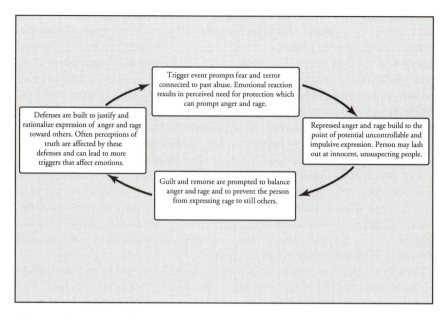

Figure 11.2 Cycle of Emotions Later in Life, Following Abuse

anger with the abuser because of their fear of them; so the emotions remained in the subconscious, seeking a way to express themselves to regain their power.

Feelings of fear and shame often do not express themselves. This is because these emotions feel too weak to express themselves. Instead, they often reside within the person and lead to symptoms of anxiety and/or depression. What often occurs to help the person cope is that a balance is developed between the amount of anger and rage, and fear and shame. Eventually, the angry emotions within the abused build up to the point where they vent them on someone else, often weaker so that they do not have to fear recourse.

Depending on the issue at hand, fear and terror may lead to anger and rage; this is because fear may come across as something that triggers memories of abusive situations. What can trigger these feelings? Triggering stimuli can range from a look on someone's face to a phrase, a smell, or even the lighting in a room. However, when the anger and rage come out, often feelings of guilt follow. As mentioned earlier, guilt is considered a weaker, negative emotion by anger since it involves remorse, but it presents itself to balance the anger and rage. As more defenses build around the anger and rage, depending on the issues of the individual, the guilt has less and less power to sway the emotions and abusive behaviors.

When someone engages in an abusive action, the subsequent guilt may grow to a point of offsetting the anger. Over time, the abuse continues to result in anger and rage, overwhelming the guilt and creating a vicious cycle. The anger and rage may only continue if they can justify their actions from behaviors in the past (the abuse they experienced) and relate abusive behaviors of the past to present events. Many triggers that bring out memories of abuse are not apparent, and the anger and rage often react in a manner that is not appropriate to the situation. For example, a particular song may have been playing on the stereo when a man beat his daughter. She may repress the experience to the point of not remembering the act, let alone the song. Years later, she may hear the song on her way to work and feel a rush of sadness and/or anger and rage, without knowing why. This pattern is often very complex. By working with clients who have developed abusive patterns as adults, therapy can reveal these underlying memories, events, and subsequent belief systems.

As the reader, you may wonder about the validity of this theory of abuse. How can I prove it? Such a theory is difficult to prove. The development of the belief system, based on the emotional aspects, stated in this book depends on the guidance of the therapist. In other words, a therapist has a very powerful role of influence with the client. Who is to say that I am not coercing my client and others to believe a delusion of mine? It is very possible that this theory is false and inaccurate, but I do not wish to defend this theory. I can only report that I am extremely careful when I do my work to make sure that I use neutral words and phrases and avoid guiding. I observe that clients have experienced many periods of rapid growth at times when they were able to understand the nature of these various emotional aspects, and to work to heal each emotional point of view.

The following example illustrates this theory and the therapeutic process used with my clients. We changed some details to protect the clients' identities. This composite client has been male and female, younger and older, African-American and Caucasian. . . . The story of abuse through generations is often the same. This combination of events and situations is as reported by different clients.

Reportedly, then, this client suffered a childhood filled with abuse. Around the house, my client's abusive parent did not allow talking back, arguing, or slow compliance when orders were issued, and my client's other siblings began to adopt some of these behaviors as this parent. As they grew older, the siblings, too, sometimes engaged in abusive behaviors toward my client. When the abusive parent was home, my client felt unsafe, especially at night, when some of the abuse occurred. Finally, my client grew into adulthood, got married, and became a parent.

As a parent, this client loved their children very much and wanted the best for them. My client was determined to avoid the mistakes and abuse that had taken place during the client's childhood. My client's marriage did not last, and the client wound up raising the children alone. In an effort to avoid being an abusive and dictatorial type of parent, my client tried to be very permissive and, from the time the kids were young, tried to avoid conflict with them. When the client did respond in an authoritative manner, feelings of guilt followed, and so the client tried to make it up to the children, often with special favors.

As the children grew older, they were hard to manage. They often ignored this client when asked to do their chores; they only responded when my client yelled and forced them to cooperate. More and more, my client felt angered by the children's apparent disrespect. Also, my client felt ordered around by the children, since they seemed to feel that they did not have to follow through on chores. My client did not want to resort to using anger and rage, because doing so would violate the vow of trying to be a different type of parent than my client's parent was.

Fear and guilt discouraged my client from addressing the feelings of anger and resentment with the children. Therefore, the anger and rage continued to grow. The only way my client had learned to deal with conflict, as a child, was to yell, hit, or demand. Because of that narrow spectrum of childhood experiences, my client felt that there were no viable choices as to how to deal with the children. My client's internal resentment continued to build toward the children (but this resentment was likely misdirected toward the children and stemmed from child-hood memories of abuse caused by my client's abusive parent), which prompted still more anger and rage. However, feelings of fear, guilt, and shame prevented my client from acting on these feelings.

As these feelings of anger and rage grew, however, my client some-times unleashed angry outbursts. Yet, these outbursts reinforced my client's feelings of guilt, shame, and fear of becoming the same type of abusive parent that my client experienced during childhood. However, the children often responded to the anger, and complied with the demands, which justified the value of using anger.

The kids' resentment toward my client increased as they grew older. They realized that they could sometimes intimidate my client if they displayed anger. This retaliation by the children led my client to confuse the kids with memories of the abusive family members from childhood. As my client's kids grew older and bigger, my client's sense of fear and terror felt threatened by the size and strength of the children. Therefore, Anger and Rage emerged to protect the Fear and Terror. Also, Anger and Rage refused to take orders from a child; the Anger and Rage commanded the authority of the client's role as a parent.

This whole cycle resulted in more and more conflict; the children became very argumentative and uncooperative. They began to adopt feelings that they had to protect themselves from my client. Unwittingly, this turn of events led my client to display some of the same abuses that took place during my client's childhood. Eventually, my client realized that by changing certain patterns of behavior, many of these conflicts could be diffused or avoided altogether.

While some of the patterns remain, it is up to the parent(s) to see their role in the exchange. In many abusive relationships, either party may sense that the other party is posing a threat, regardless of reality. I hope this example helps you to see that we each need to be responsible for trying to understand our input to any conflict.

For many people, incest is a very emotionally charged topic. Many people have trouble grasping the idea of a parent committing sexual acts with their own child or siblings having sex. Many people do not want to consider the feelings of the incestuous parent or child. They only seek to punish such people. In order to help people change their actions, we have to first understand the origin of the feelings and accept them. Before we explore this topic, we must realize that people who engage in incest often have very distorted belief and defense systems. This is just one perspective that may apply in a few cases, but nonetheless provides an alternative view to a very disturbing pattern. Most people cannot understand how someone can engage in such an unsavory act; but those who engage in such acts likely do not view their own actions so harshly.

Do you remember the types of love discussed earlier (agape, eros, and philos)? We talked about the confusion that our language's use of a single word "love" can cause. If we think about this situation, we might better understand some of the issues that may surround incest and other types of sexual abuse. Let us consider a child's development and their interpretation of language. They tend to take things very literally, and they often attach word meanings to pictures, images, and examples that they see. Additionally, instances are rare when people explain the different types of love to children. So, very few people grow up understanding the different aspects of love.

Children see many different images of love at home, on television, at friends' houses, and in church or school. As stated earlier, children see philos, agape, and eros types of love every day and may feel different types of love toward others. However, they may feel confused as to how to express their feelings of attraction. Discussing love with a child is a difficult thing to do; this is especially true when it may approach discussions about sex. Nevertheless, if we do not talk about these issues, the child's ideas, even as they mature, often may grow skewed and clouded by ignorance and confusion.

Children often fail to understand many life events that go on around them, and these events can confuse them and distort their understanding of love. As a simple example, Bobby tells his mother that he loves her, and so does his father. Bobby kisses his mother before he leaves the house, and so does his father. We may want to believe that Bobby "just knows" the difference between how he feels for his mother and what his father feels for his wife. But, how can a child understand the difference if no one explains it to him? For some people, I believe that the seeds for incest stem from childhood; however, they may not surface until adulthood when the child, now an adult, is facing their own issues of love for their child. While an adult may not want to discuss their thoughts or emotions with others, for fear of what others may think, communication often opens up the doors to healing.

Parents often want to manage or control the thoughts, feelings and attitudes of their children. But, there is no way for parents to know everything that happens in their child's life or the feelings that develop as a result. I work with many adults who suffered very traumatic events that one or both parents did not know about; I see people of all ages whose childhood included abuse by family members and friends, but the parents never knew about the events. Such things often remain secret between the two people, due to the fear and shame of both abuser and abused.

Let's return to our discussion of incest. Think back to our earlier statements of the development of the conscious and unconscious mind. You may recall the comments about unwanted or unaccepted emotions and feelings that are separate from the conscious mind and reside in the subconscious. The theory holds that if we put much energy into repressing the feelings, idea and/or events, we may block these events from conscious thought or memory. Let's pretend that these repressed feelings and events are like air inside a balloon. If we squeeze the balloon, the air must go somewhere, and if we squeeze hard enough, the balloon will pop. We may try to hold back unwanted thoughts and beliefs, but they will find a way of expressing themselves, many times beyond our control. Therefore, we fight internal battles between the need to express our feelings and the desire to repress them.

Any repressed issue may express itself in the form of a compulsion or obsessive thought pattern, and the person may feel it will linger until it is acted upon. Many people who engage in incestuous acts know that their actions are wrong. This is why they often swear their "victims" to secrecy. They know that their thoughts and desires are not in the best interest of anyone, but they often continue to work to control their thoughts, which may strengthen obsessive thoughts. Therefore, if a person felt confused about love (between philos, agape, and eros) as a child, they may remain unresolved. If they acted on their ideas of how to express the feelings, it may have resulted in either feeling punished or rewarded. Due to feeling punished, they may conclude that the feeling that led them to their actions is not good or right. If they felt rewarded by some people and punished by others for their actions, confusion may set in. This results in an even more complex internal conflict between the good and bad feelings.

In order to preserve their desire to be good or right, the child may learn how to deny, repress, or hide the events and emotional issues. The issues never went away, they were just well defended from the conscious mind. What can happen when Bobby grows up with repressed or confused feelings of love? When Bobby grows up and becomes a parent, he will deal with young children, and this may pose problems for him. He may find himself unprepared to manage and address these emotions. We may feel that Bobby's attempts to express love or closeness to others is not consistent or appropriate. These actions result from his confused child aspect.

In presenting this theory, I do not mean to condone or minimize the actions of anyone. I do believe that we all need to take responsibility for our actions. It is always within our power, at some level of our existence, to observe our feelings and beliefs and seek help for them. If we feel that no one will understand our thoughts, feelings, or actions, then we isolate ourselves from healing. I offer this theory to provide a possible explanation to explore therapeutically. For many people who engage in incest, it adds little to our understanding to simply label them as "sick"; but their thoughts and feelings certainly are extremely misguided and dysfunctional. Furthermore, the longer these thoughts and emotions continue unexamined, the more they resist change.

THE ROOTS OF FAMILY CONFLICT

As you can see, there are many issues in a family that can contribute to conflict. Power issues may stem from parents asserting too much power, or not enough. The parents may not act in a manner that is consistent with the family's belief system. When children fight, one child may feel that the other children receive favorable treatment, and they may feel many other combinations of issues. There are also instances where a family may have a black sheep (when, due to a child's actions, that child is ostracized by the parents) and/or when the parent expects their children to live out their own lost dreams. While there is not enough space in this chapter to cover all of these issues in the family, and indeed they would require a separate book, we will address some of them.

Some of the biggest conflicts in families that I see stem from inconsistencies in behaviors or belief systems of parents. Children often get sucked into their parents' conflicts, and this can create further conflict between the kids. Children, being as astute as they are, often notice this and may learn how to manipulate one or both parents. The other side of the coin is that the children, who sense that they are in the middle of the parents' conflict, may feel manipulated by their parents and feel helpless to affect the conflict.

We see that our world is one big hierarchical structure. Parents are powerful at guiding their children, and it is important for parental figures, in any family setting, to understand and accept each child's feelings. In doing so, we may come to a mutual agreement on how to manage and guide our children. In the power structure of families, it is important to resolve conflicts when one or both parents feel at odds with the status level they have gained or assumed. Parents often hold the top two positions in the hierarchy, but either may prefer to have the status of the other parent. Sometimes, a parent does not determine their own status. Instead, other members of the hierarchy determine the roles and status.

There are both subtle and obvious ways that children may decide the status level of the parents. Children respond to how much time they spend with each parent, how the parent responds to the child, and how the parents act toward each other. Children may measure power in verbal exchanges, and in body language, eye contact, and voice tone. These are only a few of the more subtle issues that may strongly influence and aid in determining status in power structures.

Many times, conflicts regarding parental status involve the working parent and the parent who stays home with the children. In this situation, the children who have more exposure to the parent at home may feel that this parent is most powerful. The parent who tends to the kids is often the parent who disciplines and rewards them. However, the parent who works to provide money for the family may view their role as powerful, since it's necessary for the survival of the family. As such, that parent may want recognition for making these sacrifices. When the working parent arrives at home, they may want the power structure to recognize their status; this can result in a major disruption to the family. The parent at home may bear feelings of both resentment (that the working parent seems to come home and take their power) and guilt (that they understand the sacrifices of the working parent). The conflict for the stay-at-home parent is often between deferring to the working parent and keeping their power as the primary caregiver. The working parent may feel the need to disrupt the normal structure of the family; this often stems from insecurity felt by that parent and a resulting need to have others feed their power. These issues with parents needing different types of reinforcement from their children can feel both confusing and frustrating to children and the spouse.

Let us consider Tammy and Jason. Tammy is a district manager and works long hours, while Jason is a writer and stay-at-home dad. The kids are home with Jason all day, and so it is his job to ensure that they act as he wants them to. Since Jason is with the children all day, he feeds them, corrects them and punishes them throughout the day; they see him as the disciplinarian. Jason often feels burdened because he always seems to be the bad guy. On the other hand, when Tammy is home, she may want to increase the feelings of closeness and likability with her children and may want to avoid punishing them. In this case, Tammy sometimes becomes the fun parent and Jason may feel resentful about always having to be the disciplinarian.

For both parents, it is important to understand that gaining respect from the children will often come before any other role played by the parent. This is especially true when the children feel the need for help or guidance. We may see that discipline does not always command respect. We looked at the nature of abuse, and there are many different opinions on child discipline. I believe that discipline should involve learning with a purpose and should take place as close to the time of the unwanted act as possible. We will look more closely at the issue of child management later. At the very least, parents need to be aware of their emotional issues that may affect their children, especially during discipline.

In today's society, it is very common for both parents to work outside the home. Many families need two incomes and cannot afford to have either parent stay at home to care for the kids. The rewards and consequences of having two working parents are not often clear. While there have been many different theories regarding the impact of both parents working, it is difficult to gauge a true cause and effect.

Working parents often have problems that result from the influence of the daytime caregiver and the amount of supportive guidance that occurs. In most situations, if we add up the hours, the child spends more waking hours with the caregiver than with the parents. Daycare is quite expensive; however, the workers tend to receive low wages and may not be a good influence on our children. We know that people who spend much time with a child tend to influence the child; this is true whether the person is the child's parent or a hired caregiver. So it goes without saying that we must be careful and consider the habits, beliefs and attitudes of the people who will care for our children. Unfortunately, many caregivers have little, if any, training in child development and may engage in behaviors that conflict with what you want your children to see or hear.

It is often wise to choose a daycare provider after watching and interviewing the workers and checking references. Many parent/child conflicts arise when the child comes home with new words and habits that they picked up from their caregiver or from other children. As parents, we may see some parts of newfound knowledge as positive and others as negative. However, the child may feel confusion if the rules at home are different from what they are at the other place where they spend so much time. It is important to keep things as consistent as possible between home and daycare to help reinforce stable behavior.

Often, when children feel confused or frustrated, they tend to become more hyperactive and distractible and/or irritable. Because they easily misunderstand some of the complex events happening in their life, children may not know how to express their feelings of confusion. Some children in daycare feel that their parents do not love or care about them because they feel abandoned. Anytime we put a child in someone else's care, it is important to take the time to explain to the child why things are the way they are. We may see that if a child feels that life is chaotic and unstable, it may decrease the child's feeling of power in his or her life. These feelings can follow a child into adulthood.

EXTENDED FAMILIES

The extended family includes grandparents, aunts, uncles, and cousins; add to this those friendships that may rival the closeness of blood relatives. How a child's parents interact with their adult siblings and parents often determines how much of a role the extended family plays in a family unit. It is more common in some cultures than in others to have grandparents or parent siblings living in the same home. There is a greater chance for more role confusion to occur when extended family lives in the home; this is especially true if the boundaries between family members are not clear. There may also be stronger family ties and closer bonds when the extended family is active with the family unit and able to aid in the growth of the children.

Issues of power may arise in extended families when it comes to discipline and child guidance. A child's parents feel that they should be the authority on correcting and guiding their child, and the family elders may want to guide and correct the parents, since they see themselves as having more experience and higher status. For the child, this can feel confusing because the child may not understand who has the true authority or status. The child can also learn to influence parents and other family members in a situation. This is common when kids figure how to redirect guidance of them into clashes between other relatives.

Parents dislike feeling that other family members do not approve of their parenting style. When a parent feels undermined in their power as a parent, it may lead to feeling many weak emotions. It is not hard to see that a parent in this situation may feel frustrated, humiliated, and disempowered. It follows that when these emotions feel threatened, the parent may feel resentment and anger. Sadly, the parent may direct these feelings of anger at the child, instead of at the family member that prompted these feelings. Otherwise, these feelings may lead to conflict between the adults, or the parent may repress his or her emotions. In this case, the parent can often sense emotions like those they felt as a child, and their "child aspects" may come forth. When the parent feels like the child, they often have a hard time parenting and making sound parenting decisions. They may respond in an effort to recover a sense of power, instead of doing what is in the best interest of their child.

The elders of an extended family do the most good when they allow the parents to act as the children's main source of guidance. If other family elders feel that the parent needs advice, they may offer their comments to the parent when the child is not present. In doing things this way, the parent's power does not feel attacked in front of their child. Elders may be wise to allow parents to learn from their errors, instead of constant correction. I have heard of cases with clients where other family elders want to punish children more harshly than the parents. Their comments can be very upsetting, and the parent may feel attacked and punished for not treating their children as other family members would.

It is not unheard of to find that extended family members may punish children regardless of whether the child's parent is around. In some cases, the parent does not approve of the punishment and does not feel that others should impose discipline on their child. When I see these things, I often see that passive-aggressiveness and power conflicts are present. In these situations, when parents feel that other members are not guiding their children in productive ways, parents always have the option to remove the child from the elder's care; the care of the child is the parent's responsibility.

No matter where a child's sources of influence come from, it is important, again, that they have stable guiding forces. For this reason, it is often in the long-term best interest of the child and parents that the adults in the home agree to a set of consistent guidelines to follow. When there are conflicts between parents and other family elders, they may find help from a professional. This can help them determine guidance and discipline of the children. But they must all accept and resolve old issues that may be affecting their current relationships.

SINGLE-PARENT FAMILIES

We know there are many causes and reasons that lead to a single parent trying to raise children. In each of these scenarios, there are different issues that will affect all parties, depending on the situation. When divorce leads to a single-parent family, many powerful forces come into play. Which forces influence the situation depends upon who has custody and how the custodial parent places blame or responsibility for the divorce.

The factors that contribute to a death or divorce in their family do not matter to children. To a child, dealing with a sense of loss involves a grieving process that they cannot simply rationalize away. As adults, we may say, "It is really sad that Rick and Kerry split up. But if he had not cheated on her, they would still be together." A child, however, does not know, understand or justify the breakup in these terms. The child only knows that Daddy now lives somewhere else and Mommy acts as if she doesn't like Daddy anymore. Children put in this situation often feel confused and weak; those feelings may increase when the adults around the child begin to use defensive emotions to protect themselves from the hardship of the events that took place. For example, a child may cry for her father, and that may lead the mother to feel hurt and then angry and upset about the divorce. But, she may misplace her hurt and anger and aim it at the child. Besides the issues directly related to the breakup, a recently single parent often contends with feelings of fear and/or stress over not having anyone with whom to share their anger and other emotions.

Being solely responsible for the well-being of a child creates much pressure and stress for a parent. A parent may often feel that one of the child's needs must suffer in order to meet another need. The parent must work to buy food, but if the child is sick, he needs to go to the doctor. The parent may fear that he or she will lose their job if they take any more time off from work. Also, they may fear that if they lose time from work, they may not be able to pay the doctor bills or buy medication. Although the parent may find that the child tries to help with caring for some of their own needs, the feelings of stress related to being the only parent may continue to feel overwhelming. From a perspective of power, a child will have problems (in the case of divorce) with understanding how he or she fills the gap between the parents. If both parents have similar power over the child, the child may feel torn about where allegiances should lie. In this case, there is neither a good-parent nor a bad-parent view toward the parent if there is only one parent living in the home.

The single parent becomes the primary decision-maker. Because there is only one parent, there is more of a demand for the children to resolve their conflicts with the parents, since the parent is the primary source of support. If both parents live with the child, the child may learn that, if Mommy says "no," ask Daddy. Likewise, if I did something that made Mommy feel upset with me, then I may avoid her and spend time with Daddy. As such, when there are two parents, the child is able to create a good parent and bad parent. Avoiding the "bad parent" enables the child to avoid resolving the conflict. Having to seek this resolution with the single parent can be very healthy, if the parent is receptive to conflict resolution. This situation teaches the child to address conflicts with others who they may feel have more power than they do.

Children in single-parent homes may also feel confused when the parent feels unable to act as the parent. A mother may decide that she simply cannot bring herself to bathe her youngest child or needs to rest, instead of doing laundry. In these cases, an older child often assumes the role of the mother and acts as a parent in caring for the younger child. In some situations, the older child may feel forced to parent the parent or to take on the role of the missing spouse and act as a parent to the younger children. While power issues can arise from this role confusion, some parents are more than willing to accept the role switch. In accepting this change in roles, the parent may avoid using parental control and thus avoid feelings of failure for things gone wrong or bad.

I often see, when a single parent has major emotional issues such as depression or anxiety, that the level of stress rises for both the parent and the children. The parent may feel extreme guilt, shame and responsibility because of their issues. The stress that often comes with these feelings may cloud the matter of resolving issues. The child may feel many emotions because of the parent's issues. Children in this situation may feel insecurity, fear, anger, and resentment toward their parent's issues. At early ages, they may also feel confused about the cause of their parent's issues. It is also common to see that the child blames himself for the parent's psychological state. Although the child may have negative feelings as a result of the parent's issues, the parent should not take the situation to heart. Instead, the parent may want to help their child understand the cause of their issues.

STEPFAMILIES

We all know the pattern: a couple marries, has children and then divorces. The parents then remarry (often to people who also have kids from a previous marriage). This pattern of marriage and divorce does several things; obviously, there will be stepparents and stepchildren in such a household. If the couple then has children together, there will also be half-siblings.

One of the main issues in a stepfamily is that the stepparent often does not have the status of parent. Given that, some of the children in the family may not want to obey the stepparent. The reasons for this lack of respect and obedience stem from many power issues. As I said earlier, in a family that develops a hierarchical power model, members of the family seek to gain and hold the highest level of status that they can command.

When a stepparent enters the family, power may shift. This shift often depends upon the level of status that the stepparent wishes to command. In most cases, the stepparent will assume the first or second position of power and may call on status power to justify their position. When the children see this stepparent has a superior role of status, then the children may feel that they are giving their own power away. This may bother the children because they may feel they had to work very hard to get the power that they now fear they may lose. Kids may also feel confused about the other parent's power (the divorced parent no longer in the household) being usurped.

The idea of family loyalty tends to confuse many kids in this situation. Often, one or both parents add to this confusion. Problems may arise if the divorced parent outside the relationship feels threatened by the stepparent. It is common to see this parent questioning the children about their stepparent and/or interfering in the relationship between the kids and the stepparent. Parents in this position may interfere, due to feelings of fear of losing status in their child's eyes, or concern for what is in the best interest of their child. Also, they may fear losing the love of their children, fear unfair treatment of their children, and may feel other fears and threats. The height of the issues related to the entry of a stepparent often prompts many conflicts over power and status within the family.

The stepparent often enters the new family with feelings of fear and unease. Even before the parent and stepparent marry, the children and other parent may voice objections through actions and/or words. Whether or not there is true conflict with the stepparent, they may sense conflict.

In these situations, it is easy for people to read things into the relationship, and this is no different for stepparents. If the stepparent senses conflict, they will likely react to protect themselves. This can lead to confusion and hostility from other family members. In addition, we cannot ignore that the stepparent may not want to act as a parent; the person may simply wish to be a husband or wife. The stepparent may have issues with self-confidence and past family matters that may cause the person to feel threatened by their spouse's relationships with the children and/or ex-spouse.

The stepparent may resent the role of acting as a parent. They may or may not express their resentment; but often children are sensitive to others' emotions. The children may see the stepparent's emotions and motivations. Children are very aware of the feelings of those around them; they may have ulterior motives in reporting conflicts related to the stepparent. The child often feels weakened by the entry of a new person into the power structure. Therefore, we must accept the child's concerns and try to find the nature of their issues. If we address the issues early in the relationship and all can reach a level of understanding, acceptance with the life changes, stress and conflict may diminish, and the family may feel more safety and security.

STREET GANGS

You may ask why I have included a discussion of street gangs in a chapter on families. The reason is that I see a street gang to be an extension of the family. The street gang is based on a hierarchy where there is typically a leader of the gang that is "in control" of the other members. Disregarding the demands of the leader can result in serious consequences, similar to disregarding a parent. From the gang leader on down, there is a hierarchy of members with different statuses that may be challenged from time to time by other members, similar to sibling rivalries. When someone becomes a gang member, there are certain rules that they are to follow, certain ways they are to dress, and certain territories that they are supposed to stay in. Gangs often challenge other gangs and then often battle each other for superiority. The gang is supposed to protect its members from outside threats. If the gang is not able to protect its members, then there are often challenges for power internally, or the members may leave the gang; however, trying to leave a gang can result in death. The ability of the gang leader to maintain an arrogant sense of control and to elicit fear in others is crucial, similar to many hierarchical parenting strategies.

Where do gang members come from? They often come from abusive or broken homes. These individuals often have poor self-esteem, feeling unloved, abandoned, and rejected from their families and society. They are looking for a safe refuge in a world that feels terrifying. They are looking for love, support, and a feeling of belonging. The gang can provide this. In order to become a part of the gang, they have to go through rituals, which often involve illegal actions and sometimes murder. In a way, these actions push the prospective member further and further away from their family and society, so they feel that they have nowhere else to go but to the gang. In many situations, the leader of the gang gets the members to do the dirty work and relies on his status to maintain control. When a gang member has passed the test, the initiation often involves a love beating, which involves members of the gang punching, slapping, kicking, and doing whatever else they feel is necessary to deem this person worthy of being in the gang. For most people who have been through a painful experience, after they have been through it, psychologically, they have to feel it was worth it, especially if they consented to going through it. So, they are often more loyal as a result.

If you think of a family, the gang is not very different from a dysfunctional family. Think of the love beating. Now, think about how many times a parent will say that they are hurting their child because they love them and want them to learn. Many people who grow up in these environments have a poor understanding of what love is and what it is not. They also have often been so demeaned and humiliated that they feel that they need someone stronger than them to take care of them. Furthermore, the parents have often taught them that they should be willing to do anything to prove their love, and the child is just an extension of the parent. They are not their own person. Gang leaders are often no different. They are looking for people to worship them and give them their power. Without the other members in the gang, they would have no power.

The bottom line is that gangs exist and are growing because our family structures are deteriorating. They have become a substitute for something that gang members are not getting when they are young. It may be more prudent to look at the existence of a gang as being a symptom of a larger problem, not the problem itself. To correct this problem, we have to start in the home and with the parents. We also have to see how our hierarchical, controlling, fear-based parenting styles contribute to the desire of our children to go elsewhere to feel loved and accepted. We all have the ability to take responsibility for what is in our home, rather than blame our neighbor for something we should be doing. My directness is not intended to disrespect anyone, including any gang, but to wake people up.

SUMMARY

I have discussed a number of issues involving families and a variety of family settings. The discussions were only a brief overview of what is a large body of information. At this point, you may have questions and feelings of frustration; maybe you are unsure about how to respond to your child or parent. Many times, when working with parents, I find that they have many questions and almost feel paralyzed as to what to say to their child without affecting them negatively. By considering the numerous issues presented in this book and chapter, I am asking that you question yourself about the motivations of your behaviors. By asking questions of others and ourselves, we challenge ourselves to grow and learn. Our children, regardless of how they come to us or how long they are with us, will still look to us for guidance and direction. For those reasons, we need to be aware of our own direction. As long as we are asking the questions, we are more likely to find the way.

As parents, we are all going to make mistakes. The only perfect parent is the one who can accept their imperfections and not feel afraid to admit them and learn from them. Some of the most powerful words a parent can say to a child are "I am sorry" when the words are followed by a sincere effort from the parent to change the undesired behavior. Apologies often lose their influence when the same hurtful behaviors continue. As we are able to acknowledge our humanness to our children, they will often be willing to acknowledge their humanness to us.

QUESTIONS

1. If you are a parent, would you be more inclined to say that your parenting style is similar, or opposite, to that of your parents? If you aren't a parent, do you feel that you would emulate your parents' parenting techniques, or would you choose a much different path?
2. How do you view the role you played in your family while growing up? How does this compare to your relationship with your family now?
3. Consider the family situation in which you grew up. Whether you lived in a household with an intact family, a stepfamily, or were a teen parent, in what ways do you feel you benefited from the situation and in what ways do your feel another situation would have been more desirable?
4. Who was the most influential person in your family when you were growing up? What lessons, both positive and negative, do you feel were the most significant of those you learned from this person?

12

Power and Intimate Relationships

Love demands infinitely less than friendship.
                    —*George Jean Nathan*
Love does not consist in gazing at each other but in looking outward
in the same direction.
                    —*Antoine de Saint-Exupery*

TEACHING OBJECTIVES

- Explain the development of conflict in intimate relationships
- Provide models for understanding core issues in relationships
- Discuss how our past experiences and beliefs contribute to conflict and cycles in relationships
- Provide insight into understanding and managing changes in relationships
- Increase awareness of relationship issues through examples and exercises

I counsel many couples who could easily resolve their conflicts and enjoy closer and more trusting relationships, and whose issues of mistrust do not come from the actions of their current partner. Instead, their issues come from past events and misperceiving their partner's actions. I often talk about people placing masks on their spouse that represent past people in their life. They often do not realize they are doing this, but, through therapy, they see more clearly how this has happened. In these cases, they base their actions on emotional memories, in an effort to try to prevent the pain of the events or feelings from recurring. This chapter will address many of these issues, and provide strategies to aid in understanding and resolution.

As we saw in the section on abuse, many people will try to compare the actions of those who could hurt them in the present and future with those who have hurt them in the past. People try to predict their partner's actions to seek a sense of power and self-control to avoid painful experiences and feelings. When they do not make these predictions and allow themselves to get hurt, they often feel that they should have known better, which can result in feelings of failure, shame, humiliation and resentment toward themselves. Let me provide a sample scenario.

Doug and Julie have been in a relationship for six months and have been having difficulties surrounding conflict. This is Doug's second serious relationship and Julie's fourth; she divorced her first husband two years ago. To provide background on both Doug and Julie, Doug's parents divorced when he was twelve; Julie's parents did not divorce, but argued and fought often. Doug's parents did not argue aloud, but when tension was present, his father would spend more time at work, and his mother would go shopping and spend money, often bringing home toys or gifts for Doug. When Doug's parents divorced, he did not remember much arguing and felt that his parents just drifted apart. When Julie's parents fought, they often yelled and screamed. On a few occasions, her parents' arguments got physical, and her mother was injured. Before her parents' biggest arguments, Julie remembered that her father would often come home late for days on end, sometimes after drinking.

Julie had married a high school boyfriend who became verbally abusive toward her and several times threatened her with physical abuse. The marriage lasted two years, and she initiated the divorce. Doug said he felt that his previous girlfriend was very needy and wanted him around all the time. He said that she ended up meeting someone else, and when he came home one day, he found a note that their relationship was over, and she moved out within three months.

Both Doug and Julie currently work in professional settings. They sometimes work late hours to catch up, and both would like to maintain their careers, regardless of the relationship. They spend evenings together after work, and weekends, as well. While Doug acknowledges that he cares for Julie very much, he also wants to feel that he has more freedom to do what he wants to do. Julie admits that she feels somewhat angry with Doug when he works late, but also understands that he is working hard to advance his career. Julie does not want Doug to feel trapped, and is conscious of not asking him to stay around if he has other things to do. She also states that he never says anything to her about wanting to do "his own thing," and she feels frustrated when he indicates that he feels trapped.

One of Julie's other complaints is that Doug has never done anything to make her feel very special. She said that Doug even worked late on her birthday. When he arrived home, he took her out to dinner and gave her a birthday card. Doug stated, regarding working late on her birthday, he had a deadline to meet and said that he would not have chosen to work late, if he'd had a choice in the matter. He also mentioned that she also seemed to "conveniently" forget that he made her breakfast in bed and detailed her car on the weekend after her birthday. He went on to say that their relationship was only six weeks old on her birthday, and he was not sure what direction the relationship would take.

According to the couple, conflicts between them often involve a period of decreased communication when there are disagreements and, as Julie reports, "tension you could cut with a knife." As the tension builds, either Doug or Julie will make a sarcastic comment that leads to other remarks that result in Doug leaving the room. When Doug leaves the room, Julie often makes snide comments about Doug leaving. Julie says that when they argue, she feels like she wants to scream and throw things in order to make herself heard. However, she feels fearful about what Doug may do if she expresses her anger this way.

Julie says that when they argue, Doug gets a look on his face that scares her. Doug reported that sometimes when he has stood up to leave the room, Julie sometimes flinches and raises her arms over her head for a moment. He also says that he leaves because he feels verbally attacked and does not want to say anything in retaliation that he does not mean. However, he goes on to mention that he often feels as if he could explode inside after becoming infuriated with the things Julie says. Neither Doug nor Julie understands how to break out of this pattern, and they both recognize that their families did not handle conflict well.

EXERCISE

In the example provided, we may see many of the major issues and contributing issues. At this time, I would like to ask you to re-read the story and relationship details, and form some ideas of how past issues and emotions are affecting both Doug and Julie and their relationship. My analysis begins with the next paragraph. It may be necessary to

1. Review the list of emotions in the back of the book
2. Consider the possible attitudes of Doug and Julie when they were children
3. Think about what each party may have learned indirectly from observing their parents

4. Find parallels between past learning and current behaviors
5. Draw conclusions about possible misperceptions of both Doug and Julie that are contributing to current conflicts

In analyzing the conflict, it is clear that both Doug and Julie have some significant issues from their past that affect their relationship. While Doug or Julie may not easily see these issues, therapy may help bring these issues to light. Both experienced some vivid learning through their parents' relationships. What Doug seemed to absorb was that when there is conflict, people don't talk about it. He also felt confused about how to deal with emotions, since neither his mother nor father expressed them.

Doug felt angry when his mother bought him gifts because he felt that the gifts were bribes to try to make him happy and make him like her more than his father. He never felt that his parents really wanted to spend time with him and often felt sad and lonely. He also felt that the gift buying was supposed to take the place of time spent together. He felt constantly pressed to prove his worth to his parents, just so they would notice him. Because of what he saw and interactions with his family, Doug developed some beliefs and behaviors that he carried into his intimate relationships.

Doug never learned how to develop a close, intimate relationship. Since he never learned how to share emotions, he avoids expressing them in favor of seeking a logical point of view. Doug's problem with expressing his emotions leads him to feel unable to connect with other people. This lack of expression may lead his partner, Julie, to think that he does not care for her; she may feel that it is her responsibility to try to draw emotions out of him. From the viewpoint of power, since he uses logic to communicate, he often comes across as being strong and powerful, which may attract women seeking a strong, supportive male. Nevertheless, once the relationship is established, women may feel excluded and rejected.

Doug never felt that his parents fully accepted him. He thought that if he lost himself in work and succeeded at his job, he would finally find acceptance and love. Although he never felt that he got the acceptance and love from his parents that he sought, he found that if he buried himself in activity, he did not feel his emotions. Doug feels driven to strive for more because he never learned to believe in his power; he feels that he constantly has to prove his worth and receive power from the praises of bosses and those in more superior parent-type roles. He feels that if he impresses people whom he feels have more power than he does, he will then feel worthy to accept love in an intimate relationship. He could not consciously see this and express his feelings to Julie, so she felt that he was spending so much time at work to avoid her.

In Doug and Julie's relationship, he began to work harder because he felt inadequate and unworthy of Julie's attraction to him. When they argued, Doug felt that it was his fault because of the many times others told him that he was emotionally unavailable. His underlying thought was, "as long as I can prove my worth to someone through my work, they will not leave me." He also felt that Julie's working such long hours ratified his belief system, "Work is good." These beliefs only resulted in placing more distance between him and Julie. When he and Julie had conflicts, Doug also felt, inside, like a powerless little child, and didn't know how to react. He wanted to shout at her and defend himself, but he felt that if he did, she would leave him. Instead of yelling and screaming, he learned that, if he worked more, he could forget about the conflicts and avoid his feelings of guilt, shame and unworthiness.

Doug's feelings about giving presents reflected his misgivings about his mother's gifts to him when she and his father had problems. He formed the opinion that giving presents was a fake way of telling someone that you care. He believed that people had to show their love through their actions, which is another reason why he worked so much. This is also why he made Julie breakfast in bed for her birthday, rather than buying a gift. When she seemed to reject this gift as insignificant, he felt that he had screwed up once more, which seemed to support his feelings of ineptness in relationships.

There was also the issue of Doug feeling trapped in the relationship. While there were some direct and indirect ways in which Julie prompted him to spend time with her, there were many more times that Doug read too deeply into her actions. What he was seeking from her was permission to do his own thing. However, he feared that Julie would leave him if he didn't spend all of his non-working time with her. (This is what he believed he observed from his parents and previous relationship.) He felt that he had to sacrifice his wants for hers. This internal conflict resulted in guilt and fear when he did do things on his own without Julie and resentment and anger toward Julie when they were together. The resentment he felt did not relate to his feelings for Julie. It reflected what he saw in his parents and previous relationship, and he then indirectly vented these feelings on Julie.

The result of Doug's experience and issues led him to feel unworthy of accepting love from others. He also internalized and repressed many emotions that he did not feel were safe to express. His guilt and shame balanced his anger and resentment, and until Doug understood the relationships between his feelings, he could not resolve them. Doug began to see that he looked to others for power, love, and acceptance, instead of believing in himself and his own worth. He remained in relationships that felt uncomfortable; he felt lucky to find someone who liked him. Beneath his façade of confidence and strength, he felt largely unlovable and unable to have a relationship that felt good to him. The way he acted in his relationships unwittingly supported his belief systems.

Julie also formed many faulty beliefs and behaviors about relationships from watching her mother and father. First, she seemed to believe that people arguing and yelling proved that they cared for each other. This belief came from what her mother told her after many of her parents' arguments. Julie's mother said that the reason that her parents argued so much was because they loved each other so much. Through gaining insight, Julie started to see that her mother likely told her this in order to explain and justify her and her husband's actions. In doing so, Julie's mother avoided the fear of feeling unloved by her husband and denied feeling guilt and confusion about their arguments.

During arguments, Julie often felt an underlying fear of physical harm. This fear stemmed from the few times that her parents' arguments had in fact resulted in violence; she felt that if she asserted her feelings too directly, she could be hurt physically. This learning resulted in her repressing many of her resentments over a long period of time, which built into intense feelings of anger and rage. When she did argue with others, the anger and rage (stored from previous arguments) would build to the point where she felt as if she could explode. Instead of saying what she really wanted to say, she would make sarcastic comments, which disguised her true emotions. Fear offset her anger and rage, preventing it from coming out, and it lay in hiding until the next conflict. In this manner, she never felt as if many of her concerns were resolved, and the emotions continued to build.

The times when Julie's father came home late, she often felt fear that a big argument would take place and, many times, one did. Often, she also feared that he would never come home. When her father worked late, her mother became short-tempered and often vented her anger (likely her hidden feelings of confusion, helplessness and fear behind the anger) toward Julie and her siblings. Julie then developed feelings of anger and resentment toward her father for working late, and felt unloved by him. She believed that if he really cared, he would be at home to protect them from their mother's anger. Her anger protected fears of feeling unlovable, unworthiness and shame. The other message she seemed to pick up was that if she worked like her father did, maybe he would love her, be proud of her and, finally, take care of her. When Doug worked late, for the reasons discussed previously, Julie's feelings toward her father surfaced, and she felt as if Doug was avoiding her because he did not love her.

Doug had issues about showing others that he cared about them, and Julie had issues that added to her feelings about Doug never doing anything special for her. As was stated, Julie seemed to overlook the fact that Doug made her breakfast in bed for her birthday and detailed her car (although it was after the date). These were only a few of the things that Doug had done that Julie seemed to forget or not acknowledge. Julie's parents, siblings, and some of her past boyfriends called her selfish. This was a very sensitive issue to discuss because Julie grew tearful and felt defensive when any comment related to selfishness came up. Julie said that she felt deeply wounded when others referred to her as being selfish; she often felt that she had made many sacrifices for others and always tried to be helpful.

As we further discussed their issues, Julie realized that she often did things for others with an underlying hope that they would return the favor. She often felt betrayed by others, especially her siblings, and felt unappreciated. Julie seemed to feel that people did things for others to get something back. But she did not want to admit this to herself because she felt guilty about expecting things in return. Julie wanted to feel like a giving person. However, feelings of anger, resentment and fears of people taking advantage of her held her back.

Issues of trust also entered into her issues of giving. She seemed to feel that she either trusted without reservation and ultimately "got screwed" or did not trust at all. She seemed to waver between trust and mistrust with Doug, and Doug's behavior often had no bearing on whether or not she deemed him trustworthy. In her relationships, Julie always felt an underlying sense that she would be hurt and/or abandoned. She never allowed herself to accept the good things that came to her. She feared abandonment and mistrust. Someone could take these things away from her, leaving her with a sense of powerlessness.

Julie never felt truly loved and accepted by her father; this added to her seemingly selfish attitude. Many times, children misread the actions and words of their parents. Young children tend to be egocentric or self-centered (not to be confused with selfish) and are not privy to know or understand their parent's life before they were born; they often over-attribute their parent's actions to themselves. Because of these things, many children attribute a parent's attention, or lack thereof, to their own feelings of worthiness or inadequacy. Children then often repress these feelings of inadequacy and act them out into their adult relationships. In Julie's case, she never realized that her father likely had his own issues and, although he loved her very much, he may not have found ways to express it to her due to his own feelings of inadequacy, shame, failure, guilt. . . .

Several factors make dealing with lingering childhood issues very difficult. One is that many parents are not willing to discuss their own personal issues with their children, no matter what age they are. Many times, parents are not fully aware of their issues and the impact they had on their children. Julie did not discuss these issues with her parents; in most therapeutic situations, it is unnecessary. When working with clients, we try to resolve emotions, not verify their accuracy. People's emotions and belief systems commonly affect their recall of childhood events. For this reason, much of what people remember about their childhood may be factually inaccurate. Therapeutically, I do not want to blame parents or anyone, I want people to understand each other.

Julie's apparent selfishness came from questioning her worth, value, and power in the eyes of others. As a child, she felt that she had to take what she could get from others. She also developed feelings of resentment toward those from whom she felt she had to assert her needs. Julie justified her needs, and it appeared to others that she expected to receive certain things. Julie indirectly demanded attention and acceptance, and beneath that was the fear that she would never find love and never get what she truly needed. Her demands for time and material items could never substitute for the love and affection that she craved.

When Julie understood what created her behaviors, she saw why she had had so many troubles in past relationships. As Doug learned the dynamics that prompted Julie's actions, he found it easier to have patience with her; he learned that when she acted demandingly, she needed to know how he felt about her. He also would take the time to talk about the behaviors that bothered him.

In many ways, Doug and Julie's issues complemented each other's, in the sense that one's issues often evoked a characteristic reaction from the other. I firmly believe that, like Doug and Julie, many couples are involved with the person that can benefit their growth the most. When conflict erupts in relationships, we have a choice; we may either point the finger at the other person or look at the three fingers pointing back and take the time to look at ourselves.

Doug and Julie's issues, in various forms, are very common with couples. Both were somewhat dependent on the other for love and attention; both had issues related to feelings of weakness that prompted behaviors that looked powerful. Neither party wanted to feel that they needed the other for acceptance and worth, since those needs prompted feelings of weakness, worthlessness, and inadequacy. They both felt that they needed to be strong, confident and capable to be worthy of the other's love. Each felt that the other person would leave them if they knew how they felt inside. They both sought out materialistic ways to find their worth and hide feelings of inadequacy, instead of taking the time to believe in themselves.

RELATIONSHIP MODELS

The issues presented in the previous example show some common issues that affect the power of each person and the relationship itself. There are various ways to think about relationships in regard to power and energy. If we consider these different views, they may help us to understand some of the ongoing conflicts we have in our own relationships. We may only think of bonding as something that occurs between two people. Nevertheless, these models can include any number of people that make up a given relationship. As such, we form bonds when two or more people interact. Furthermore, if we remain in a relationship, we increase the chances of affecting someone's power. For our purposes, we will mainly look at intimate relationships.

Figure 12.1 represents a variety of relationships based upon an overlapping or sharing energy. In this case, each person shares part of their energy with their partner. In addition, it implies that each person may have varying amounts of energy to use for him- or herself. This energy depends upon the feelings and interaction of both people in the relationship. As shown in the models, the personal power of both parties may be the same size, or they may differ. The amount of power relates to the feelings and beliefs of each person in the relationship. In most relationships, there is a difference between how each person perceives

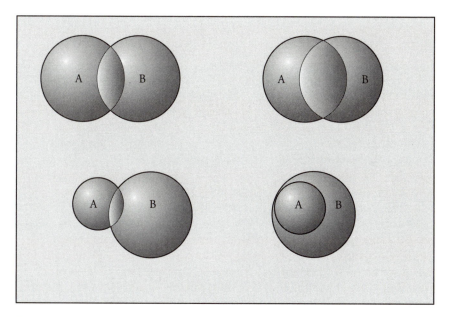

Figure 12.1 Examples of Overlapping Energy Relationship Models

their own power and how others perceive their power; however, power perceptions of each will likely vary.

The amount of shared energy a couple has can affect the relationship. The belief system of each partner also affects this sharing of power. In Figure 12.2, Person "A" (we'll call her Alice) has sunk her energy into Person "B's" (we will call him Bart) energy. This is most likely due to her belief that she needs other people's power to survive. This example shows that Alice does not believe in her own power; she tends to develop very dependent and clinging relationships.

Bart may end up feeling drained of his personal power and "sucked dry" over time, because Alice never feels that her needs can be met. Bart may enter into the relationship to rescue Alice. This enhances Bart's own feelings of power and worth, but, as he feels drained of energy, he senses that he needs to get out of the relationship to save himself. There are as many possible models of the overlapping circles as there are relationships. Furthermore, each person in the relationship may have different perceptions of the dynamics and the way that each person sees the energy in the relationship may change by the hour. The point is that each person has their own view of how they see the relationship, and seldom do both people in a relationship see it the same way.

Figure 12.2 represents one sense of what happens when a relationship ends. Often, after a relationship ends, people feel that they have some-

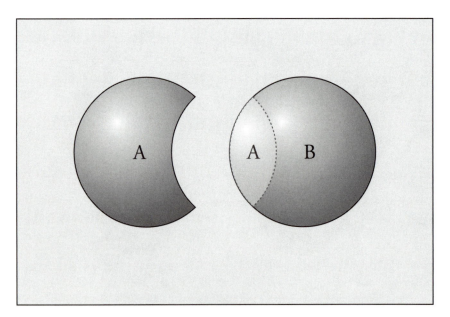

Figure 12.2 Perception of Power Lost by "A" in an Ending Relationship

how lost something or that the other person took some part of their self away. We will see, however, that this belief is inaccurate in truth. However, if we feel that we shared a part of our energy and the relationship ended in an unhappy manner, it is likely we may feel that we lost part of our energy and that becomes our reality. Therefore, we will believe that we have less power to share in the next relationship and may either feel that we have to hold on to ours tighter and/or see what we can get from the next person.

The crescent in the figure next to the circle denotes energy that Alice feels she lost, while, to her, Bart remains whole. This idea of lost power is in the mind of the beholder. Many in failed relationships do not see that both people in the relationship feel that they have lost something when the relationship ends. Since both people feel that the other person took some of their power, neither feels that they have access to it any longer and, as a result, carry the feelings of hurt, bitterness, resentment and betrayal with them. While the roots of these views begin in childhood, we often take them into each relationship. In Figure 12.3, we see the emotional effects of feeling a loss of power when a relationship ends. Such feelings of loss can occur repeatedly, until a person may feel they have nothing left to give. By looking at this model of shared and lost energy, you may see why there are so many issues related to trust in both intimate and casual relationships.

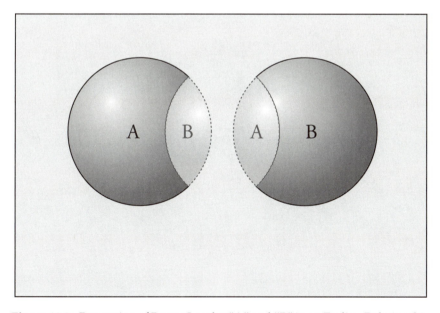

Figure 12.3 Perception of Power Lost by "A" and "B" in an Ending Relationship

This second model of relationships includes a third entity that forms when two people interact. We may think of this third entity as "The Relationship." In this model, the Relationship is a product of the interactions of two people. Figure 12.4 shows two people in a relationship, where the exchange of energy (denoted by the arrows) breathes life into the relationship. This model offers a healthier situation, since it does not involve sharing power. Instead, this model involves an exchange of energy that creates a new entity. In this case, the two partners share the power created by the relationship, while keeping their own power.

If we enter a relationship with our power intact and realize that we do not have to give our own power away, then we will likely feel less risk of losing power. We may then see more potential of gaining from what the relationship has to offer us. The interaction in this relationship model depends on the amount of power that each person puts into the relationship, but not so much on what they give to each other. We see that, in this model, a relationship ends without either person losing any power. In fact, it allows these two people to end the "dysfunctional" aspects of the relationship to create a more functional relationship, often through therapy. I describe this situation to couples that I work with. I tell them that sometimes an ailing relationship has to die so that a healthy one can be born in its place.

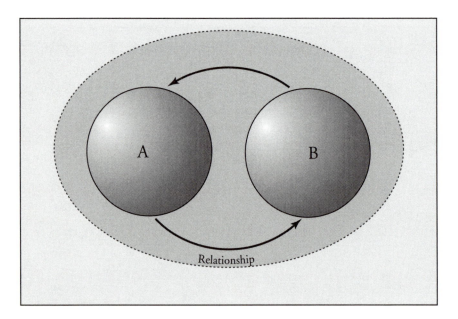

Figure 12.4 A Relationship as a Separate Entity

You may question the value of this relationship model; you may wonder how people share with each other when they appear to be giving to the relationship, not to the other person. In this model, the arrows indicate the energy that passes between both people. It is not that people are giving in the name of the relationship. The main point is that they are always preserving their personal power and do not have to feel that they are giving of themselves for the other person in the relationship. It creates a different perception of what the relationship is so that they do not have to feel that they are losing, or are even at risk of losing, anything.

The situation represented in Figure 12.4 decreases the chances that one of the parties will enmesh himself with someone else—and now we need to talk briefly about "enmeshment." People's boundaries often become blurred and in the process, they become too involved with the other in the relationship and their energy overlaps or is subsumed in both parties. We call this event enmeshment. A couple in an enmeshed relationship often tries to fulfill each other's desires and dreams, rather than their own. Because of this, emotions such as guilt and shame are easily manipulated. Enmeshed relationships may often occur between parents and children. People in enmeshed relationships usually do not believe that they can be successful on their own. These people tend to believe that they need their partner to survive. They are also commonly rescuer-victim relationships. The sense of one's personal power in an enmeshed relationship is low; this is why they form such a strong need for others. They may either be the person who wants adoration or the one who receives nurturing. The initial overlapping energy relationship model discussed before typifies an enmeshed relationship. There is an overlapping of the individuals' energy. As we saw earlier, members of the enmeshed relationship fear that the overlapped energy is lost if the relationship ends. The second relationship model serves to show that people have a right to maintain their own power and psychological health.

Many couples who seek counseling fear that they may end up apart, and feel that their days together are numbered. People often feel that if their relationship isn't working now, it never can or will work. I work with many couples that care very much for each other and could have a powerful and positive relationship, but, as we saw with Doug and Julie, people bring personal issues with them into the relationship, and these issues may prevent the success of that relationship. Through therapy, I try to help each person understand what aspects they may want to change to help their relationship become more positive.

EMOTIONAL SHORT CIRCUITS

Refer to Figure 12.4, showing relationships as a separate entity. We may see that the relationship suffers when the energy is reduced or misdirected. You may think of the bond in a relationship as a string of Christmas tree lights. The number of lights that remain lit affects the intensity of the bond. The more lights that remain lit, then the stronger the bond, the more that get burned out, the weaker the bond. I want to help people find these "electrical shorts" that burn out the lights.

For another example, we could think of someone whose car battery keeps draining. They took the car in for repair twice. The mechanic installed a new battery and checked the electrical system in the car. But, two weeks later, the person again has a dead battery. Upon further questioning and exploration, the mechanic finds that when the person turns off the car they leave the parking lights on. The energy required to run these lights drains the battery. How does this metaphor tie into relationships? "Emotional shorts" in people are unresolved emotional issues that divert our energy from the present and prevent us from objectively seeing and responding to an event.

For example, on Monday nights, when Doug came home late, Julie felt very angry. No matter what he said, she reacted very coldly and occasionally tossed a sarcastic comment. She did not understand why she reacted in this manner, but felt her mood change coming throughout the day. We learned that, when Julie was a child, her father sometimes left for business trips on a Monday and would not come back until Friday. Many times, he would not tell her he was going to be gone, and she often felt hurt and abandoned. Julie's old feelings of hurt and abandonment flared up when Doug worked late. We may see, therefore, that part of her feelings of anger and rejection were not wholly because of, or even related to, Doug.

The cause of Julie's emotional short was hard to find and understand. Nevertheless, it had a definite effect on her relationship with Doug. Julie spent her energy unconsciously on this past event, and it affected the potential success of her current relationship.

We see from the example that energy diverted or "shorted out" by past events can present problems in the relationship. This short affects the amount of energy available to Julie to put into the relationship. The drained energy affects the feelings and interactions of both people. The causes and effects of these emotional shorts, elusive as they may be, can put a huge drain on relationships.

Julie's reaction to Doug's working late is just one emotional short or unsettled issue. Many of us have many emotional shorts in our past and present that affect our current relationships and day-to-day living. Some of these problems are easier to detect than others. Emotional shorts that affect relationships are the same as issues that affect other parts of our life. These shorts may take the form of emotional aspects that seem to take over during conflicts. They may also consist of attitudes or ideas that affect how we respond to interactions.

Sometimes, the most difficult issue regarding these shorts is whether the person wants to see the issue and be accountable for it. Many times, it is easier for someone else to recognize, from a little distance, the patterns of emotional shorts.

In Figure 12.5, you may notice that emotional shorts can be ascribed to people in the past (mother) or to unresolved emotions (fear and mistrust); there may also be a single event or many events (abuse). A person must resolve the issue that is responsible for the short in order to release it. After this release, a person is more emotionally present in the relationship.

In the example with Doug and Julie, Julie's anger related to issues with her father and the feelings that arose as a result. In the history of Doug and Julie, it was clear that Doug also had his issues in the past that were responsible for his working late. His actions, however, evoked in Julie the emotions related to *her* past. This complex interaction of past issues and feelings that affected both Doug and Julie exists in most relationships. The past relationships resulted in various emotional shorts that grounded out the energy that could have been devoted to the success of the relationship.

Although the couple may know what the conflicts stem from, even in Julie's situation, she was not able to let go of the anger. She first had to resolve the feelings around the initial issue that related to her father's

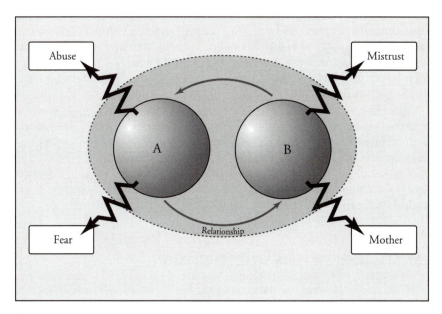

Figure 12.5 Emotional Shorts in a Relationship

travel. When she accepted the old issues with her father and resolved these conflicts of her past, she found that she could redirect her energy toward her relationship with Doug. It is crucial for couples to focus on the present and live less in the past.

Too often, we feel that once we understand our issues, they should be resolved. However, for many people, the issue continues to affect their lives and the lives of those around them. It is true that if we can understand our issues, our knowledge can help us to change our behavior. Behavior management can help to alter these patterns. But, many times, hidden below the surface, many people still either feel the desire to act on their emotions, or they find another behavior to express the same emotions. Substituting one behavior for another that is related to the same issue is called symptom substitution. While this can happen in any facet of a person's life, it is important to discuss this in the context of relationships. Many people want to think that if they change how they act, that the pattern of behavior has ended. Often, if we look closely, we find that either the pattern goes on in another way or it crops up in another relationship.

Gary has a history of yelling at Dawn, his wife. In therapy, we address the issues of yelling, and Gary finds other ways to express himself. Although Gary reports feeling an initial reaction to want to yell, he chooses to use the new methods of expressing himself that he learned. Gary and Dawn begin to relate better and the issue appears to get better. Within a few months, Dawn calls and tells the therapist that their relationship is well and there is less yelling between them. But, Gary is now shouting at the children and has less patience with them. In this scenario, Gary learned strategies to manage his expression of anger toward his wife, but the anger and its causes were still present. Gary then began to vent his anger toward the children, since the anger still needed an outlet.

Gary changed the way he treated his wife, but now vents his feelings of anger on his children instead. Further counseling with Gary should focus on the causes of the past emotional short that lead him to express this anger in the present. In similar client cases that arise, I find that anger usually comes from events during childhood; it comes from a time when the child did not feel able or was not able to express anger without fear of retailiation.

CYCLICAL RELATIONSHIP PATTERNS

Many times, during the process of therapy, clients will ask, "Why do I keep ending up in relationships with the same type of person time and again?" The other most common realization is the statement, "I married 'my mother' or 'my father.'" Clearly, the person did not really marry one of their parents; they married someone who "mirrored" similar issues to them as their parent(s). There is no simple answer as to why these trends seem to occur. There are many issues to take into account in this somewhat common trend. One of the easiest answers is that people often prefer someone who seems familiar to them. When people feel that they know what to expect, no matter what their experience, their life seems safer, because it's more predictable. In other words, some people choose to be with those who behave in ways they recognize. Unfortunately, people who received abuse as a child all too often simply expect abuse as an adult, even if they resented the abuse and know that it is unproductive.

The second reason that people seem to fall into a cycle of similar relationships time after time is more complex. This issue involves subconscious choices and belief systems. The term that describes this subtle occurrence is projective identification, which is related to object relations theory in the field of psychology.[13] Projective identification occurs when someone subconsciously expects or believes that they deserve certain interactive patterns in their relationships; because of their own subtle behaviors or styles of interactions, the interactive patterns recur. The person's behaviors create a self-fulfilling prophecy. In most situations of projective identification, the individual who expects the reactions of others is not consciously aware of their choices, behaviors, and actions. The best way to explain this is with the following example. Although this will be an extreme example, it does occur and it is my hope that it will prompt you to examine your own underlying beliefs in relationships.

The example involves a woman who received physical abuse. This person has experienced abuse in four different relationships. She has been in six relationships and her shortest relationships were the two that did not involve abuse. As a child, her father physically abused her, and her mother was sometimes verbally abusive. In her most recent relationship of six months, her boyfriend had slapped her on two different occasions. The first occurrence was four months after they started dating.

In questioning her boyfriend, he reported that he had never hit anyone before, and no one physically abused him as a child. He had been in relationships in the past and never felt like slapping any previous girlfriends. When asked why he had slapped her, he admitted that he could not understand why, but he felt that when they argued, she was unyielding, and he felt a rage silently building within him for some time. On the first incident, he felt that something snapped and next thing he knew, he hit her. He apologized profusely and even wept afterward. He stated that he promised he would never hit her again after that. After the second incident, he felt that they needed to get some help; he was very motivated to understand their behaviors.

On the part of the boyfriend, there was a great deal of guilt regarding his actions. While the woman felt very hurt and mistrustful because of his actions, she seemed resigned that what had happened was "par for the course." Deeper exploration with the woman found that there was an aspect of her that believed that she deserved abuse. In her behaviors, there were very subtle behaviors she engaged in, and she often felt that a conflict was not over until someone hit her. It was not until she understood this aspect of herself that she began to realize how her actions, although subtle, resulted in the behaviors toward her.

I do not excuse his abuse, regardless of her actions, subtle or obvious. He had the choice to settle the matter without violence, to walk away and take a break during the argument when he felt his feelings of rage building. If he felt that she was provoking his behaviors, he had the choice to end the relationship. While there is much more to examine in looking at their history in understanding the escalation of behaviors, this example provides a situation where the person's underlying belief systems prompted another person's behaviors.

Other examples of behaviors that involve projective identification can involve verbal abuse, relationships ending, losing a job, or feeling abandoned. . . . However, people often refer to projective identification in regard to negatively viewed behaviors; we may see that it can also involve the promotion of these positive belief systems. When people who may subconsciously use projective identification are questioned about their actions, they will deny any knowledge, and indeed they are truly unaware of their actions and belief systems; this is by definition an unconscious process.

We can understand the issue of projective identification by considering the individual power issues that occur within each of us. In some manner, the conscious mind felt the need to suppress the belief system, and the belief system found a way to express itself (without conscious knowledge), undermining the power that the conscious mind was seeking to command over this belief system. As was explained in Chapter 10, on internal power struggles, many times we experience very complex internal power dynamics that create a number of internal conflicts.

Another issue that results in cyclical relationship patterns is the perceptions of the individual in the relationship. People often see what they want to see in life, and what we see often depends on our belief systems. For example, people who believe in the existence of spirits or ghosts are more likely to believe that they have seen ghosts. When people have certain perceptions about relationships, they may acknowledge some behaviors and ignore others. For example, someone may believe that someone else will abandon them. They can justify this by stating that every relationship that they have been in has ended. In making that observation, they neglect to state that they ended more than half of the relationships, and the other relationships often ended when they distanced themselves from the other person. Many people do not take the time to realize that if they are currently in a monogamous intimate relationship, every previous such relationship had to end. In other words, to be in a relationship, one must have had a 100 percent failure rate in previous relationships, if you define failure as the end of a relationship.

Many times in relationships, people will only focus on what goes wrong or what happens to hurt them. For both parties, this can result in a very helpless and frustrating feeling. Many times, the accused party will try exhaustively to help the "afflicted person" to see all of the positive aspects of their relationship, and may seek to convince them that they shouldn't feel the way they do. Sometimes these efforts to convince the other person of the positive aspects result in a stubborn adherence to their negative belief systems. Too many times, the individual with the negative belief systems will frustrate the other party to the point where they may begin to adopt a similar belief system and/or end the relationship to save them. The resulting end of the relationship often serves to reinforce the other person's negative belief system, which will then likely be a continuing factor in the next relationship.

From the aspect of conflict, it is important for us to consider the underlying power dynamics of those who choose to focus on the negative aspects of relationships. Their perceptions can both be protective and result in a continued victim mentality. The manner in which their perceptions can be protective is that more negative perspectives prevent us from getting too close to someone or expecting success (if we don't get our hopes up or let ourselves feel happy, then it won't hurt as much when—not if—we are abandoned or feel sad). The manner in which perspectives contribute to a victim mentality is that if someone believes that people will always abandon them, then they are giving up their power to believe that they can have a positive, productive relationship. In this manner, we have given up our rights to see life as a positive experience, and we have become a victim to negativity. In most situations, if we choose to focus on the negative aspects in our lives, that is what we will see.

Another reason people seem to find themselves in similar relationship patterns refers back to the idea that life is a mirror. Concerning relationships, I think that we all end up choosing or finding the person that can teach us most about ourselves. However, we may not be willing to look close enough to acknowledge our growing points, and/or may choose to play the victim role and feel that life happened to us, not for us.

Time after time, when working with couples, I help them to realize how many different ways they can learn from each other. Often, when they are able to see the connections, their relationship can continue to grow and evolve, or they can acknowledge that they are not ready for it to grow in that direction. We are the only ones who can choose to recognize our life patterns and learn from them. Although we may sometimes feel helpless to change aspects of our lives, especially in relationships, no one else can do it for us.[14]

Are you interested in examining the relationship(s) in your life? Do you want to find the emotional shorts and unproductive cyclical patterns that exist? If so, you may explore these perceptions with someone who knows how to dissect these issues from an impartial point of view. People often need to have some distance from an issue to be able to see it objectively, and often family and friends are too close to the issues, since they often care about us and may subjectively misconstrue facts for or against us through their own interpretations.

WHEN RELATIONSHIPS CHANGE

What happens when the energy shifts in a relationship, and the relationship can no longer survive? There are situations when it is best for a relationship between two people to end. The people may have different interests and priorities, or one person may have outgrown the other and/or life circumstances may have changed. In any of these situations, I feel that it is integral for any couple to explore their issues with a therapist to examine the issues behind a potential breakup.

As was just discussed, most relationships have the capability to survive or change when both people understand how they are contributing to issues in the ailing relationship. However, when a relationship does not work, many people want to feel that the relationship was a waste of time and/or energy, and they want to distance themselves from the other person and the perceived failures in the relationship. As I have indicated, I tend to consider that every relationship we form in our lives, no matter how short, can teach us something about ourselves. Each person we meet can be of value to us. We can choose to focus on what was bad about the other person or the relationship, or we can choose to focus on what we can learn from them about ourselves.

One of the most important issues to understand when a relationship ends is the concept of love as an emotion, and how the different aspects of love (philos, agape, and eros) may have contributed to the success or end of the relationship. Many intimate relationships go through cycles of eros, or romantic love, throughout the years. However, if the relationship does not have powerful components of philos and agape that carry the relationship through the low points of the cycle, the relationship may have trouble. Often when a relationship is based solely on eros, it will not survive the test of time. Often, balancing the different aspects of love is an important key to achieving a prosperous intimate relationship. However, even when a relationship starts in balance, the balance can shift, if attention is not paid to maintaining the relationship. Similarly to raising a child, if one thinks of a relationship is a form of living entity, it too needs nourishment, nurturing, and attention. If the relationship does not receive what it needs, it may die a slow death.

An example of a relationship that changed and slowly died is that of a couple who had been dating since high school. They felt an intense attraction for each other (eros) and admired aspects of each other including kindness, intelligence, athleticism, appearance . . . (philos and agape). As the relationship continued over the years, they both graduated from high school and decided to marry. The husband began his career working in construction and, within a few years, started his own business. In order to start his own business and insure its success, he worked many hours, often six days per week. His drive to work as hard as he did was motivated by his perception that he needed to be the financial provider in the family, which had been the trend in his family for generations. His wife worked part-time and took classes toward fulfilling her dreams of a college education, with the ultimate goal of having a professional career.

Issues began to arise in the relationship when the wife became more interested in her education and her husband began to feel threatened by her increased knowledge and changing interests. As she met more people in her college classes, she began to spend more time with them, since he spent so much time working. She admired her husband's hard work (contributing to her feelings of philos and agape for him), and part of her motivation to obtain a college education was so that she could contribute to the financial stability of the family. Part of the motivation for the husband to work so hard was because of his love (philos, agape, and eros) for his wife and wanting to provide her with financial stability. Because they both worked so hard in their respective interests, they were not able to put the effort into sustaining the energy and interest in the eros aspect of their relationship.

Throughout the relationship, they continued to admire each other, but the husband's continuing insecurities about his wife growing away from him with her newfound knowledge continued to drive a wedge of insecurity in their relationship. The wife sensed the husband's feelings of insecurity and, while she understood why he might feel threatened, she felt that she could not sacrifice her dreams for his insecurities. She felt that if she sacrificed her desires, she would feel a great deal of resentment, which could also have devastating effects on the relation-ship. The more she continued to progress in her education and the more her husband continued to work, the less time they spent together, and the more time she spent with her college friends. The less time the couple spent together, the more they felt the eros aspect fade.

Even though there was conflict in the relationship, both the wife and husband continued to deeply care for each other and felt admiration for the other's hard work. However, the husband began to realize, more and more, his internal need to be the breadwinner in the family because of the feeling of power he believed that it brought him. He was not willing to look at the causes of his underlying insecurities that contrib-uted to his need to make more money, which prevented the couple from resolving their issues. The wife was feeling stuck because of her need for personal growth and fear of losing her first love.

Through soul searching and discussion, the couple began to realize that the balance of the love in their relationship had changed. Neither person was willing to change aspects of the relationship that could help to resolve some of the issues (the husband not wanting to address his insecurities, and the wife not wanting to change her aspirations). They both felt increasing feelings of resentment toward the other's actions, and there was no longer any physical attraction. They spent time together on weekends and took some trips to see if they could revive their attraction (eros). However, the underlying issues continued to contribute to the distance between them. There was a constant tension between them, and arguments would start over small issues.

As the unproductive pattern of communication continued, both began to feel that the only way to save their friendship (the philos and agape aspects) was to end the marriage. After they made this decision, the relationship improved and the conflicts decreased. While the con-flicts decreased, they began to feel some hope, and the couple flirted with the idea of reviving the eros attraction through periodic intimate interactions. After these periods of intimacy, the underlying issues would resurface, which helped to convince them that they had made the best decision to separate.

In this example, there are a number of issues to discuss. First, this couple experienced some conflicts, but their pattern of resolution was very mature, and they continued to communicate directly with each other throughout. Most relationships do not end so smoothly.

Second, this relationship did not have to end. Each person brought their own issues that contributed to the problems with the relationship. Some of their issues were unproductive to their own growth and some of their issues helped them to grow, but were counterproductive to the relationship they had established. The wife was justified in pursuing her aspirations for an education and career, but although the husband had the right to feel insecure, his unwillingness to resolve his insecurities placed an obstacle in their lives. It is very likely that if he had worked through his issues, they could have developed a more powerful bond. Furthermore, although the couple decided to end their relationship, there is still a possibility of them reconciling after they spend time apart and learn more about themselves. Because they continued to admire and care for each other (philos), there is a better probability of them forming a healthy relationship after their current relationship dissolves, instead of suffering through a breakup rife with bitterness and anger.

Third, this example helps to explain that intimate relationships require more than one aspect of love to survive. The bond began with an eros attraction that grew into a deep philos friendship and had aspects of agape. The eros, philos, and agape aspects of the union continued to grow, but when neither party put much energy into maintaining the intimacy between them, the eros faded. As the eros faded, intimacy continued to decrease. The strong aspects of philos and agape carried the relationship for some time even after the eros faded and contributed to a peaceful resolution. The couple had grown in different directions, having different interests, which made it difficult to rekindle the eros aspect.

Fourth, the couple did not have children, which made the decision to break up a little easier. Often, once people have children, they feel that their options to part ways are greatly limited. I have worked with many couples with children who continued their relationship only because of the children. Both parties had significant issues that prevented them from resolving their relationship issues. Additionally, each person's feelings of resentment and anger may lead them to take their frustrations out on their children, directly and indirectly. In these situations, when children are involved, I often explain to the parents that they should think about the affect they may have on the children if they remain together despite their dysfunctional relationship.

The couple needs to consider what they are teaching their children about relationships, as well as about their own right to feel happy in their life. Many times, children would rather see their parents feeling happy and separated than sad, miserable, and married. When parents stay together in an unproductive situation, the children often learn that marriages are not supposed to be positive, happy, and loving, but ultimately end up being wrought with anger, frustration, and sadness. Granted, most couples go through cycles, but many have a difficult time finding the upswing. There are situations when, after discussing the options of splitting up and what is truly in the best interest of all, tension is relieved, and the couple is able to begin to resolve some long-standing issues.

SUMMARY

This chapter has covered a number of issues related to intimate relationships. While it can feel that there is more at stake in intimate bonds, many of these dynamics can occur in almost any relationship, but may not feel as risky. There are also an endless number of examples that could be used to explain the nuances between different aspects and dynamics. Each relationship is unique in that it brings its own subtleties to light, and there is no way that I could capture all of those subtleties. The key points to apply involve examining the relationship models (overlapping energy versus the relationship as an entity) to see how you may be conceptualizing your own relationships. It is important to understand how your perceptions and power dynamics contribute to your relationships and you should be willing to accept the possibility that you may have some subconscious aspects that have different priorities or perceptions at work that you may not consciously realize. Allow this chapter to be a beginning guide to examining issues relative to your relationships, and to yourself, and begin to write your own chapters in your book(s) of life.

QUESTIONS

1. Can you identify a pattern of cyclical intimate relationships in your life?
2. If you reflect upon discord in your intimate relationships, have you ever considered how you may have contributed to the conflict and how you may have been able to help resolve the matter in a more productive manner?
3. Have you ever felt that an undue amount of energy in one (or more) of your intimate relationships was being consumed by conflict, instead of being applied toward nurturing the relationship?

13

Power in the Workplace

> Some see private enterprise as a predatory target to be shot, others as a cow to be milked, but few are those who see it as a sturdy horse pulling the wagon.
>
> —*Winston Churchill*

TEACHING OBJECTIVES

- Discuss power issues in office settings
- Explain the hierarchical nature of business and how it contributes to conflict
- Provide scenarios and examples to explain concepts presented
- Provide a framework to begin to resolve individual power issues in the workplace

Power struggles in the workplace are probably more common than anywhere, except maybe in the family; however, power struggles in the workplace are often more subtle and indirect. Direct threats to power in the workplace often meet with direct resistance. Why? As mentioned earlier, such conflict may seem threatening to those with power. This chapter will provide a very brief overview of conflict in the workplace and the issues of power that accompany the conflict.

Conflict in the workplace is one of the hardest to navigate of all areas of conflict. This situation is often complicated by how others view emotions in the workplace. In business, many believe that image is everything, and a major part of image involves coming across as strong and powerful. Many people feel that emotional expression has no place in a business setting. So, one has to be very careful to monitor their expression. If you ask almost anyone in business, their worst fear is probably crying in front of their boss.

The irony here is that there is often a feeling of fear that pervades a business environment. These fears relate to keeping our job, advancement, demotions and other hierarchically related issues. We may try to please the right people, "make the numbers," and jump through many other hoops. Many feel that it is wrong for workers at any level of business, to allow personal issues to affect their job. We often hear, "Things at home should stay at home and things at work should stay at work." However, no matter how hard we try to limit the effects of our personal life at work, it is nearly impossible to shut our emotions down when we walk into our place of work. If we look closely at our work relationships, we might realize that they are another reflection of our personal issues. This chapter will discuss some of the obvious issues related to conflict in the workplace that affect us daily.

I will keep this chapter brief, in light of the number of conflicts and power issues that occur in business settings. In this chapter, I hope to introduce you to some of the issues to consider within the power structure of any business.

THE CORPORATE LADDER

Most businesses are rife with power structures. Throughout time, businesses have functioned with differing levels of status within a business. They do this to provide structure and order to make sure that tasks are completed. Business relies on the notion that it needs leaders and followers, directors and "go-fers," visionaries and doers. Many times, employers tie job titles to status, and higher status generally means higher income. However, some companies give job titles and power, but do not offer pay that is on par with the responsibility. In some cases, the employer hopes the title and power are reward enough, without a salary to match. Banks, for example, often give titles of status without an income to match; many banks have a large number of vice presidents. However, the salary structures vary and, with these promotions, sometimes there are no changes in salary, just a change in status.

We could probably think of many reasons why power structures are so common in business. Often, the goal is to allow each employee to put their best skills to use in their job with little interference or minimal supervision. Businesses often prioritize the skills they need in order to thrive. In turn, they give varying degrees of power to those in these jobs.

Structure is a major part of the success of any business. Is it necessary to define levels of power to the degree that it exists in most corporate structures?

For example, in a software company, the programmers may have a higher status than those who package the software. Still, we must ask, what is the importance of marketing the software, compared to creating the software? A company might have a great product, but, without effective marketing, no one will know it is available. If the packaging looks flimsy or cheap, people may doubt the reliability of the product. In addition, if the product's packaging is poor or sloppy, the result could mean damage during shipment. This results in unhappy customers and needless expense to the business. Most of us have received a parcel that looked as though someone used it for a football. My point is that, although some positions may have a higher profile within the business, all employees must perform as members of the team. Each person is important to the success of the business. An even more tangible example: is it likely that you would buy this book if it were a loose collection of paper written by hand? If I wrote the most important book in the history of the world, but it was poorly packaged, few would give it a chance. I, as the author, carry the message, but it requires the effort of editors, marketing people, typesetters, artists and many others, all of whom were crucial in seeing this book through to delivery.

Remember, the presence of a hierarchy often increases the chance for dissent and conflict. We each have our own gifts to bring to our professions. When we concern ourselves with rising through an organization to establish our status and worth, we might find that we are doing things we neither have the skills for, nor enjoy. Some may lose their jobs because they cannot perform at an acceptable level in the position they have assumed; they outgrew their skill set.

In life, we may feel pushed to increase our skills and keep growing, evolving, and moving upward, to gain more power. Growth and challenge can be very positive things, but we also need to respect our limits. However, out of all of the areas in our lives that can experience growth, many of us emphasize growth in our careers; it's no secret that we often measure our success in monetary value and changes in career status.

What happens when we only emphasize personal growth in the aspect of our career? Commonly, other areas of our lives suffer, and we feel the unbalance caused by focusing too heavily on one aspect. If we lose sight of our goals in other areas of our existence, we can become lost in life. However, we each must have the courage to say, "I am lost and need some direction." I've lost track of how many business executives I have worked with who felt they had no life direction other than in their work.

Even in our work and finding our skilled areas and weaknesses, there is balance. Most managers know that they may lose some of their best employees when the employees feel pressed to grow beyond their skills to gain status and power. However, if management does not promote a person who does wish to rise through the hierarchy, they risk the chance of losing them, too. The business then must learn to help their employees to feel powerful and valued in the jobs at which they are most skilled.

What seems to happen when people rise through the ranks of a corporation and find themselves at the top of their organization? They often take precautions to hold on to their newfound power. In a position of power, they have the ability to control the workplace and keep things in their favor; they may thereby protect their power through unsavory means. Some say that IBM lost its market position due to the hesitancy of those who controlled the company to change with the industry and/or be willing to allow others with new and different ideas to step in. This was the same with the auto industry, and likely, the trend will continue in different venues.

There is no shortage of stories about all the people who refused to step down from leadership roles, even if they were inept or doing a poor job. Regardless of the scope of their power, managing a convenience store or running a country, these people often cling to their power in similar ways and for many of the same reasons. In these situations, the passion to keep control often comes from a fear of loss of control and/or fear of the loss of status, and thus perceived power. Those who grip their kingdom too tightly may end up being the king of nothing. For example, what if Fidel Castro allowed the citizens of Cuba to travel anywhere they chose? Is it possible that large numbers of the population would emigrate elsewhere? In today's society, many business owners and managers find themselves forced to share the control they once held and involve others in the decision-making process. Consider the role of arrogance and vanity in someone's reluctance to let go of status.

In the last ten to twenty years, many companies attempted to reduce the layers of power and promote a more lateral structure and team philosophy; but the road to reaching these ideals has been rocky. Clearly, when someone who feels they have a position of status senses a loss in status, they tend to feel threatened; therefore, they may try to sabotage the people or situation that prompted this sense of loss. Once again, our insecurities and fears may prevent even very good ideas from succeeding.

Some of the changes within businesses, in the last ten years, illustrate that these team approaches take time to enact and do not assure long-term success. In addition, some companies find themselves in a state of constant change; they keep searching for the magic formula that will finally "turn the company around." I tend to think that the team concept can work, but the process often suffers setbacks caused by those in the structure who have not learned to work in teams. Many still seek attention as an individual in order to gain more powerful roles and status.

When co-workers do not trust each other and/or managers, the team faces a dilemma. Often, employees who feel a loss of power also feel that things will change, eventually. These employees may realize that if changes do not increase the company's profits, those in charge will react and change things again. These continued changes (made out of feelings of fear that we sometimes confuse for logic) may restore power to those who feel they lost out in the previous changes. In such cases, final decisions in business fall upon management; it then reverts to a hierarchical power structure and removes the power from the team.

OFFICE POLITICS

It is important to realize who influences power structures and how. Many times, management is not as involved in dictating the structure and hierarchies as are those at lower levels who want to increase their own sense of power. Many needless power structures come into being, due to people bringing their own personal issues into the workplace. Many workers may try to justify their actions and the informal structures in the name of their job duties or functions. However, it is likely that people seek out positions that reflect their own personal issues; this helps them to cling to their life perspective.

Let us look at a brief example of an informal hierarchy that came about through a practical joke. A group of co-workers told Travis, a new worker, that it is a company tradition for new workers to take their team members out to lunch with his first paycheck. In this example, Travis likely feels insecure in this new job, as well as with his co-workers, and wants to fit in. Travis's co-workers seek to exploit his vulnerability and exercise their power to manipulate him. This is an abuse of power. If confronted about this "tradition," they would dismiss the event by calling it a joke. In playing this joke on Travis, his co-workers may cause feelings of mistrust that may surface later in their working relationships.

I don't mean to imply that I dislike humor. I do think, however, that we should consider how our intended humor could affect others. I also believe that using humor to boost our sense of power is unfair and often harmful. We can use humor, especially in the workplace, as an effective tool to build relationships and create a sense of unity. But many times the humor we use has the intent of undermining someone else's power and status, which creates an imbalance of power.

OVERSTEPPING BOUNDARIES

We will now consider an example using someone I will call Terry. Terry created needless power structures that wound up leading to conflict in the company, rather than harmony, and which only served Terry's needs. This example comes from a hodge-podge of my direct experiences, as well as different people and stories, but the details are true. Terry was an office administrator and was in charge. Terry managed the daily operations of the business so managers could take care of business growth. Terry had a number of self-created policies and procedures for employees. When new employees started, Terry met with them for the first hour to inform them of the policies. While meeting with a new employee, Terry also briefed them on the office politics, which the new employee should keep between the two of them.

Terry set work schedules for the employees that included break times, lunch schedules, working hours, etc. However, Terry took many breaks to talk to others and sometimes came in late. Terry also created a policy for reporting problems to management. This policy stated that all suggestions and feedback had to go through Terry; no employees under Terry's supervision were to "interfere" with management being able to perform their jobs. Failure to follow this policy could cost the violator their job. In short, if an employee had an issue with a salesperson, they had to discuss it with Terry. The employee could not address the salesperson. When an employee quit or terminated, Terry conducted the exit interview and sent the report to management.

Terry often wrote office policies and procedures and asked management to sign off on them in order to save time. Terry maintained that writing all the policies would make the managers' jobs easier. Terry's managers liked this ambition and happily agreed with the proposals.

Terry was inconsistent in dealing with others in the workplace. Terry was often very agreeable and friendly to managers, salespeople, or new employees, but unkind and often rude and abrupt with those working under them.

Employees often griped to each other about Terry's treatment of them, but they sometimes feared that a co-worker might be an informant to Terry. This fear created an air of mistrust, so some felt that they should avoid and/or reject new employees if they appeared to be too friendly with her. The staff felt that there was no point in trying to make suggestions on changing policies. In the past, when others made suggestions, Terry offered them to management as an original idea. People in the office feared talking directly to other managers about her; they thought that they could lose their job by going over the administrator's head. They also feared that whatever they said could get back to Terry. Many employees felt that they needed to protect themselves and keep quiet to keep their job and status. The result was that trust between coworkers continued to diminish.

Many issues are common in the workplace. The first issue that you may have recognized is the manner in which Terry has tried to seek control of so many aspects of the workplace to increase a personal sense of power. Terry wanted to be a cornerstone in the operation to both the management and the employees. You may see right away that these attempts to gain power likely stem from some feeling of powerlessness and inadequacy in Terry. Terry made policies, met one-on-one with new employees, functioned as a go-between for workers and management and even monitored break times. . . . Yes, it may have been necessary for Terry to perform these duties, and they may even have been part of the job description. Even so, we need to look below the surface at the manner in which someone carries out these duties.

One subtle way that Terry asserted power lies in the attitude she expressed toward others. Managers may view her position as being one that respects power, and in her policies to talk to new employees about office politics, she could appear warm and welcoming. Yet, in doing so, she tried to color their opinions in ways that served a hidden agenda. This was done in part by threatening dire results if they violated the office policies that kept Terry informed. In this manner, she could screen and head off any problems, without drawing a manager's attention. By forbidding her employees from talking to her superiors, Terry sought to create a sort of closed environment wherein the employee had no real recourse to air their problems. She wrote policies that were not part of the office manager's job description. In doing so, her sense of power increased while leading the management to believe that this was simply a timesaver for them. She talked the managers into affording her the power to write policies by selling them on the idea that it would make their job easier. In this example, her job functions likely reflect some serious personal issues. The way Terry carried out these job functions were likely an extension of deep-seated power issues and a way to manipulate a sense of inadequacy.

In this example, Terry played a large part, both directly and indirectly, in the conflict patterns in the office setting. Still, she is not solely to blame for these conflicts. She commanded a great deal of authority; but those in management could have noticed the patterns and made sure there were checks and balances in place to prevent anyone from abusing power. Furthermore, other employees could have tried to understand her views and chosen not to react in such a mistrustful manner. However, given that other employees were at a lower level of status, they felt unable to manage the conflict, since they did not have the power to resolve it.

In thinking about the previous example, do you see how a single person can have such a very profound effect on the actions of others and on the operations of business?

Issues to keep in mind regarding this situation are that Terry did not act out of malice; it is more likely that she acted with the intent to insure survival and that fear motivated her actions. People often feel pressed to do almost anything to keep their job and their sense of financial safety and security. In the example, she felt forced to make decisions based on feelings of insecurity, fear, and/or powerlessness. . . . It is not likely that Terry, or many of us, would see the true motivations of their behaviors or our own in the same position. Also, some people know that they may say cruel and damaging things to others; but many often justify their comments, and still others do not realize the impact of their actions and comments on others.

In this example, I would like you to see that, although Terry may come across as controlling, ruthless, and malicious, her actions did not come from anger, bitterness or rage. The vulnerable emotions (fear, insecurity, mistrust) prompted Terry's actions. Still, we need to take responsibility for our actions. We may or may not understand or accept our issues, but rejecting our issues does not reduce our capacity to do damage. In Terry's case, we see how people's personal issues often intrude into the work setting. It is indeed naïve to think that we can separate work life from personal life.

SUMMARY

This chapter discussed only a few examples of power issues that occur in the business world. There are certainly many other issues that I could address, and likely will in future volumes. I hope that this discussion offered some insight into power issues to consider in the business world; my hope is that this may help you to apply these concepts to your own personal issues.

To resolve power struggles in business settings, there are some problems to overcome. Resolution of power struggles in business settings are probably more difficult than in other settings. Why? Because there is often not as much motivation to resolve power struggles from those who have higher levels of status. Some managers take the my way or the highway attitude. As a result, employers or co-workers may decline to work on some power issues. In these situations, many people feel that they need the income from their job and often remain in difficult and stressful situations. The reality is that we always have choices in our lives.

It is always our choice to try to see what we can learn from our interactions with those in business and any other situation. It is also important to see that we always have the options to look for a more respectful and supportive environment to work in. How often do people find themselves in the same predicament in job after job, just as in relationship after relationship? I know that there are people in business settings who seem to continue to run into the same conflicts without realizing how they promote the rise of the conflicts. It has to be up to each of us to understand why, just as it has to be up to each of us to learn from our experiences. When they are able to truly understand their contribution to the conflict, they will probably find that the pattern ends.

Remember the discussions throughout this book which mention that life is like a mirror, and our own issues reflect back to us in all areas of our life. While we often do not think that our own issues will affect us at the office, it would be in our best interest to look closer.

QUESTIONS

1. If you work outside your home, do you feel discouraged or ill at ease about expressing emotions at work? Do you sense that your coworkers have similar feelings?
2. What emotions, if any, do you commonly avoid while in your workplace? To what degree do you feel that these emotions affect your attitude?
3. To what extent do you feel that your boss's attitude affects your attitude? To what extent do you feel that your attitude affects your job performance?

14

Understanding Power Struggles and Conflict

The degree of one's emotions varies inversely with one's knowledge of the facts—the less you know, the hotter you get.
—*Mark Twain*

TEACHING OBJECTIVES

- Provide a visual framework for understanding conflict escalation patterns
- Explain the relationship between perceptions of power and emotion in conflicts
- Provide an example of a conflict to illustrate conflict patterns
- Increase awareness of conflict management

After reading to this point in the book, you know where power comes from, and you've seen many examples of situations where we are likely to run across conflict and power struggles. I have purposely avoided talking about resolving conflict, up to this point. Until now, my intent has been to prompt you to become more aware of the issues surrounding your search for power and how it plays into discord; I also wanted to give you the opportunity to ponder and develop conflict resolution strategies of your own. Most who are reading this book are hoping to get answers to resolving conflict. Sometimes, however, when we try to come up with our own answers, it helps us to find our limitations in order to grow even more when we learn. While we see how power affects many different scenarios, the path to resolution of most power struggles is the same.

MOTIVATIONS FOR CONFLICT

Finding answers to resolving power conflicts means asking some questions. A crucial question is, What is my goal in a power struggle? Other questions are, What am I feeling at the various stages of a power struggle? Why do conflicts escalate as they do? Does anyone really win in a power struggle? If you answer these questions honestly, you may understand what motivates you and resolve the issues affecting power struggles in your life.

The first question, What is your goal in a power struggle? is a key in the process of resolution. For most of us, the answer depends upon what we expect from society and what we feel society expects from us. Since we tend to emphasize keeping a sense of strength in our culture, we often try to appear strong in a conflict. We want to appear strong, so the goal of most power struggles is to win, sometimes at any cost. Why are we driven to win? Let's consider society's outlook on sports. Please note that sports represent only a single example of this must-win attitude. In 1996, the Olympics took place in Atlanta. The sponsors and other companies flooded the city and surrounding areas with advertisements. In fact, the International Olympic Committee criticized the Atlanta Committee for over-commercializing the Olympics.

Regardless of the criticism, a billboard from a well-known sports shoe company caught my attention. The slogan on the sign said, "Second Place is First Loser" in very large letters. What I take from that billboard is a notion I consider nothing short of outrageous: that every athlete at the Olympics who did not win a gold medal is a loser. First, there is no question that only the very best athletes in the world even gain the honor of participating in the Olympics. Most of the athletes dedicate their lives to their chosen sport. Should any Olympic athlete come away from the event feeling like a loser? Second, think of the millions of people who saw the billboard, not the least of which were impressionable children. Many of the kids who saw this sign were likely wearing shoes made by this company. Most of us realize the impact that commercials have on children's beliefs and attitudes. In addition, we see the impact of the sport shoe industry with their high-paying endorsements from top athletes. This billboard sent a very negative and harmful message to the world. This one billboard reflects symptoms of the underlying belief systems that reinforce our current ideas about power and our feeling of need to win.

Many of our power struggles come down to an issue of win or lose. We are often fighting to be first to make our point or to be the last to get a "dig" in. In doing so, we do not seek mutual understanding or resolution, and we may not want to consider the other person's point of view. Why is this? We commonly hold an underlying fear that others might see us as weak or vulnerable; this is often true even when we recognize that their point is valid. In order to win, we have to appear as good, strong, and right as possible. In a conflict, we may base emotional and unemotional responses on logic (to explain our way out), humor (which often becomes sarcasm), irritation, arrogance, flippancy, sarcasm, defiance, anger, hatred, and/or rage. When conflicts escalate, the progression of emotions often follows the order presented in the list.

When we think of win versus lose, we may see this dichotomy as the most important. In some ways, it is because it determines the ultimate outcome, and in our minds the ultimate outcome of the measure of our life. I, however, see it differently. Of the three remaining dichotomies discussed earlier in the book, which one do you think becomes the most important one in determining who wins or loses: good/bad, right/wrong, or strong/weak? Before I give you the answer, seriously consider this question. . . . Still thinking? The answer is: strong/weak.

Strong vs. weak is the most important dichotomy in a conflict. History, experience, and in many ways common sense tell us that if we are the strongest, we will win. Along with being the strongest comes the luxury of defining what is good and what is right. Therefore, in a conflict, I can try to make my argument, but it is often to prove that I am stronger, so I can win.

Conflict often begins when one or both parties perceive a threat. Therefore, in order to express any of the emotions I just listed, we must first feel at least threatened by another party. It is important to know that the purpose of the above anger, rage, arrogance, flippancy, defiance, sarcasm, and hatred are to protect us or the other party we are protecting. If we understand this, we can often choose to respond differently to an escalating conflict. If the conflict is escalating, the other person is likely feeling at least as threatened.

Clients often state that conflicts seem to take on a life of their own. They find themselves saying things and acting in ways that they can't understand. Even those, like teachers, counselors, therapists, who know that people use some emotions for protection sometimes find themselves reacting to preserve their power when they are in conflicts. Even when we know better, I strongly believe that while we are socialized into hierarchical systems of power, the need to protect ourselves when we feel threatened is almost innate. We will be inclined to react to conflict by protecting ourselves. However, I also think that we have the wisdom to manage our power and understand why we are reacting as we are.

We might answer the other above questions, related to our emotions and patterns of conflict in power struggles, by closely viewing and evaluating the natural patterns of our power struggles. Now that we have identified the most common goal of power struggles, which is to look strong so that we can win, we can start to consider the process of how the parties in the power struggle try to reach their goal.

The first step in examining a power struggle is to break it down to exchanges of power. A power exchange can occur with both verbal and non-verbal communications. In fact, we may often engage in power struggles by non-verbal methods. Silence can sometimes be the most powerful form of expression in a power struggle. We may use silence in an aggressive manner if we withhold information, attention, or affection. When used tactically, silence can be the most effective communication tool of all.

SAMPLE CONFLICT

Before we start to dissect a conflict, we have to identify a conflict. Parents and children often have conflicts over the completion of homework. This is probably truer now than ever before. When both parents are working, they are less apt to be around as often to help their child manage their time. When working parents cannot monitor their child's choices after school, as well as other time constraints, they may feel stressed about their child's learning even before any discussion begins. Whether or not the parent is aware of their underlying stress is another issue, but it is an influence regardless. I will number each exchange in the conflict for later discussion.

1. The conflict about homework often begins when Dawn, Jim's mother, asks Jim, "Did you do your homework yet?"
2. Jim replies, "Uhh . . . when I came home, I was too busy doing my chores to get to it."
3. Dawn replies, "I don't see that any of the things I asked you to do are finished."
4. Jim states, "That's because when I let the dog out, he ran off, and I had to go all over the neighborhood looking for him."
5. Dawn responds, "I saw Mrs. Smith on the way home, and she said you were having a great time playing with Tommy this afternoon."
6. Jim replies, "She doesn't know what she's talking about; I went over there to ask him a question about my homework."
7. "For an hour?" Dawn asks accusingly.
8. "It took a long time for him to explain . . . and why are you always checking up on me? You never believe anything I say," Jim says, in angered exasperation.
9. "If you ever did anything I asked you to do, I wouldn't have to check up on you. Frankly, young man, I am sick and tired of having this discussion every day when I come home from work."

10. "You don't care about me; all you do is work," Jim yells.
11. "I don't want to hear it anymore. You are going to sit down and do your homework. When your father gets home, he is going to handle this."
12. "I don't care what you do or what Dad does. I hate you both. I wish I was dead. Then, you'd be sorry!"
13. "Get out of here, and do your homework. I'm done talking to you!" Dawn screams.
14. The conflict seemingly ends when Jim stomps off and opens a schoolbook.

In this conflict, there were fourteen exchanges of power, and each person attempted to steer the other person's emotions and responses with each exchange. Both parties had a choice of how to respond to change the outcome of the conflict.

Let's examine this conflict by looking to the *power exchange diagrams* to better understand the course of the conflict. Figure 14.1 denotes a range of Low to High perceived power and each communication exchange. The mid-point shows the point of resolution for the conflict, where each person feels understood, and that they resolve the conflict. In each exchange, both parties feel emotions that affect their perception of power that we can graph. The graph shows emotions in terms of a

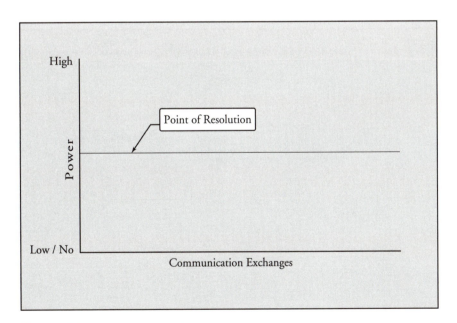

Figure 14.1 Power Exchange Diagram

level of power that the person feels as it relates to their perception of power when they feel that emotion and/or combination of emotions. It is important to be aware of the stronger emotions we present, instead of the underlying weaker emotions; these "weaker" emotions create the reactions that we may defend either emotionally or logically.

Let's start at step 1 (Figure 14.2). A conflict starts when a person perceives a threat. A hidden factor in this conflict arises later in the argument. If Dawn had not spoken to Mrs. Smith, Dawn might talk to Jim about his homework in a totally neutral tone. However, since Mrs. Smith told her about seeing Jim playing with Tommy, she probably expected Jim's response and prepared herself for battle. Because of this, it can be argued that the conflict started even before she got home. However, for the purposes of this discussion, we will assume that her question was neutral and merely to seek information. In the diagram, I denoted "Step 1" on the bottom. Jim's feeling of power appears as a grayed dotted line and Dawn's is the dashed line. When Dawn asks her question, Jim knows the answer and likely feels guilt, shame, and embarrassment and may have felt stupid if he didn't understand how to do part of his homework. Since his mother's statement was neutral, she does not have any particular emotional or power loss/gain. The conflict could have ended at this exchange if Jim stated, "No I haven't done my homework yet. I did not know how to do part of it, and other

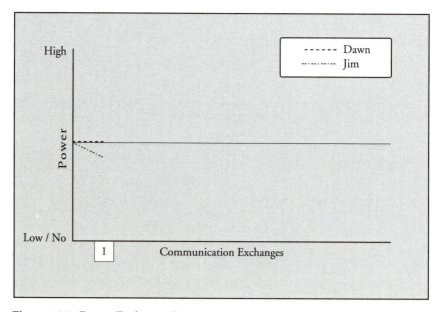

Figure 14.2 Power Exchange Diagram—Step 1

things distracted me when I came home. I will work on it, and can I ask you about the questions I have?" That communication exchange did not happen.

After his mother asked him the question, Jim's response at "Step 2" (Figure 14.3) sought ways to avoid discussing his homework and his feelings about his homework. At the core, his response was an attempt to regain his power and put his mother on the defensive. By saying that his mother had too many other things for him to do, Jim attempted to place the blame on his mother, on the hope that she might feel guilty and back off. His response was mostly from a logical standpoint of making a statement to challenge her perceptions, and he left some room for the conflict to escalate while trying not to offend his mother too much.

Dawn's reaction to his response was likely a series of emotions: frustration, manipulation, confusion, threat, doubt, and maybe a twinge of guilt. If she trusted what he said, then she may have stated, "You are right. I have given you too many responsibilities, and I am sorry about that. Let's see what I can do to help you out." At that point, Jim would have avoided the homework issue, and his mother would have tried to give Jim more time to do his homework. If his mother understood why Jim was avoiding his homework (fear of failure), she might have stated, "You know, when I was your age and even some-

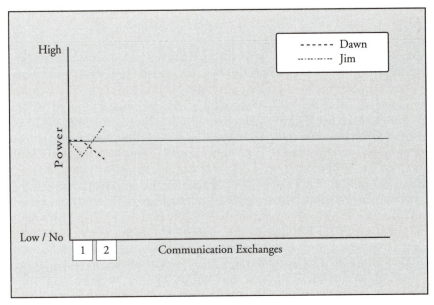

Figure 14.3 Power Exchange Diagram—Step 2

times now, there are things that I have to do that are hard, and I don't think I can do them. In the past, and sometimes still, I looked for other things I could do to avoid doing what I should do. As an adult, I am often fearful that I may fail, and when I was a kid, I often feared that my parents would feel disappointed with me if I didn't do as well in school as they thought I should. Could that be part of what you are feeling?" In this statement, Dawn is helping the child to see that she understands or is willing to understand why they are avoiding their homework. In this statement, Dawn is also sharing her more vulnerable feelings with Jim. This means he will probably feel less of a need to overpower his parent in future interactions because there is more understanding and a balance of power.

Dawn's actual response in step 3 plays into what the child just stated about having too many tasks to complete. While the parent is trying to catch the child in a lie, there is also a defiant, "prove it to me" intent made by the mother in the statement. At this point, the child may feel that they have no other choice but to defend themselves, because they know they are caught, or find another route to distract the conflict from the topic of homework.

Dawn's reaction to her feelings of manipulation and frustration comes from a logical, yet irritated, viewpoint; it is an attempt to try to re-establish her power. However, her response could range from calm and relaxed to sarcastic and disapproving. Voice tone is a driving force in many conflicts. Although a person may not intend to express negativity in their voice tone, they often do so without realizing it. In this example, Dawn's voice tone was somewhat disapproving, which drove the conflict to the next step.

In step 4, Jim tried to divert attention from his homework by bringing up the matter of trying to find the dog. Jim's comment about searching for the dog sought to elicit empathy and support for his efforts. If the dog got out, it was probably due to Jim's actions; but also, this comment might seek to place blame on Dawn or another family member. If Dawn felt sorry for Jim and responded with empathy, she would take on the role of "rescuer" instead of the "persecutor" to Jim. It is likely that the event never happened. It is likely that Jim made up the story to try to divert his mother from the subject. However, the comment contributed to the conflict because his mother mistrusted him.

There is a range of emotions that Dawn may have felt from Jim's comment about the dog. While she likely felt mistrust, she probably felt further frustration, confusion, and doubt. If she believed Jim's story about the dog, she may have felt guilt about jumping to conclusions, which might shift the course of the conflict.

In step 5, Dawn indirectly challenged Jim's story about the dog running away, instead of confronting him about the story. She mentions seeing and speaking to Tommy's mother who informed her that she saw Jim playing with Tommy. Dawn's comment on this matter was likely a passive way to let Jim know that she realized his story was a lie; however, she does not directly call him a liar. She may not bring the conflict back to the subject of homework. We see, however, that the effort to distract her with the dog story fails.

As the conflict builds, it escalates into an unproductive exchange that moves further from the initial topic. Dawn's response likely resulted from her effort to make a logical retort to his story. As such, there may have been a tone of arrogance and sarcasm in her voice, and Jim likely realizes that his mother knows of his lie. Because of Dawn catching him in a lie, Jim probably feels vulnerable, threatened, and fearful. He may feel guilty and shameful about lying, and confused as to how to get out of the conflict, as well as why he told the lie. Since she did not stop the conflict, he probably feels frustration and possibly humiliation, since she passively caught him in the lie. At this point of the conflict, Jim has some choices. He can own up to his lie and be responsible for not doing his homework; he can keep avoiding responsibility and escalate the conflict, or choose several other responses.

In step 6, Jim chose continued avoidance. To protect his vulnerability and other emotions, Jim uses a defiant and angry tone, and he tries to detract from Mrs. Smith's credibility (diminish her power). He tries to do this by saying that she does not know what she is talking about. In saying that he went to Tommy's house to ask a question about his homework, he tries to present the idea that he sincerely wanted to do his homework. Jim's comment about Mrs. Smith is also an attempt to play the victim, insisting that, through ignorance, she falsely accused him. If his mother feels sufficient doubt about his purpose for being at Tommy's house, then maybe she will get off his back.

Because of Jim's previous lie (in step 5) his mother is feeling manipulated, and she will doubt most of what he says. As Dawn's frustration and confusion increase, she is likely to feel hopeless and helpless about resolving this issue peacefully. In most conflicts, there is an underlying, growing feeling of fear and threat that continues to feed the escalation; this conflict is no exception. Jim's mother feels threatened and fearful about her son's insolence and disrespect toward her in her role as a parent. It is common for parents to feel fearful about the morals and values that their children are adopting. This fear will often drive a very powerful and over-controlling reaction in the parent's treatment of their children. However, as Dawn feels more threatened by her son's disrespect, she feels a greater need to try to retain her personal power. At this point, the initial dispute becomes secondary to the issue of power.

When we feel that someone is lying to us, we often feel that the other person must think we are stupid. In this manner, we often do feel stupid, as well as disrespected. When we feel that another person is trying to make a fool of us, the object then becomes to make a fool of the other person. If Dawn feels that Jim believes she will fall for his stories, then she may attempt to retaliate.

At this point in the conflict, it is important to call attention to the element of balance that underlies most conflicts. You may ask yourself, "Balance? What is balanced about this conflict?" The balance lies in the extremes of the emotions, both the seen and the unseen. As the intensity and number of underlying weaker emotions increase, there is often a counterbalancing of the more "powerful" emotions that we express outwardly.

Figure 14.4 shows the exchange of power in the conflict between Jim and Dawn. The power exchange diagram helps to explain that the expressions of power increase in response to a sense of loss of power; we feel this through emotions that are more vulnerable.

Another hidden emotion that can contribute to balancing conflict and moderating the extremeness of the reaction is confidence. Having confidence in a conflict is not easy and often confidence turns into arrogance. However, if I am able to maintain a confident attitude during a conflict, it will keep me from using extreme emotions such as anger and/or rage. In other words, if I feel confident that I can win the conflict,

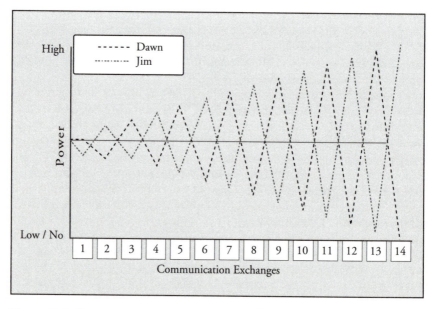

Figure 14.4 Power Exchange Diagram—Steps 3 through 14

I will often manage my emotions and wait for the other person to give in or see their side of the conflict. It is also important here to avoid confusing confidence with arrogance. They are not the same, and arrogance is an additive emotion in a conflict that we sometimes use to inflame the other party and advance our own position. Especially as children mature and learn how to push their parent's buttons, they arrogantly enter into conflicts trying to tear their parent's power down so that they can feel a sense of power.

In this conflict between Jim and Dawn, however, both parties feel more emotions as the conflict goes on and the intensity of those emotions increases; Jim and Dawn are battling more for a sense of power and self-protection than for understanding and resolution. Looking at conflicts from this point of view is helpful. In doing so, we may easily see why so many conflicts end fruitlessly with both parties feeling misunderstood and hurt.

It is important to remember that these exchanges in a conflict take place in the span of seconds. It's a bit like a ping-pong match wherein we may not have a lot of time to think about what is coming toward us, and we often just react. This whole conflict between Jim and Dawn lasted maybe two minutes. You, as the reader, may wonder why I made such a detailed analysis of this conflict. You may feel that I have over-analyzed it. We often do not believe that people are quick-witted enough to respond thoughtfully during an argument. We are not considering thought and logic as much as emotions and learned behaviors.

Research has proven that dream sequences can occur very rapidly, but our mind perceives them in real time. What this means is that while we may feel that a dream may last all night long, it probably only lasted a few minutes. We should remember that our brain often operates at many different levels of consciousness and subconsciousness. The human mind is like a very complex computer. We may only be able to pay attention to a limited amount of information, but our brain is often processing a lot more data than we are aware of. All of this information enters into our output, whether we realize it or not.

In step 7, the parent continues to remain diverted from the issue of homework and seems more invested in the lies Jim is telling. She likely realizes that his stories are continuing to grow, and with her logical questioning, she is trying to break him down. Once again, voice tone is important in this conflict. With his mother's mounting frustration, she responded with a sarcastic and arrogant "Do you think I'm stupid?" tone in response to his story. Her hope may have been that by demonstrating her superior understanding of him, he will miraculously admit that he had been making up a number of stories to try to cover himself, and he was sorry that he had wasted her time.

With the response he received from Dawn, Jim will feel more desperate to try to reassume his power. He knows that his mother has him cornered, from a logical standpoint, and his feelings of guilt, shame, fear, threat and humiliation continue to mount. He also fears the result of his behaviors that he may almost feel are out of his control, which will affect his self-preservation. He may feel that his mother thinks he is stupid and may feel confused as to how she truly feels about him. Jim likely feels failure for his inability to talk his way out of this conflict. This sense of failure may foster feelings of hopelessness and helplessness.

In step 8, Jim still feels the need to try to justify the amount of time he spent at Tommy's house. Stating that the question took a long time to answer keeps with his statement about being confused. In addition, it makes sense that a lengthy explanation would reduce the amount of time he could devote to his schoolwork. In doing this, he tries to add an element of doubt to his mother's arrogant comment. After all, it is possible that he was trying to work on his homework; if that was the case, then his mother must risk feeling very guilty if she assumed that he was lying to her when he was truly trying to do the right thing.

Another aspect of Jim, or his logical aspect, is probably reacting to the realization that he will not likely talk his way out of the argument. With this realization, he may believe that he needs to cause Dawn to feel more guilt, by implying that she unfairly mistrusts him. If Jim can elicit sufficient guilt and shame in his mother, then he feels that she may back off, if she feels that she has done something to him that she needs to make up for. We may see that Jim tries to prey upon various emotions to get Dawn to ease up or end the conflict.

Dawn might feel various emotions after his comment. If she identifies Jim's effort to try to shame her, she can decide that it does not, or she can feel angry about her feelings of manipulation and respond to that. If Dawn does not recognize the tactic, she may feel shame, guilt, doubt and failure in her role as a parent; she may also feel sad, rejected, frustrated, and hurt. Even if she understands Jim's tactic, she may feel a twinge of the emotions, but she may fend them off as quickly as they appear. The issue that started out about homework may promote Dawn's feeling of hopelessness. She likely feels that Jim does not understand her efforts or why she feels upset about the situation.

When a parent asks their child about schoolwork, it is often because they care about the child's success in school. However, parents may often feel baffled by the stiff resistance the child poses when asked about homework. Parents may fail to see the strength that their looks of disapproval and judgment have on the emotions of their children. Children desperately want approval from their parents; so, kids may feel hypersensitive to any signs of disapproval from their parents. For these reasons and others, children do not take parental displeasure lightly. If a child gets a sense of rejection or disapproval from parents, it often leads to feelings of shame, guilt, insecurity, worthlessness, failure, and other, more painful emotions. If a parent did not learn how to deal with feelings of disapproval from their own parents, they may create the same issues in their children. Many parents may not fully grasp how deeply they affect their child's emotions when they are still stuck in their own issues.

In step 9, Dawn's response reveals that she probably took his comment personally, and is trying to shame him back so he will feel like she felt. Dawn feels that she is the mother and should not show vulnerable feelings; so she reacts with more strongly perceived emotions. Dawn might sound a bit ferocious; she seems to have lost track of the fact that she is talking with her child, who actually seeks love and acceptance from her. Since she feels guilt, shame, and hurt, her comment about being sick and tired of the discussions could be her way of trying to end the conflict. Furthermore, she holds Jim responsible for the conflict because, in her mind, if he would just be quiet and do his tasks, she would not have to go through these hassles.

If Jim hears what she is saying, he should see that Dawn is coming to a point where the conflict will end, or she will explode. Up to a point, Dawn was patient with Jim's efforts to manipulate her. Beyond that point, her patience wore thin and her angry, irritated tone reflects her fatigue and vulnerability. The conflict strayed from the homework issue, and although Dawn came back to the homework conflict, the dispute focused more on attacks and personal issues.

Because of Dawn's comment about him never doing what she asks, Jim is probably feeling personally attacked and rejected by his mother. He may feel that he can do nothing right, which reinforces the underlying reasons that he did not do his homework. His feelings of guilt, shame and humiliation continue to build, as his feelings of failure and stupidity surface. He may also see that the conflict is not turning out to his liking, regardless of his attempts to divert it from the course; his mother is trying to return to the original issue. If Jim admits to any of his feelings, he believes that he will lose the conflict, and, at the very least, he will have to do his homework. Further, because of his comments to his mother, there may be additional consequences that he wants to avoid.

In step 10, Jim keeps avoiding the homework topic in favor of exploiting the morsel that his mother left for him in bringing up her work. Since he feels somewhat desperate to maintain his power in the conflict, he grabs hold of anything he feels he can use against Dawn to distract her. Jim hopes to prompt guilt in his mother by saying that she cares about her work more than she cares about him. In addition, as Jim feels more desperate and vulnerable, his tone grows louder and angrier.

The discussion of work between parents and children often pulls a number of strings within the parent. Often, the parent feels guilty about working, but for financial reasons, may feel that there is no choice but to work. When children have behavioral issues, their parents often feel guilty for being away from home. They often feel that their absence may contribute to the child's issues. Working mothers often hear comments from their parents, friends, or neighbors who are not aware of their personal or financial issues.

As the parents feel more and more guilt, helplessness, and failure, they often become less and less patient with the child; the child's issues continue to bring up the parents' emotions. In some cases, parents do care about their job more than about their child, and the child's behavior seeks to get their parent's attention. When we find ourselves in an argument, and someone makes an unkind comment that has a ring of truth, it often prompts a strong sense of need to protect ourselves. If we feel guilt and/or shame in regards to something about ourselves, and someone hits this "nerve," we may lash out in an aggressive or violent manner.

When comments such as Jim's occur, it is important to discuss the point of view and feelings of that person—but later, so that it does not distract from the issue at hand. When Jim made the statement about his mother's work, she could have said, "I understand that you may feel upset that I have to work, but now is not the time to discuss that. I can continue that discussion later, but let's keep on track with our discussion about your homework."

In the conflict between Jim and his mother, Dawn probably feels that Jim is continuing to cloud the issues by bringing up her work. She may feel manipulated by him, but she may also feel guilt and frustration. These latter feelings may come from a sense of failure as a parent in that she may question her ability to meet Jim's needs. She may also feel continued confusion as to how to resolve this conflict without so much pain. It is also important to remember that the emotions evoked throughout the conflict continue to linger through each exchange.

In step 11, Jim's comment appears to strike a chord within his mother. Her comment to him about not wanting to hear it anymore, is her way to disengage from the conflict. She spoke in an angry manner, and meant to try to control Jim's outburst. The other half of the comment about his father handling it when he got home, sought to pose a threat to Jim, meaning that if she could not control his behavior, then he should fear what his father may do. At the point when Jim's mother makes the statement about letting his father handle the situation, she has given all of her power away. Additionally, while Jim knows that he has to endure the consequences with his father, he may feel that he has won the battle.

Dawn gave away some power by bringing Jim's father into her showing of force. In doing so, she let Jim know that she feels powerless to win the conflict. When a person appeals to someone else for help in a conflict, I call this getting other people's power (OPP). When someone, especially a parent or teacher, gives their power up in this manner, it is very difficult to try to win conflicts in the future because the other person will drive the conflict until their adversary gives in or until they get OPP.

Many of us remember hearing (or saying) "Wait 'til your father gets home." I believe this has been one of the most often used clichés used by mothers, grandparents and other family members. Teachers, educators, and daycare providers may fall into this conflict, either when they send the child to the principal's office or the teacher calls the parent. There are many more issues related to school and daycare settings and getting parents involved. That is likely for another day and another book. However, understanding the nature of OPP issues can explain later conflicts between the same people.

Through waiting to resolve the conflict and deferring to OPP, we raise a number of issues that can set difficult precedents. As stated earlier, when a person forfeits their power, they let the child, or other person, know that they cannot handle the conflict. For another example, we might think of two young boys arguing. One boy may say, "You'd better leave me alone or I'll get my big brother to beat you up." Similar to Dawn, this boy admits that he does not feel that he can fend for himself. However, in issuing the threat of calling upon a stronger, more powerful person, the boy hopes to get his rival to back down. If we admit that we do not feel the strength or power to end the conflict, the other party, especially children, will often act up even more, until the more powerful person arrives. A child may wonder, "Why should I obey this person if this person doesn't have the power to do anything?" The child often feels that since they are already in trouble, they might as well "take off the gloves."

Returning to the conflict between Jim and his mother, how does he react to his mother using the OPP tactic? In step 12, Jim tries to use flippancy and anger as a defense by stating, "I don't care what you do or what Dad does." If his mother thinks that he doesn't care about any consequences, then he may still have a chance to win the conflict, even after his dad gets home. He also tries to reject his mother by telling her that he hates her, and then tries to elicit fear and guilt in his mother by stating, "I wish I was dead. Then you would be sorry."

Children may use the classic "I wish I was dead" tactic to pull at the emotions of parents, and this sometimes may work by getting the parent to respond. It is also an attempt for the child to challenge how much their parent cares for them. The child often thinks that if their parent does not react to these statements, then they must not love them or care about them. So, Jim makes this statement to try to challenge his mother, and to see if she still loves him when he is bad.

Parents often recognize the "I wish I was dead" tactic as an idle threat and do not respond; but not responding also protects their own emotions. Still, it is true that some children may ultimately respond to their own threats, feeling cornered into following through with their threat. It is always important to discuss these statements, when made, after the conflict has cooled down. This lets the child know that you care about them, but that you will not react to statements like that. You may tell them that if they ever really feel that they want to cause harm to themselves, you hope that they would be able to talk with you or someone else they feel they could trust. The underlying issue with threatening suicide is the same as (but more extreme than) taking a toy away from a child when they are in trouble. "If you can take something away from me when I do something you do not want me to do, then I can do the same to you."

Remember that in step 11, Jim's mother gave up her power when she said Jim's father was going to handle the situation. She did this to try to disengage from the conflict, but with Jim's statement about killing himself, he pulled her back in, emotionally. When she gave up her power, she felt helplessness and powerlessness, and these feelings will continue through any other interactions they may have. Because of Jim's comment, Dawn is probably feeling rejection and failure as a parent, as well as fear that she may push him to hurt himself, which then prompts feelings of intense guilt, fear, and failure.

In step 13, her response to Jim seeks to help protect her from her underlying emotions. To respond to Jim rejecting her, in desperation, she states, "Get out of here and do your homework." She then officially disengages from the conflict when she states, "I am done talking to you."

In step 14, Jim walks off, probably feeling that he may have won part of the battle. However, in doing so, he has effectively rejected his mother, which elicits his fear of rejection, shame, guilt, and failure. At the point when he walks away, his mother may feel that she won part of the battle in getting him to be quiet. Even so, her painful feelings will continue to affect her under the surface.

This conflict is not over yet, and it probably began long ago. The feelings expressed by both Jim and his mother began long before this specific conflict, and they will continue to grow and evolve long after this incident. Also, Jim still has to deal with his father when he gets home, while his mother must still deal with her feelings of failure and inadequacy. The conflict was not resolved between Jim and Dawn, so the common emotional threads will continue through other conflicts. How the father involves himself in the conflict, and the feelings that he has regarding their conflict, and about himself, his wife, and his son, is still another issue.

The question is, "Did anyone win this argument? And for that matter, does anyone ever really win an argument?" When emotions become involved in conflicts, the true goal is not about who was right or wrong, but becomes about feeling understood by others. Please review Figure 14.4 and observe the exchanges of power. Here are some questions to ask yourself:

1. What emotions were communicated to each person in the verbal and nonverbal exchanges?
2. What emotions were concealed or hidden from the other person?
3. Why did each person avoid discussing what he or she felt inside?
4. How aware was each person of the other person's underlying emotions?
5. How aware was each person of his or her own underlying emotions?
6. Did each person have some validity or truth in some of their comments?
7. Could they avoid this conflict?

If you review the conflict diagram that contains all of the exchanges, the emotions expressed are on the peaks (those seen as higher power levels) on the diagram. They did not express the emotions in the valleys or (seen as weaker) on the diagram. Dawn and Jim avoided expressing these feelings, for fear that showing these emotions viewed as weaker would cost them the conflict. In most disputes, it is likely that people do not know of their own underlying issues, let alone the other person's feelings.

As I demonstrated in the previous example, often both parties feel pressed to react to the other person and protect their power; this sense of need often takes a higher priority than the desire to consider the emotions that occur within us. It takes a long time and practice to truly evaluate emotions and step back from conflicts. We learn patterns of expression, and they develop as habits similar to learning to put away toys or do homework. Productive communication and effective ways to resolve conflict aren't things that most of us develop naturally. So, a person must learn these skills. It takes years to develop certain patterns, it takes time to unlearn them.

At some points in the conflict, both Jim and Dawn made valid arguments. In most arguments and conflicts between people or groups of people, both sides make some valid points. That's one reason, among others, that the conflict continues. However, we cloud many of those points with emotion and/or disregard them as manipulation tactics; neither party truly considers those points of view.

If we take a step back to consider the emotions that we did not express, the effect that they have within the person is very powerful. As I said, we avoid these emotions because we fear that others may see them as weak and vulnerable. It is our societal viewpoints that lead us to label emotions as strong or weak. However, any emotion we feel can be powerful and have strong effects on us and those we share them with. If both Jim and Dawn could step back and discuss what they were truly feeling under the veil of flippancy, anger, arrogance, they could bypass the need for conflict. Understanding would be the outcome. Thus this conflict, as with most, was preventable.

Many readers are probably thinking, "This looks good on paper, but it doesn't work in the real world. Conflict has existed forever, and this stuff is not going to change the world." I do not profess that this information will change the world overnight. I do believe that we have to be responsible for changing ourselves, and if we change ourselves, one by one, for our own reasons, then the world will have changed.

The following is an example of a decade of change that has affected the world. In the eighties, researchers, universities and the government were the main users of the Internet. A very small percentage of people had access to the Internet and not many people cared. To most people, the Internet was an intimidating and unwieldy waste of time. But, over time, its appeal changed, as programmers and businesses made it easier to use and easier to access. One by one, as more people have "logged on," the Internet has changed the way the world interacts.

In the context of the world's population, the percentage of people using the Internet is very small. The changes it has brought, however, affect even those who have never heard of the Internet, or a computer for that matter. It took the individual efforts of each person to log their computer onto the Internet for it to grow to the monstrous proportions it has attained. Some people went kicking and screaming, and others couldn't wait for the chance. For those who made the investments of time and resources in the beginning, there were no guarantees that other people would follow. This is also true when it comes to making changes in your life. For us to make the most of our choices, they must be motivated from within.

SUMMARY

Independent of your thoughts about conflict and resolution, I would like you to see that it may be a mistake to try to label our emotions as "weak" or "strong," "good" or "bad," "right or "wrong." As I said in Chapter 6, each emotion has a positive, powerful reason for existing. If we can use each emotion for the purpose each was created for, then each emotion becomes strong and powerful in its own right. From this standpoint, we can erase the labels that some choose to place on our feelings and see them for the purpose for which they exist.

QUESTIONS

1. Do you feel our society has an unhealthy preoccupation with being strong, right, good and/or winning?
2. Have you ever been in a conflict that transpired in a way that parallels the one described here? Can you identify the points in the conflict that changed the tone and direction of the exchange?
3. Which of the dichotomies (good versus bad, right versus wrong, etc.) do you feel most motivates you?

15

So, What Do I Do Now? Conflict Resolution Strategies

Argument is the worst sort of conversation.
—*Jonathan Swift (1667–1745)*

TEACHING OBJECTIVES

- Discuss strategies to approach life issues which will aid in conflict resolution
- Provide exercises to resolve power issues in a variety of settings
- Increase awareness of power issues and how to seek internal and external resolution

This is the moment you have been waiting for—maybe you even skimmed through the earlier stuff to get to the good part. Many different strategies can help to resolve conflicts to the mutual satisfaction of all parties. Some may work better than others for different people. We are all different people and have different levels of understanding and insight. Also, as we all learn more about what is driving our conflicts, we may realize that some strategies are more effective in different situations.

In this chapter, I will talk about conflicts and their issues and ways to resolve them internally, within families, in intimate relationships, and in the office. We will look at several topics, and each discussion includes a different strategy. I will use previous examples to illustrate the exercises, and these will come from the conflict between Jim and Dawn, discussed in the previous chapter. These exercises apply to most conflicts or power issues in our lives, and different exercises will appeal to different people. I only ask that you try each one more than once, to see which one(s) you feel work best for you. Feelings of success may not come the first time that you employ each of these techniques; it may take practice and discussion to understand how and when these techniques may work best for each of us.

The following are some general points to consider when trying to resolve conflicts.

1. Overall, the most important fact to remember is that resolution is not about winning or losing. If you feel that the goal of a conflict is to get your point across to the other party without hearing their point, then you have created a win/lose situation. This often results in both parties falling into and being stuck in a conflict. If we think about the conflict between Jim and Dawn in Chapter 14, both tried to gain or win something. (Dawn wanted her son to do his homework, and Jim wanted to avoid homework.)

2. It is unrealistic to think you will avoid emotional input. I would hope that by this point in the book, you realize that it is nearly impossible to avoid emotional input in conflicts. Emotions may hide in the logic of one or both parties; if there are more direct expressions of emotion, remember that the emotions help us understand ourselves and each other.

It can be quite hard to take the risks in the beginning. But, discussing emotions can help to more quickly resolve conflicts; however, this discussion of emotions does hinge on the other party as well. Keep in mind that just as we must practice to learn how to speak a language, learning how to convey emotion effectively also takes some instruction and practice. In Jim and his mother's conflict, they discussed many points, and there could have been different and/or better emotional communications by both parties.

3. Always, always, always remember why we have protective emotions and what they are for. Do you need a refresher as to which ones are the protective emotions? Here they are: anger, rage, arrogance, flippancy, defiance, sarcasm, hatred, and irritation; these emotions come to the fore to protect feelings of threat and vulnerability of either party. Each emotion may protect others or ourselves in different ways and may attempt to cause harm to others or ourselves. However, the goal of those emotions is to protect in some manner. When either party realizes the purpose of their emotions, they have the choice and power to change the course of the conflict. Both Jim and his mother used these protective emotions liberally. There were points where they each used emotions to cause pain in the other person, but the underlying purpose was to protect the self.

4. Look for the logic in each emotion experienced by each party; even more importantly, be willing to take the perspective of the other party. Many times, in conflicts people will assume that someone is not making sense or will make comments such as, "That is ridiculous . . . what a stupid idea. . . ." Sometimes, we may even think to ourselves, "What was I thinking when I said that?" If the person making those comments felt that their comments were stupid or didn't make sense, they probably would not have said them. Also, remember that sometimes we, and others, may make a comment like that to try to diminish the other person's power, in order to protect ourselves.

To some aspect of us, there is some sense of logic that motivates us to communicate. Just because we think or do something does not mean that our logic was rational or well thought through. We can sometimes help others to reconsider what they say. We may ask, "What did you mean by that?" or "Have you really thought that through?" Those questions can help us and the other person think through their comments, but if seen as judging, they can also inflame the conflict. Because we often learn to react to emotions, we quickly learn about the logical aspect of each emotion, such as fear and anger or love and hate and how they interact.

5. Don't rush through the conflict. Take time to be willing to consider the issues of both parties. If there is not enough time to finish the conflict before doing something else, offer to discuss it later—and set a time. If you do not keep your word on discussing it later, don't be surprised if trust issues surface and future conflicts escalate more quickly. When working with children, as well as when forming new relationships with people, it is important to take the time to resolve conflicts and develop open paths of communication. If we develop these pathways, then it is easy for open, honest dialogue to continue throughout the relationship.

6. Be willing to give some power to get some in return. Do not create your own impasse. Too many times in our culture, people fear giving away a perception of power because they fear that they will lose respect or status from other parties in some way. This issue is especially prevalent between parents and children. Parents often feel that they are supposed to have a higher level of status, so they believe that they are supposed to maintain control of the direction and outcome.

Many times children will de-escalate a conflict if they feel they can express themselves honestly and have some say in the consequences. However, in doing this, parents should not allow the child to divert from or redirect the conflict. Remember that we evaluate our personal sense of power through our perceptions. We can choose to allow others to negatively affect our perceptions and disempower ourselves; or we can believe in our own power and the power of others.

In the conflict between Jim and his mother, his mother could have asked him questions early in the conflict, such as, "What do you feel that you could do to help get your homework done? Is there anything I can do to help? I am not sure if you understand why getting your homework done is such an important concern."

7. Try to express to the other party what you think they may be feeling, through your own experiences. In many conflicts that escalate, each person tends to hold on to their position and ignore or discount the other person's perspective. When one or both parties try to summarize what they hear the other person saying, the other person doesn't feel that they have to keep trying to express their feelings and can, instead, listen. Then, if someone is confused in what the other wants to express, clarification is possible.

Besides restating the other person's words, we should also try to read between the words to the underlying emotions. In the conflict between Jim and his mother, we may see many approaches that could have changed the course of the conflict. Jim's mother could have made statements during the conflict such as, "It sounds like you are feeling frustrated with your homework; is their any way I can help?" Or, "It sounds like you feel that I don't trust you. From the choices you have made now and in the past, can you understand why?" Jim could have made statements such as, "Do you feel like I let you down?" Or "I'm sorry that you feel frustrated with my choices. What can I do differently?" In the beginning stages of learning to listen to the other person, these statements do not come easily. It takes time and patience to learn to listen. Remember that when making comments about emotions, they can result in emotional reactions by other parties to protect vulnerable feelings.

8. Provide reflective feedback to the other party regarding what you feel their point is before trying to state your case. This differs from reflecting feelings; you are trying to present the gist of what is being said, rather than discuss underlying feelings directly. However, if feelings do not enter into the conflict, they may come up in the feedback. Reflective feedback often comes during longer discussions or after several exchanges.

In the conflict between Jim and Dawn, it would be difficult to provide reflective feedback because of the many diversions and short, explosive exchanges. However, Jim's mother could have said, "It sounds like there are many more issues than the homework here. It sounds like you feel overwhelmed, mistrusted, frustrated, and uncared for. I can understand if you feel that way, but I also feel that you are trying to avoid taking responsibility for what it's in your best interest to do. Can you understand where I'm coming from?"

When a parent takes the time to make statements such as this and discuss them with their child, the child can learn the same skill. It may still feel risky to make reflective statements and to summarize emotions. This is especially true when the other party may try to divert away from the subject matter or become emotionally reactive. Discussing the issues and being patient will help in the end. In addition, as we learn to understand what we are trying to say, ourselves, it often becomes easier to do the same with others.

9. Explore all options to resolve the conflict, not just the initial points considered by both parties. Put your heads together and brainstorm other outcomes. Many times, conflicts deteriorate when one of the parties foresees an outcome or result that they do not like. The conflict may often continue because the other party persists in trying to avoid the "inevitable" outcome. This commonly happens with children when they eventually may be forced to do what they do not want to do. So, they will do what they can to avoid and divert.

It is often helpful to explore different possible outcomes to a situation and be willing to entertain input from the other party. However, it is important to keep in mind what the ultimate outcome is and make sure not to totally avoid it. The conflict between Jim and his mother is a perfect example of such a conflict. Jim is trying to do all he can to avoid doing his homework. However, there could be many different reasons for his avoidance. It could be fear of failure, laziness, and/or feeling overwhelmed, Jim may need time to unwind after school, and/or other reasons. If they only focus on unfinished homework, then they cannot find solutions that are equitable to both. The conflict between Jim and his mother may find resolution if he gets help from a parent with his homework. In addition, Dawn may develop a schedule for Jim to follow. In doing so, he has time to play when he gets home before doing homework, and his parents offer a window of time each evening to help with homework. . . . The point is that we all must consider other options to outcomes so that all can feel empowered.

RESOLVING INTERNAL POWER STRUGGLES

As I mentioned earlier, most power struggles and conflicts in our life stem from internal issues and our own power struggles. Our internal power struggles often shape our outlook and belief systems. The best way to resolve our personal, internal power struggles is by being honest with ourselves. However, sometimes the most difficult thing that we may do in our life is to be truly honest with ourselves. At this point in the book, I hope you can see all the different ways we use emotion. We may use emotion to mask and manipulate our emotions, behaviors, and beliefs, not only from others, but often from ourselves.

As I have reviewed my own life and my own power struggles, I find that the biggest factor that prevented me from being truly honest with myself was fear. Fear of my own truth, fear of failure, fear of success, fear of rejection by others, fear of getting what I really wanted. Remember that fear underlies guilt, shame, insecurity, inadequacy, and most other emotions. To understand the fears, we must look at them and find where they come from. To look at ourselves with such a level of honesty can sometimes feel like a painful task.

How do we begin this process of looking within? There are many different self-inventories out there in various books or other settings. Each often presents a slightly different way to look at others and ourselves. Always remember that when doing any of these self-exploration exercises, we have to be willing to look with honesty to find our truth. The following list provides some questions and observations to start with when looking within and around you.

1. Look at your relationships with friends, family, spouses, children. What are some common interactions, conflicts or arguments that occur with these people? Do the same types of conflicts happen with more than one person?
2. Listen to what others say about you and your behaviors. Ask people to give you feedback about how they view you. Also, when you ask, understand that they may have a difficult time being honest with you for their reasons (fear, shame, guilt . . .). Be willing to respect that.
3. Assume that in everything you do in your life, you have had a choice. Examine the reasons why you chose your career, your house and neighborhood, the car you drive, your spouse, the number of children you have. . . .
4. Do you have illnesses often? If so, what kind? Colds and flu? Allergies? Muscular? Arthritis? Are any illnesses chronic? What part of the body do your illnesses affect? What illnesses run in your family? Is there any history of addiction?
5. Do you ever feel happy and proud about your accomplishments?
6. Do you ever feel happy for others and their accomplishments?
7. Would others say that you are critical of others or complimentary?
8. Do you have a tendency to be grouchy and irritable? If you are grouchy and irritable, do you always feel like you have a reason when you feel this way?
9. Do you feel that you should always be upbeat and happy?
10. Do you feel that most people tend to look out only for themselves?

11. What are you like when you drive? Passive? Aggressive? Rage-ful? Vengeful? Calm?
12. If you were a friend of yours, what would you like about you? What would you not like about you?

These are just a few questions to help you get started. I hope that from this list, you can come up with more questions of your own. I would encourage you to write down the questions you ask yourself, as well as your answers. You may want to talk to someone close to you about the questions and answers you came up with after you have completed this task. They may be able to provide you with additional feedback and insights. I will not provide any interpretation of answers to these questions, because I think that we may all have slightly different issues to consider. Sometimes, when we begin to take an internal inventory, we begin to feel the underlying emotions and may not know what to do with those emotions.

If you find this exercise difficult, you may want to think about talking with a professional about some of your life issues. Obviously, I do not think that we should look at counseling or therapy as a negative thing. Just because someone sees a therapist does not mean that there is something wrong with them. Granted, I am a therapist and I am obvi-ously going to be biased, but there were times in my life that I had to admit to myself that I needed help and guidance . . . and those times still occur.

There have been some trends toward changing the image of therapy. Some of the most enjoyable and motivated clients that I have are professionals in the business world who are looking for more in life and want to smooth out some rough spots and find more direction in their life. Too many times, people are looking for more meaning in their life, but feel too embarrassed to ask for help. Remember, this is your life, and there is no need to feel fearful of how others view your choices. You have the power to ask for help. Therapists have begun referring to themselves as coaches and consultants, and I am sure that more marketing-oriented terms will emerge. I hope that we all remember that just because we may be "adults," that does not mean that we have to have all the answers in our life. Furthermore, there is a very profound realization that I have made in my life: That is that age, experience, maturity and wisdom are all independent issues. Think about it.

If you choose to seek counseling, be sure to check into the credentials of your therapist. It is not common that you can ask for references from the therapist, due to confidentiality, but you may be able to call the state licensing boards to see if they have had any complaints. Finally, inter-view your prospective therapists over the phone, if possible. I think it says a lot about a therapist, if they are willing to take a few minutes out of their day to answer a few questions for a prospective client.

RESOLVING POWER STRUGGLES IN FAMILIES

We all know that family interactions are a hotbed for conflicts and power struggles. Conflicts can occur between almost any members in a family. In many situations, groups of family members slip into the conflict, so they may choose sides. Sometimes, family members may even lobby for support from others in the family to back them up through the conflict. There are many challenges to resolving family conflicts; often, this is because of the hierarchical structure of the family. Also, the extended family (grandparents, parents, uncles, aunts, children, and/or grandchildren) may get involved in a conflict. Therefore, there are often too many power issues to easily address. When this happens, the conflict becomes a fight for survival, instead of a quest for understanding. During a family-wide conflict, members tend to pick a side and resist changing their opinion or seeing any other point of view. This tends to happen due to their belief in and desire to be good, strong, and/or right.

Parents often try to hold on to their higher level of status, and avoid letting it go. Also, in conflicts and protests toward their parents, children (of all ages) often hold on to their perceptions, because they do not want to appear weak or vulnerable and/or feel tired of losing. Parents often feel that they must stick to their decisions, or else they may appear weak. Many times, parents make snap decisions, but later realize they may not have been fair. They may reconsider their feelings at some point, but many would prefer to stick to the original decision, rather than appear to waiver. A parent's willingness to review the issue involves several things. How they feel about themselves at the time and the importance of the issue often determine whether they will reverse a decision.

It may or may not surprise you to know that many family conflicts continue for weeks, years, even decades—or generations. Family conflicts can drag out for long periods for the same reason that other conflicts linger: we do not want to appear weak or vulnerable, and we do not want to lose. If we believe we are giving in, we may feel that we surrender our power and pride. If we are wise, however, we may see that "saving face" or clinging to our arrogance is often not worth the hard feelings or damage we may do. These long-term, unresolved conflicts can distance and divide families. There are too many stories of people who feel sorrow, guilt, and regret when a family member dies and the conflict was not resolved.

Often, the key to resolving long-term power struggles and conflicts involves one or both people looking at their own issues. After dealing with these inner conflicts, both parties need to think about the other person's point of view. Without mutual efforts to resolve conflicts, they cannot reach a solution.

Fear is often the most powerful emotion involved in family conflicts. Too many times, neither person wants to admit their fears to the other; this is because of how they feel it may affect their power. I feel saddened to see the many conflicts between parents, children, and siblings that continue because of one or both people's fears of losing something. Nevertheless, what they fear losing is something that no one can ever truly take away: their power. We often shroud these fears in arrogance (often confused with pride), stubbornness, anger and hatred. We may also use rationalization, sarcasm, defiance, and many other defenses to protect us from our fear. I think that family conflicts tend to run so deeply because, as children, we depend upon our family for acceptance, love and approval. Because of the risk of rejection and the deep damage to trust that can occur in families, wounds can be very deep. While many times, it would be ideal to be able to resolve our conflicts with others in our family, sometimes we are still, in part, led back to finding our own resolution within ourselves.

As children, our parents and families are the first people that we turn to for love and acceptance; so, there is much more pain involved when we feel that we cannot get that love and acceptance. We then work very hard to hide this pain from others and ourselves. When we try to work through the hurt with the people who we feel caused some of that pain, we feel we become vulnerable to being hurt all over again. So, many of us feel that it would be better to bury the pain and "write off" those who hurt us. If we can learn to take care of our own emotions, then the risk of feeling hurt again in future interactions with that person is less. In doing so, we can realize that we do not lose anything, but only gain from the possibility of re-establishing our relationship with that parent or sibling.

POWER EXCHANGE DIAGRAM

We may better understand our conflicts by visually breaking them down into pieces and parts so we can often get a better idea of what each person was feeling at each stage of the conflict. Two or more people can also discuss the interactions, emotions and thoughts together while they graph or diagram a conflict. When both parties can step back and visualize their ideas, thoughts, and feelings of power and how their actions affected others, they may avoid future conflicts. Creating some type of visual tool to explore conflicts can be effective in families, especially with children. With practice, they find it easier to understand visual depictions of conflict that can assist with problem solving. In doing this, children and adults can see how the power shifts during the conflict and begin to understand why this happens.

The power exchange diagram can be a powerful tool in understanding your conflicts and helping you to seek successful resolution. The power exchange diagram that shows the conflict between Jim and Dawn is a good example of using a graph to "see" what happens in a conflict. It takes practice to use the power exchange diagram. You may want to start by trying it for yourself on some past conflict. If you are doing this alone, diagram what you think the other person's emotions and power levels may have been by putting yourself in their role, and make educated guesses based on what you have learned in this book.

To do this exercise, you will need at least an 8.5" x 11" piece of paper, and preferably, three different colored pens or markers. Graph paper is not necessary (you will be making rough lines and sketches). This is not artwork. I use a dry erase board when I do this exercise in my office. The board is big and easy to make corrections on. It may also be helpful to have the emotion list at the back of the book at hand as a reference.

The first step is to identify the communication exchanges that you will later graph. When identifying the communication exchanges, it is important to be able to note when and how each communication exchange occurs. It may be a good idea to write down the conflict as close to word for word as you can remember and label each exchange; this is similar to what I did in the conflict between Jim and Dawn.

Remember, besides using words, we communicate in a number of other ways. We express ourselves with facial expressions, gestures, grunts, groans, and silence. In the heat of battle, we may use as much body language as verbal language. We often cross our arms, walk away or toward the other party, sit down, stand up or do any number of things. Whether or not a person meant to use an action to communicate something, if you take something as an expression of power, then you should include it in your exchanges. Why? This is because if someone had a reaction to it, it may have contributed to the escalation (or de-escalation) of the conflict. For example, sometimes, when people feel fatigued they may sigh, but a well-timed sigh can be a sign of frustration; this can result in an emotional reaction and/or retaliation from others. In the learning stages, you will probably miss a few exchanges, but, as you continue to practice and work some through with others, it will become easier.

The next step is to create the graph for the diagram. This is very easy. Refer to Figure 15.1. Draw the axes with one color marker (or pen), and label the graph on the side (High–Low Power) and bottom

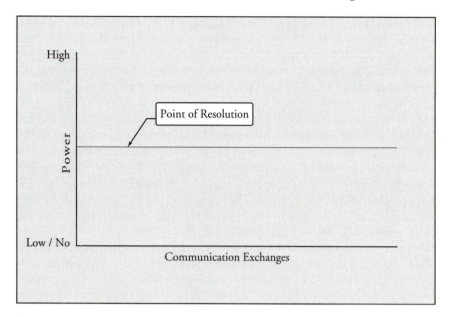

Figure 15.1 Power Exchange Diagram

(Communication Exchanges) so that those doing the exercise will understand what they are looking at. Always remember the point of resolution line (the line in the middle of the graph) so that all people in the exercise will be mindful of resolution and balance, which you should be seeking. You are now ready for the next step, which is to diagram the exchanges.

Mark an exchange by drawing a line up or down, to note a change in "perceived power"—or sideways if there was no change. Use a different color to indicate each person in the conflict. At each exchange, all people should have a line drawn to mark the exchange. Refer back to the conflict between Jim and his mother for a visual reference of a conflict drawn out using the Power Exchange Diagram.

When you diagram an exchange, think of how power*ful* or power*less* the person appeared externally, even if you do not know what they were thinking or feeling on the inside. Remember that their powerful action is often a reaction to what they were just feeling. So, if you don't know how they were feeling, look to their reaction to the next step as an indicator. When plotting the exchanges, always remember that each exchange affects each person's feeling of power. Often the rule "what goes up, must come down" and vice versa applies. Whenever someone has a more powerful exchange, remember that it is probably because they are reacting to a more vulnerable internal emotion.

Try to see if you can think of more than one emotion that the person may be feeling at each exchange. Refer to the list of emotions at the back of the book for help. Sometimes, conflicts escalate because the person feels overwhelmed by all the many different emotions they are feeling. They may also try to frustrate people by trying to manipulate different emotions.

When you graph the conflict, try to be aware of how the conflict is getting "hotter" or "cooler" and see if you can figure out why. Sometimes, a very simple response can ease a conflict; but neither person may realize how it worked until they can step back from the conflict. It is important that the diagram represent the escalation patterns, so that you can see the trends in power. Being able to see the graphical changes in power is a visual teacher to those involved in the conflict, and can definitely aid in resolving future conflicts.

When you feel that you have diagrammed each exchange in the conflict, see who you think "won" and who "lost," and identify why you believe that. As I said before, too many times people in a conflict feel that there was a winner or a loser. Remember, that almost as many times, we usually want to be the winner. That is why conflicts drag on as long as they do. Remember that, although someone may have the last word, they still often feel the same underlying emotions that they felt just before the conflict. As I have stated numerous times, I feel that often no one really wins a conflict. I say this any time neither person made the effort to understand the other, and; the true underlying conflict will probably continue later under different circumstances.

After the Power Exchange Diagram is complete, review each exchange and ask yourself the following questions:

1. How could the conflict have changed course if someone would have said or done something different? (There are several possible answers to this)
2. Do I understand what the person was trying to say in this exchange? Could they have said it differently or better?
3. Did they communicate what they were truly feeling?
4. Could this conflict have been resolved at this step if I would have responded differently?
5. What can I learn about myself?
6. What can I learn about how I feel and react to this exchange?

This exercise may take some time to complete (45 minutes to 1 hour). However, you may find that the more often you follow it, the easier it gets; and, therefore, the sooner this understanding and resolution within yourself, and with others, may occur. Although it may take some time to walk through it with someone else, you may be saving yourself a lot of time in the end, if the conflict no longer occurs.

RESOLVING INTIMATE RELATIONSHIP STRUGGLES

As I said in the chapter on intimate relationships, many relationship conflicts come from issues that go back to childhood and/or other relationship patterns. Other times, we may see that a relationship spawns specific conflicts that may drag on and on. These can slowly contribute to a breakdown in the communication and in the relationship as a whole. If the parties involved can step back and consider the other person's point of view, they may be able to see why the conflict happened and how to resolve it.

When looking to resolve struggles in intimate relationships, the key is for both parties to make an effort toward resolving the problem(s). I often see that one person is ready to address problems before the other is. One person in a relationship can understand the issues that lead to a conflict, and this can help that person avoid pouring fuel on the fire. But both people have to be willing to resolve the conflict for it to be resolved.

The following example discusses what may seem to be a minor conflict to most. However, conflicts such as these can lead to larger problems and issues further down the line. They do this by creating a sense of underlying mistrust and insecurity that is difficult to restablish, if the issues are not resolved. Sometimes simple arguments begin a snowball effect that may take years to get out of control.

Chuck and Lori are boyfriend and girlfriend. They often have arguments about calling to let each other know when they get home after being out late at night or driving home from the other person's apartment. Lori often fails to call when she gets home, but she feels upset when Chuck doesn't call her. Chuck doesn't like calling her, and he feels resentful and fearful when Lori doesn't call him. Lori becomes very defensive when Chuck brings it up. Chuck is willing to talk about it, but he feels that there is a double standard on Lori's part; still, he will often avoid discussing it, because he doesn't want to deal with the conflict. Chuck will still call Lori when he gets home, and he expects that Lori will not call him. However, he will often go to sleep worrying about her, and this feeds his feelings of resentment. In this example, they do not discuss this conflict, and it remains unresolved. Instead, Chuck tries to deal with it the best he can, but it is likely that his resentment may continue to build, and other conflicts will arise as a result.

It is rare for two people in a relationship to resolve their conflicts without the help of someone else. I am sure that by now, you understand that people in relationships feel fear rejection, abandonment, and misunderstood by their significant other. Therefore, it is very difficult for them to be completely honest with each other and themselves. Often, if they will involve a neutral third party and let them filter through the emotions, history, issues, and concerns, the third party can help people to see each person's side more clearly. However, it is crucial for this third party to remain neutral. It is not a good idea to involve parents or best friends, and especially bad to involve children in the conflict. Often, the best course is to find someone trained in conflict resolution, such as a therapist, counselor, or a member of the clergy.

Before seeking help from a third person, it is important to make sure that both people feel comfortable talking with this person. I think it's best to interview this person with both people present. Both people should ask questions that they feel are important to them, and if something doesn't feel right, discuss it with this person, but also look elsewhere. If you consider talking with pastors and priests, remember that their religious beliefs may guide their viewpoints, and therefore they may not be impartial. It is important to know that we all ultimately have the power to heal ourselves; however, we still have to trust and respect the person who helps us to find the willingness to heal.

Many times, money is an issue that prevents people from seeking help from professionals, due to the cost of therapy. I do believe that we can all benefit from some type of professional counseling, and talk to someone that can help us to step back from our lives. But, sometimes financial and other issues result in us having to make do with what we have. Writing in the form of journaling, poetry, and lists and even just putting our thoughts down on paper can be a very powerful tool to help us explore our own issues. When we write, we can look at what we wrote later, when we are not stuck in the emotion, to gain a better perspective. In addition, when we want to share our thoughts and feelings with others, the other person can digest them at their own rate, by reading what we wrote. I feel that if couples can write down their concerns and fears and share them with each other, they may reduce many conflicts. The following exercise is a writing exercise that any two people can do, and it is not limited to the use of couples. You can do the exercise by yourself, if necessary, but it is most effective if everyone in the conflict does it together.

CONFLICT RESOLUTION EXERCISE

To understand the nature of the conflict, sometimes it is helpful for each person to write down the issues that they feel feed into the conflict and prevent the conflict from being resolved. Since both parties often have differing points of view, the next step is to write down the issues that they feel the other person may feel contribute to the struggle. As each person writes down the issues, they should also look for what role their own issues play in maintaining the conflict; also, they should look for solutions that they feel they could provide to resolve the conflict. After each party has done this, they should sit down together and discuss each perspective.

Now, how do you get started? Start by discussing the other person's feelings first, so that the person listening can hear what the other's thoughts are and, therefore, can help them feel understood. When someone feels that someone understands them, they are more likely to listen to the other person's feelings. The other reason to communicate the other person's perspective is to make sure that you both can feel that their issues are perceived accurately. When both people finish presenting their thoughts, then both people should try to generate or brainstorm solutions to the conflict. It is important to not criticize any ideas in brainstorming because criticism will discourage responses. After brainstorming, both should evaluate the options to find the best solution.

Here is an example. Robert and Jenny often have conflicts about what they are going to do on Friday nights. Most Friday nights, Jenny likes to stay home because she's feeling tired from a long week at work. However, Robert likes to burn off some energy and frustration by going out to a happy hour, dinner, or movie. By Thursday mornings, the stress of the impending weekend is already setting in, and the couple starts getting short-tempered with each other. Due to months of fruitless conflicts, Robert stops off at a bar with friends for happy hour and does not come home until 8:00 p.m. or later. As a result, Jenny will eat something at home, turn on the television and give Robert the cold shoulder when he gets home. They seldom talk about their frustrations anymore. If both followed the exercise and wrote down their feelings about the situation and what they think the other feels, they might come up with the following solutions.

Jenny's Notes

I feel very tired after working all week and would like a night to relax. I work all week long, I wake up early, I work late some days, and he doesn't seem to care about how hard I work. I feel angry, resentful and trapped when Robert wants to go out on Fridays, because I feel that if I don't, he will feel upset with me and will not want to be with me. Also, it seems that Robert doesn't want to spend time with me, because he would rather be out with other people. I enjoy the time I spend with Robert, but not when there are so many other people around to distract him from me. I want his attention, and I feel that we have very little quality time together. I often feel lonely in crowds, because it seems that no one wants to talk to me, and I feel nervous and shy. I often don't know what to say when meeting new people and feel very insecure. I feel very angry when Robert tries to force me to do things I do not want to, which makes me even less cooperative. Although I think that he doesn't care about me, he probably doesn't understand, because I often do not tell him what I am really feeling.

I think that Robert works very hard and likes to unwind at the end of the week. He probably likes the noise and atmosphere of being around other people. He seems to like activity, and he always does ask me to go along with him, even if it is at the last minute. He may feel that I am trying to control him by keeping him at home, and it is possible that he feels resentful and trapped, as I do when I want him to stay home. He may feel more uncooperative toward me, when he feels forced to do something that I want to do. He has always been an outgoing person, which is one thing that I like about him. He may not feel that I understand where he is coming from, and he often has difficulty talking about how he feels. I notice that when he is stressed, his activity level increases; whereas when I feel stressed, I want to sleep more.

Robert's Notes

I work very hard during the week and would like one night to unwind. I don't think that it is too much to ask, but I feel resentful and guilty when Jenny wants to stay home, and I want to go out. I feel like I can't win. If I go out, and she is with me, I know she does not want to be there, and I feel guilty and stressed, because I feel responsible for her. If she stays home, I feel selfish since she is at home alone and resentful, because I want to relax with a nice evening out. If I stay at home with her, I feel resentful, angry and controlled by her, and even though I enjoy the time I spend with her, I still feel angry inside for the rest of the evening. I feel very frustrated because I feel trapped and overwhelmed, because I sometimes feel that she expects me to take care of her. I have felt, for a long time, that if I tell her how I feel, then she will get upset, and I will feel guilty again. I think that I have been holding these feelings in for a long time, and they have been building. I feel a great deal of fear and apprehension about talking to her about this, and I am not sure how to handle the situation.

I recognize that Jenny likes to be at home, and she works some late nights during the week. She probably feels very tired by Friday nights. She might feel some resentment about me wanting to go out on Fridays, and some nights, we have stayed out late because I ran into some friends and wanted to visit with them. She may have felt angry about staying out late and may not trust that we will come home when I initially agree to.

I know that she likes to spend time with me, and I appreciate her loyalty to our relationship and dedication to spending time together. She seems to feel hurt and neglected when I want go out, and when she comes with me, she seems very quiet and distant. I feel like she is trying to punish me, but I have to remember that she is somewhat shy and probably feels uncomfortable in crowded settings. She does seem to enjoy going to movies every now and then, probably because it is just the two of us. I think that if I did not want to go out every Friday, then she may not feel so frustrated. However, the more that I feel that she doesn't want to go out, then the more that I seem to want to go out. I think that I need to understand myself better. She probably feels pressured, trapped and frustrated, as I do, and may also not know how to talk to me about it.

The Discussion

Jenny and Robert get together to discuss their notes, and either may agree to go first. If Robert went first, he would start by discussing his notes about Jenny. He may or may not choose to read his notes, as he wrote them, because he may not feel comfortable talking about everything he wrote. When he finishes talking about how he thought she was feeling, he would then talk about his notes regarding his feelings. After he finishes, then Jenny would discuss her notes, starting with her notes about Robert, and then discussing her notes about her own feelings.

After each person discusses their notes, both may want to talk more about helping each to understand their feelings and observations. After both feel satisfied that they understand the other person, then they begin to generate ideas to help resolve the conflict. In Robert and Jenny's conflict, the following list was generated:

1. Alternate going out on Friday nights, one Friday go out and the next stay in.
2. Robert can go out with friends one Friday each month.
3. Robert and Jenny go out together on either a Friday or Saturday in a weekend.
4. Robert can go out with his friends four evenings per month, but only one Friday.
5. Robert and Jenny will agree to a time when they will come home before they go out.
6. Robert can make more effort to introduce Jenny to friends, and Jenny will try to have a better attitude toward meeting people.
7. Robert and Jenny will make efforts to go out with other couples so they will both feel that they have someone to talk to.
8. If Robert or Jenny feels pressured or trapped, they agree to discuss it together so it does not build into resentment and anger.

9. Robert and Jenny will make a list of activities that they can do together at home and out that they can select from, if needed.
10. If Jenny wants time alone, she can tell Robert so that he can make plans to do something else.
11. Robert and Jenny can make a wish list of things they would like to do together and apart and use that as a reference on future occasions.

This brainstorm brought up more than enough ideas for Robert and Jenny to use. They may choose to use a combination of different ideas in the list, or may use just one strategy. In most situations, many ideas come up that you can use in resolving the conflict. The list of ideas helps each person to understand the other. Also, many of these ideas take both people's needs into account, and resolution is easier to reach.

Some tips to pay attention to when doing the conflict resolution exercise are:

1. It is important that each person can talk about their list without interruption. Both people will probably feel very emotional when talking about their feelings. As such, it often helps to let them say what they are feeling so they do not get lost in other emotions and forget their point.

2. Both people may feel nervous or defensive while reading their list. As I said earlier, these defensive feelings want to protect other vulnerable emotions. If one or both parties feel criticized during their part, then the discussion will likely fall apart and could become an argument.

3. Hang in there, and be patient while the other person speaks his or her mind. After each person discusses their notes, both will likely have a better grasp for how each person felt, as well as where they each may have made incorrect assumptions.

4. Be open to realizing that you may have felt things that you did not realize. When couples and families do similar exercises, they often find that one person may discuss feelings about the other person that they had not thought about. When all parties felt more able to listen, they all learned more and many productive discussions often resulted.

5. This exercise may feel very risky to anyone involved. Part of the difficulty about doing an exercise such as this is that there is a great deal of risk involved for both people, and therefore, many chances for conflict to arise.

6. It may help to do this exercise with an impartial friend or a therapist or counselor who can keep both people focused on the issues; also, this third party can listen to both sides without having emotions interfere.

RESOLVING POWER STRUGGLES AT THE OFFICE

As I discussed in Chapter 13, resolving power issues at the office is often hard, due to issues of position and status and the structure of most companies. Many times when counseling individuals on work issues, I find that their childhood issues are surfacing. Often, their supervisor can take on the character of their parent(s) and co-workers can take on sibling roles. In such a case, the employee then plays out their childhood emotional conflicts with their boss and/or co-workers. This sometimes even happens with the people that they manage. If you think that you are immune to this, you may want to look more closely at yourself.

The keys to resolving power struggles in the office involve:

1. Look at yourself and see how you may be contributing to the conflict.

2. Try to examine how powerful or powerless you feel in this conflict.

3. Examine how powerful or powerless you appear to be to other people in the conflict.

4. Look at the others involved in the conflict to see what role the people in your past might be playing (mother, father, competitive sibling, supportive sibling . . . etc.).

5. Given what you may know about others that you work with, what roles might you be playing that come from their past (mother, father, competitive sibling, supportive sibling . . .).

6. If you see that the conflict is more about you and your past, see if you can resolve the conflict without getting others involved.

7. Do not try to fix other people's problems or solve their conflicts. You can be a resource to talk to, but avoid handling issues with others for them.

8. Do not try to turn others against bosses or co-workers. It can backfire.

9. Try to find someone outside of the situation that you can talk to about the conflict—someone who can be more objective.

10. If you have a problem with someone you work with, try to resolve it directly with them.

11. Do not let conflicts remain unresolved. One of the biggest problems that I see in poor work habits is that people do not air their concerns and issues at the office; as a result, their motivation and performance decreases. Here are several common symptoms of unresolved conflict at work: Passive-aggression, increased illnesses, angry outbursts, apathy, and avoidance.

12. Try to use some of the exercises listed earlier in the chapter to help you understand your role and view of the conflict.

If you are going to try to resolve your conflict directly with the person, you may want to try to keep the following points in mind.

1. Schedule time to meet with the person in advance and give them an idea about what you would like to discuss.

2. Write down your issues, emotions, and reactions on paper before you meet with them so that you do not forget them when you are discussing the conflict (You may want to follow the guidelines discussed in the conflict resolution exercise).

3. Be willing to see their point of view, and be willing to share some responsibility for the conflict (in other words, you have to be willing to give some power to get some in return).

4. Try to avoid responding defensively, and be willing to understand that they may be feeling defensive. Keep in mind that anger, defiance, arrogance, sarcasm . . . often protect more vulnerably perceived emotions. Also, remember the cognitive defenses: rationalization, justification, denial, projection, transference. People sometimes use these mechanisms to protect themselves from feeling emotion.

5. Be willing to discuss the issue with a mediator if you feel that it could become emotionally charged. Someone in Human Resources or even a supervisor that you both trust may provide some benefit. Offer this suggestion to the other person in the conflict and see who they may suggest.

6. It is crucial to observe your voice tone and body language. Also, observe the other person's voice tone and body language during the conflict resolution to see if it is affecting you.

7. Believe in your right to express your concerns and issues in an assertive manner (avoid being aggressive). Discuss your emotional reac-

tions and avoid behaviorally expressing them in a work-related conflict. If you feel angry, do not yell; if you feel sad, do not cry. Save the expression of your emotions for someone that you trust outside of the conflict. You may feel that this is counter to what I have been discussing throughout the book, but work is still work and there is still a prevalent belief that emotions do not belong there. This is different from how you would communicate in other conflicts, outside of office settings. It is my hope that this would ultimately change, but at this time in our evolution, most office settings are not ready for emotional "truth."

8. Understand that you are communicating with a human being who has feelings and emotions. Even if they are your boss, they breathe, eat, and feel too, and are seeking power and respect, love and acceptance, just like you.

This is not an exhaustive list of guidelines and, depending on the dynamics and personalities of those involved, some suggestions may not be appropriate. Fear is probably the biggest emotion that prevents people from resolving conflicts at work. Some thoughts based in fear are: "What if I get fired or demoted for trying to address this conflict? What if nothing changes? What if everyone else finds out about my feelings? What if they laugh at me or think I am complaining?" Sometimes, these are very realistic concerns. If they are realistic concerns that you have, based on the previous experiences of others, you may want to consider whether or not you want to continue to work in such an environment.

SUMMARY

This chapter included a number of different strategies to help you to resolve conflicts. Many of the strategies involve an element of looking within to find your role in the conflicts; this is always the first place we should look. In any conflict, whether it is with a family member, spouse, friend, or co-worker, we must try to see where our responsibility lies.

I applied each conflict resolution strategy to a certain circumstance; but we can employ each strategy in a variety of settings. Each strategy will appeal to people in a different way. While I would ask that you try each one, you will probably find that some of the strategies work better for you than others. As you continue to try to resolve conflicts with others, flexibility will be very important because strategies that work well for you may not work as well for the other person(s) involved in the conflict. Be willing to respect their differences if you want them to respect yours.

Just like learning to ride a bike, using these skills takes practice and you may fall a few times before you feel comfortable utilizing some of the conflict resolution strategies. You are also going to have a tendency to revert to old habits before you can adopt the new ones. Just because you may feel upset and yell while you are trying to resolve a conflict doesn't mean that you can't stop and apologize, and pick up where you left off in a more respectful manner. It takes a great deal of courage to take responsibility for our own actions and then continue to work on resolving the conflict. Remember, there is no failure; it is only an emotion that tells us when it is time to learn.

16

Putting It All Together

In the game of life it is a good idea to have a few early losses, which
relieves you the pressure of trying to maintain an undefeated season.
—*Bill Vaughan*

During the course of this book, we explored much material on a variety
of topics. It is my hope that by understanding conflict, power and the
roles of the victim, persecutor, rescuer and instigator you will choose to
take the path to become a champion for your own success. This is a lot
to digest. We looked at different systems of power and the pros and cons
of each. We also explored the purpose of our emotions and how they
relate to our sense of power in conflicts. I spent some time discussing
the ways in which emotions and feelings of power affect conflict in
various parts of our lives, and some ways to resolve power struggles.

It took me some time to develop and mold the ideas presented in
the contents of these pages. Also, I would expect that it will take you
some time to fully digest this information and mold it into your belief
systems. I believe that you may need to return and reread parts of
the book as you may see concepts come to life within your life. I
hope you will see this book as a resource guide to return to time and
again, as needed.

Let me be the first to say that understanding the nature of power and
emotions can benefit anyone; but not everyone is ready to embrace the
concepts or put them to use. We each need to respect our own time
frame for growth, as well as the time that others need to change. If they
are not willing to change in a way that we feel helps us, then we may
have to consider our choices to remain in that relationship.

As mentioned throughout the book, fear often prevents us from trying things that we do not feel safe about or feel a lack of confidence in doing. Many of the ideas presented in this book are probably different from what you learned in your life. What I most want you to take from this book is the idea that we all need to be responsible for our own sense of power; we do this by understanding the feelings that affect our belief in our personal power. This book provides the avenue for each of us to pursue that quest.

So how can you use this book in your everyday life? I hope that you will take as much of the information from this book and use it to create your own understanding of the world. By no means is this an exhaustive record of conflict or of the use and misuse of power; nor is it a complete discussion of emotion. This merely provides the building blocks for what you may need to construct in order to take it further. I feel that it is crucial to appreciate the importance of the hierarchical versus equity models of power and how we employ those different models in conflict and throughout our lives.

As we come to understand when and where we may choose to use our status to our advantage or to seek equity, then we can better see how we use our emotions. The next phase is to look at how we use these concepts of power and emotion in the different segments of our life: within our families, within ourselves, in our relationships, and at work. As we explore these areas of our lives, we can then seek to answer more challenging questions in our lives. It is difficult to figure out how to truly change our life if we don't know what makes us who we are. Finally, the previous chapter on resolving power struggles provides a framework for finding peaceful and mutually beneficial strategies to end patterns of conflict that have affected our lives.

My hope for you is that this book will prompt you to consider how you have played the victim, persecutor, rescuer, and the instigator by seeing how conflict and your perception of power affect all the various facets of your life. Remember that the goal is to live an equity-based life in a hierarchical world. Allow this to be a springboard for you to examine and explore the nature of your relationships and life choices from a different perspective so that you can see that you can be victorious in the manner in which you deal with the world. I wish you luck in your travels and hope you are able to find and fully embrace the infinite power at your disposal. Use it wisely.

Appendix

Comprehensive List of Emotions

When you are experiencing a conflict, remember that it is related to your sense of power, which will trigger many emotions. Take the time to review this list and identify *all* of the emotions you may have been feeling so that you can obtain a better understanding of the conflict. Always remember that you choose to feel the feelings; no one can make you feel anything.

Abandoned	Assured	Content	Discouraged
Abused	Attacked	Controlled	Disdain
Accused	Awed	Criticized	Disgraced
Acknowledged	Awkward	Crushed	Disgusted
Admired	Bad	Deceived	Disheartened
Afraid	Baffled	Defeated	Disillusioned
Aggravated	Betrayed	Defensive	Dismal
Agitated	Better	Defiant	Disorganized
Alarmed	Bewildered	Dejected	Displeased
Alienated	Bored	Delighted	Disrespected
Alive	Bothered	Demoralized	Distant
Ambivalent	Burdened	Depressed	Distracted
Angry	Cheated	Deserted	Distraught
Anguished	Cheerful	Desperate	Distressed
Annoyed	Coerced	Despised	Dominated
Anxious	Comfortable	Determined	Doubtful
Appalled	Concerned	Devastated	Drained
Appreciated	Condemned	Directionless	Dreadful
Apprehensive	Confident	Disabled	Ecstatic
Arrogant	Confused	Disappointed	Elated
Ashamed	Constricted	Discarded	Embarrassed

Empty
Encouraged
Energized
Enraged
Enthusiastic
Envious
Exasperated
Excited
Exhausted
Exploited
Exuberant
Failure
Fearful
Flattered
Flippant
Flustered
Foggy
Fortunate
Frantic
Frustrated
Fulfilled
Fuming
Furious
Good
Grateful
Gratified
Great
Grievous
Guarded
Guilt
Happy
Harassed
Hateful
Helpless
Hesitant
Hopeful
Hopeless
Horrified
Hostile
Humbled
Humiliated
Humorous
Hurt
Ignored

Immobilized
Impatient
Inadequate
Incensed
Inconvenienced
Insecure
Insulted
Intimidated
Invigorated
Irritated
Isolated
Jealous
Joyful
Jubilant
Justified
Lonely
Loved
Loving
Mad
Manipulated
Marvelous
Miserable
Mistrust
Misunderstood
Mournful
Neglected
Nervous
Offended
Old
Optimistic
Outraged
Overwhelmed
Pacified
Panicky
Patient
Patronized
Peaceful
Peeved
Perfect
Perplexed
Perturbed
Pessimistic
Petrified
Pitiful

Pleased
Powerful
Powerless
Proud
Protected
Provoked
Puzzled
Rage
Rebellious
Regretful
Rejected
Relaxed
Relieved
Reluctant
Repulsed
Resentful
Resigned
Resolved
Respected
Reticent
Ridiculed
Right
Sabotaged
Sad
Sarcastic
Satisfied
Scared
Seething
Shaken
Shame
Shocked
Shy
Skeptical
Smothered
Sorrowful
Spiteful
Stagnant
Startled
Stifled
Strangled
Strong
Stubborn
Stunned
Stupid

Suppressed
Surprised
Suspicious
Swamped
Tense
Terrible
Terrific
Terrified
Threatened
Thrilled
Throttled
Timid
Tormented
Torn
Tranquil
Trapped
Troubled
Trust
Unappreciated
Uncared For
Uncertain
Uncomfortable
Undecided
Understood
Uneasy
Unloved
Unsettled
Unsure
Unwanted
Upset
Uptight
Used
Valued
Vengeful
Vindictive
Violated
Vulnerable
Weak
Wonderful
Worthless
Wounded
Wrong
Young

Notes

1. Hillman, James. *Kinds of Power.* New York: Currency Doubleday, 1995.

2. Mandel, Faye. *Self-Powerment.* New York: Penguin Group, 2002.

3. James, Muriel. *Born to Win.* Reading, Mass: Addison-Wesley, 1971.

4. Berne, Eric. *Games People Play: The Psychology of Human Relationships.* New York: Grove Press, 1964.

5. Gray, John. *What You Feel You Can Heal.* Mill Valley, Calif.: Heart Publishing, 1984.

6. Mellin, Laurel. *The Pathway: Follow the Road to Health and Happiness.* New York: Regan Books, 2003.

7. Manz, Charles C. *Emotional Discipline: The Power to Choose How You Feel.* San Francisco: Berrett-Koehler Publishers, 2003.

8. Hillman, James. *Emotion.* London: Routledge and Kegan Paul, 1960

9. McKay, Mathew; and Fanning, Patrick. *Self-Esteem.* Oakland, Calif.: New Harbinger Publications, 2000.

10. Watkins, John G.; and Watkins, Helen H. *Ego States: Theory and Therapy.* New York: W. W. Norton, 1997.

11. Tavris, Carol. *Anger: The Misunderstood Emotion.* New York: Simon and Schuster, 1989.

12. Phillips, Maggie; and Frederick, Claire. *Healing the Divided Self: Clinical and Ericksonian Hypnotherapy for Post-Traumatic and Dissociative Conditions.* New York: W.W. Norton, 1995.

13. Sandler, Joseph. *Projection, Identification, Projective Identification.* Madison, Conn.: International Universities Press, 1987.

14. Seligman, M. E. P. *Helplessness: On Depression, Development, and Death.* New York: W. H. Freeman, 1992.

Bibliography

Gray, John. *What You Feel You Can Heal*. Mill Valley, Calif.: Heart Publishing, 1984.

James, Muriel. *Born to Win*. Reading, Mass.: Addison-Wesley Publishing Co., 1971.

Mandel, Faye. *Self-Powerment*. New York: Penguin Group, 2002.

Manz, Charles C. *Emotional Discipline: The Power to Choose How You Feel*. San Francisco: Berrett-Koehler Publishers, Inc., 2003.

McKay, Mathew; and Fanning, Patrick. *Self-Esteem*. Oakland, Calif.: New Harbinger Publications, 2000.

Mellin, Laurel. *The Pathway: Follow the Road to Health and Happiness*. New York: Regan Books. 2003.

Watkins, John G.; and Watkins, Helen H. *Ego States: Theory and Therapy*. New York: W. W. Norton, 1997.

Index

About the Authors

ERIK A. FISHER is a licensed psychologist in Georgia. He has dedicated his career to the advancement of human potential in the physical, mental, and spiritual realms.

STEVEN W. SHARP is a freelance and technical writer. He lives in Alabama.